More praise for
A God Who Looks Like Me

"A powerful antidote to the still-pervasive conviction that only the masculine and the mind are sacred.... [It] steeps women and men in simple deep healing."
—Carolyn McVickar Edwards
Author of *The Storyteller's Goddess*

"A practical and inspirational guide to the feminine aspect of divinity, empowering women with many helpful exercises and personal stories."
—Corinne McLaughlin
Coauthor of *Spiritual Politics*

"An excellent resource."
—Values and Visions Reviews Service

"The persistence, courage, and integrity of Patricia Reilly's personal journey, combined with her extraordinary scholarship and teachings, are an inspiration."
—Dr. Marilyn Jean Hauser
Clinical Psychologist

A God Who Looks Like Me

Discovering a Woman-Affirming Spirituality

Patricia Lynn Reilly

BALLANTINE BOOKS • NEW YORK

Grateful acknowledgment is made to *Five J's Songs* for permission to reprint an
excerpt from "Flowers Are Red" on page 33. Copyright © 1978 *Five J's Songs*.
Used with permission. All rights reserved.

Library of Congress Catalog Card Number: 95-95008

ISBN 0-345-40233-2

Cover design by Ruth Ross
Cover art: Detail of Dante Gabriel Rossetti's *The Bower Meadow*, courtesy of
Manchester City Art Gallery

Manufactured in the United States of America

First Trade Paperback Edition: March 1996

10 9 8 7 6 5 4

I dedicate this book to my mother,
Kathleen Patricia Diehm Reilly (1927–1993),
  Daughter of Catherine Tyndall Diehm,
  Granddaughter of Anna Neville Tyndall,
  Great–granddaughter of Catherine Kelly Neville,
In gratitude for her ongoing inspiration.

Blessed are you among women, dear Mother.
  I grieve your wounds.
  I celebrate your courage.
  I honor you in every word of this book.
Together we tell the untold stories of a lifetime.

Contents ❧

List of Exercises, Meditations, and Rituals ⇜

Acknowledgments 🦢

I acknowledge with gratitude my creative mentors, who have inspired my life and work. They are the feminine face of God to me.

Carla De Sola, liturgical dancer and gentle healer, facilitated the release of my childhood memories through movement, dance, and sacred drama. As a result of her healing work, my creativity began to unthaw. In the subsequent years I have written, drawn, and danced the creativity of a lifetime. Barbara Lyon, joyful dancer and wise crone-guide, taught me to dance toward wholeness through her life and work. By her example, I am learning to celebrate the accumulation of my years and wisdom, and to honor the changes in my body and life. Jean Hauser, skillful therapist and guide, was my first escort into the rich reservoir of healing images within me. She taught me to trust my inner life, to discern its intricate design, and to listen to its healing truth. Many of the meditations, prayers, and stories in this book have as their source the creative reservoir untapped in our work together.

I acknowledge with gratitude the women of the Open Windows Community, who accompanied me through every stage of the writing process. Many of their stories appear in the book.

The Bible I read daily as a child, adolescent, and young adult was filled with men's words, stories, and interpretations of the divine. As I have interacted daily with women's stories, their words have become an alternative Scripture to me. Immersed in the truth of women's lives, I have received the courage to bring more of my own forgotten stories out of the silence. Together we have freed ourselves from the crippling effects of religious myths. Together we have reclaimed our original goodness, power, and divinity. Thank you, dear women, for sharing your stories and lives with me. Many readers will be blessed by your words. Thanks, too, for your practical support along the way—meals on my doorstep, rituals to encourage me in challenging moments, careful readings of the manuscript, and wise feedback at every stage of the book's evolution.

I acknowledge with gratitude the male professors, priests, and ministers of my early years.

This book was born out of the talents, skills, and rebellion inspired by these men. They groomed me to be articulate and persuasive, and yet there was no room for me in their religious world except as wife or assistant. Only the boys could be world changers. So in the roundabout way that life works, they co-created the book with me. They instigated my rebellious search for a God who would support me to take my rightful place beside men, naming my own gods, designing my own life, and expressing my gifts fully in the world. I wish them well across the distance of years and divergent life paths.

I acknowledge with gratitude the support of my beloved friends and family, who have consistently anointed my wounds, listened to my frustrations, and celebrated my gifts.

Daily I heard their words of support. Daily I was inspired by their courage to step across thresholds into the unknown of unfamiliar challenges and uncharted creative, financial, and vocational adventures. Daily I am filled with gratitude for our friendships. Thank you, Sharon, Allen, and Douglas Vandegrift; Erin, Moizee, and Savoi Stewart; Maggie Sasha Rose and Michael Smith; The Middleton Clan; Wendy and Richard Barry; Karen Schneitz; Ferrel Rao; Sharyn Peterson; Ginny Logan; Mary Kapper; Karen Heide; and Carolyn Edwards.

I acknowledge with gratitude the support of Ballantine Books and my editor, Cheryl D. Woodruff.

Our contact has been challenging and productive. I have grown and deepened as an author through our creative partnership. I appreciate that they listened to my suggestions and welcomed my participation in every aspect of the book's unfolding. I appreciate their commitment to finding "middle spaces" that worked for all of us.

I acknowledge with gratitude the support of my agents Ling Lucas and Ed Vesneski, Jr.

I appreciate their ongoing belief in my work and gifts, their skillful navigation of the twists and turns of publishing, and their wise feedback and guidance. I celebrate the growth of their business. How fortunate are those of us who have found our way to Nine Muses & Apollo!

A God Who Looks Like Me

*Discovering a
Woman-Affirming
Spirituality*

Introduction

Beginning Our Journey

> Our search for a God who looks like us begins in our own lives. She will be found there.
>
> —Patricia Lynn Reilly

Whether shouted at women in the religious institutions of their childhoods or whispered to them in the culture, the religious words and images of Father God, of judgment and punishment, of unworthiness and shame, of a sinful Eve and an obedient Mary linger in women's memories. Whether recited weekly in Sabbath School or experienced daily in the design of their parents' relationship, the religious myths of the exclusively male God, of Original Sin, and of the necessity of a male savior are deeply ingrained within women's lives. These remnants of our religious past pursue us into adulthood and interfere with the development of a self-defined spirituality. In the company of women, our imaginations will be freed from the crippling effects of these childhood myths and our courage will be awakened as we name our own gods and design our own woman-affirming spirituality.

A God Who Looks Like Me: Discovering a Woman-Affirming Spirituality is not a theological argument nor an intellectual discussion. Spirituality, by its very nature, flows from our lives and stories and is spoken in our own voices, not those of theologians or other "experts." The stories of women will play a critical role in our explorations. We cannot explore our religious past or develop a personal spirituality apart from our stories. Even the most abstract interpretations of religion are rooted in the life experience of those who are doing the interpreting. Since most of these interpreters were men, their explanations have very little to do with our lives as women. Women's stories challenge and redefine religion from a woman's perspective.

A Personal Story

Several strands of my own personal story are woven into the explorations in this book. It has been necessary for me to pay close attention to my religious background. I have experienced the impact of religion in every aspect of my unfolding life.

I believe that we hold every memory, impression, image, word, event, and formative belief of childhood within us. Nothing has been lost or forgotten. For years I ignored the past in order to get on with my life. In college I reclaimed my full birth name, Patricia, in an attempt to distance myself from "Patty" and the first twelve years of "her" life. Nevertheless my past kept insisting on being acknowledged through unexplained seizures that erupted from the depths of my childhood pain, and through disturbing eating binges that threatened to swallow my present life. Eventually I had no choice but to acknowledge my past's continued presence within me and to listen to its stories.

I choose to call the aspect of myself who remembers the early years "The Girl-Child I Once Was." She has been a faithful companion on the journey into my religious past. She has given me access to the names, images, and understandings of traditional religion that were deposited within her heart, body, and memory. In an effort to retrieve more of the stories of childhood, I wrote the piece below. It is titled "Wish as Hard as I May, Wish as Hard as I Might, God Didn't Change Daddy Tonight."

> Mommy is different. She seems happier. She reads to us from a Bible storybook filled with pictures—Moses at the burning bush, Moses parting the Red Sea, Jesus with the little children, Jesus flying up to heaven. I like the pictures. Kind people pick us up on Sunday mornings to take us to church. Mommy is a Christian now and says things will be different. One day we went to her new church. She was dressed in a white

robe. The minister dunked her in a pool of water. I was afraid. Was she going to die? And then he lifted her out of the water. She had a big smile on her face and she was all wet. I wish my daddy would change. He is mean and drunk and he hurts Mommy. I wish the God they talk about, the one in the Bible, would change my daddy. He needs more changing than my mommy does. I don't think God hears my wishes.

My mother was "led to Christ" by a co-worker at a Los Angeles hospital in the early 1950s. My father's alcoholism and our violent family situation remained untouched by religion. My parents eventually divorced. Mother learned to drive, packed up my younger sister and me, and drove us cross-country to settle with her family in New Jersey. After a year the pressures of her life plunged Mother into the throes of her own alcoholism. One day my sister and I were taken away from her and placed in a children's shelter, and then several months later we were put into a Catholic orphanage.

There I received my First Holy Communion and attended daily Mass. I was confirmed, catechized, and immersed in pre–Vatican II Catholicism by the Sisters of St. Joseph. This is where I met Mary, the Queen of Heaven. She was the one I prayed to if a friend was sick ("Make her better, Mary"). Or if thoughts of my long-lost father crowded by mind ("Protect my daddy, Mary"). Or if I wanted some hope that I would see my mother again ("Please bring us together again soon, Mary"). For me Mary was healer and protector. She worked miracles for those who loved her. It was clear to me that Mary was God, or at least equal to the King of heaven. But the nuns and priests kept telling me she wasn't. She was the mother of God, they said, not Mother God. There is a difference, they assured me.

My sister and I lived in this self-contained Catholic community for several years, rarely venturing out into the world except for monthly visits into the homes of Catholic families who sponsored us, or to the homes of relatives—motivated by either kindness or guilt—who found out about our plight. My mother, newly recovered from alcoholism, settled in Newark, New Jersey, where she found comfort and support among a loving group of people in a Protestant church. After my graduation from eighth grade Mary worked her miracle, and my sister and I were released from the orphanage into our mother's care. This time we moved from our self-contained Catholic community in rural New Jersey to the big city. There we were expected to attend my mother's Protestant church. It became our next surrogate family.

They never talked about Mary at Calvary Gospel Church except at Christmas. She was the young girl who gave birth to Jesus. After his birth she was seldom mentioned in the Protestant Bible. It was God the father who was King of Kings and Lord of Lords in our new church. And he had no queen, only handmaidens. I had to go into hiding with my love and devotion to Mary. Other things were confusing as well. According to the teaching of the nuns, all Protestants were going to hell, and now the Protestants sought to convince us that it was the Catholics who were damned.

I finally figured out what I had to do to be accepted into this new religious community, and I "asked Jesus into my heart." Born again at age twelve, I was taught to go out and convert the world, and I became active in church youth groups, prayer meetings, and open-air evangelism. God was my loving and demanding father. I was under his care and sought his direction through daily Bible reading and prayer.

I attended a Christian college atop Lookout Mountain, Tennessee. Returning to Newark after graduation, I worked as Director of Religious Education at my home church. My recovery journey began during this time. Engaged to a recovering alcoholic, I attended Al-Anon so that I could better understand him and his needs. I was not aware of my own need for healing and recovery. A binge eater from orphanage days, my eating spun out of control after we were married. When our marriage ended after three years, I attended daily Al-Anon meetings. In the Twelve Step program, I found the Christian version of God. The Our Father, a Christian prayer, was said at the close of most meetings. The "God" of recovery was very familiar to me. I had no trouble turning my life and will over to "him."

In transition after the divorce, I enrolled in Princeton Seminary. It was here that my healing journey in Adult Children of Alcoholics began. The Al-Anon of my married years had not touched the wounds of my childhood. It offered support to the spouses of alcoholics. Since that time, however, Al-Anon has recognized the particular needs of adult children of alcoholics and developed a program of support for us. At the same time, Overeaters Anonymous gave me the tools of self-care that I had not received in my childhood. Its suggested food plan freed me to "show up for my life" and to deal with the feelings that surfaced as more and more of my childhood memories emerged.

My studies at Princeton initiated my search for a God who looks like me. Mary had been effectively dethroned in early adolescence. And yet her memory was awakened one day as a professor explained to us the meaning of "inclusive language," a term I was unfamiliar with. He reminded us of our earliest lessons about God; that God was a Spirit and could not be contained within any one image. He suggested that we experiment with alternate names and images of God and listed a few, including "Mother God."

This was a revolutionary suggestion to me. It launched me on the first phase of my journey toward the feminine face of God. I became suspicious of all I had been taught in religion's name. I wrestled with the names and images of God, the stories and myths of traditional religion, and the concepts of sin, savior, and salvation that had permeated my religious past and that pursued me into adulthood. While sorting through this religious baggage, I began to view the recovery program through the lens of my own unfolding spirituality.

After receiving my master's degree from Princeton, I worked at Boston City Hospital in a chaplaincy program and then studied at the Women's Theological Center in Boston. Inspired by the courageous women I studied among in Boston, I created personal rituals and meditations in which I imagined a Woman God who looked, felt, and experienced life as I did. Her image reached lovingly into the depths of my self-hatred. She coaxed my incest memories out of hiding. She awakened my anger. For a time I even left the Church, angry at God the father, angry that my reality had been denied, angry that God had protected my drunken father while all along I had tried to be such a good daughter to both.

As I gathered together the fragments of my own forgotten story, I began to search out the stories of women in my religious past. It became apparent to me that recovery involved both retrieving my personal stories from their hiding places within the family memory, and retrieving the collective story of women from the margins of history and religion. I wove each of my discoveries into rituals, performance pieces, retreats, workshops, and sermons. I traveled throughout the United States and Canada telling the untold stories of women to circles of women. As the women of old—Eve, Lilith, Mary, The Divine Girl-Child, The One Who Shed Her Blood, The Wounded Healers, and The Wise Old Woman—extricated their stories from the all-encompassing story of the male God, modern women received the courage to tell their own untold stories.

In circles of women I have searched for and found a God who looks like me. In circles of women I have come to love and accept myself as a woman. In a circle of women I made the decision not to be ordained as a minister within the Church. Instead I chose to facilitate spiritual community among women. I offer a variety of support services, including weekly spirituality and recovery groups, monthly retreats, spiritual-growth facilitation, and ongoing support in times of crisis and celebration. In addition I am committed to an ongoing conversation with the religious and recovery communities. Through my work I remind these communities of the stories of women they have neglected to tell and of the truth of a woman's life that they have not acknowledged in their principles and theologies.

It is this personal story, permeated with intense trouble and surprising resources, that has given birth to my work among women. My commitment is to offer all women an opportunity to sort through their religious past on the way to creating a self-defined, woman-affirming spirituality. *A God Who Looks Like Me* was born out of that commitment.

Telling Our Stories in Community

Woven into this book are the stories of women who have attended the workshops and retreats I facilitate and with whom I have worked regularly as a spiritual-growth facilitator. Their stories unfolded during a three-month-to-one-year communal exploration of the materials included in this book. Our community continues to build and deepen at Circle of Life Women's Center through weekly small-group meetings, monthly potlucks and healing rituals, and periodic retreats. We support each other in crisis, questioning, celebration, and healing. We have become the feminine face of God to each other.

The women range in age from twenty-five to fifty-five. They are

African-American, Asian-American, and European-American. Among them are hairstylists, computer programmers, child-care providers, teachers, secretaries, graduate-school students, and drug counselors. They are mothers, grandmothers, single, partnered, married, lesbian, and straight. Their childhood religious backgrounds include: Catholic, Lutheran, Jewish, Methodist, Baptist, and Buddhist. Some have no formal background at all in religion; its images and stories were whispered to them in the culture.

The women whose stories you will read share a common commitment to acknowledging the truth of their personal history as it relates to the communal history of women. They have sorted through the lingering religious images and stories that reside within their memory and have developed a woman-affirming spirituality that flows from their experience, strength, and hope.

They have given permission for their stories to be used in the book. I have not censored these stories in the editing process, nor have I interpreted their stories in the text. I believe that the simple act of storytelling is deeply healing. Much as we do in a women's support group, a self-help meeting, or a counselor's office, each of us will "show up and tell the truth" of our lives on these pages. We trust that you will receive the courage to bring your own forgotten stories out of the silence as we journey together.

An Overview of the Book

A God Who Looks Like Me provides a clear overview of the religious baggage women bring with them into adulthood and a practical guide to sorting through this baggage. You are invited to discard what is harmful and to use what is woman-affirming in your unfolding spirituality. The book is arranged in four sections.

The Introduction, "Beginning Our Journey," lays the groundwork for the exploration of our religious past and the development of a woman-affirming spirituality.

Part I: Women's Religious Past

Chapter 1, "Religion's Far-Reaching Effects," examines the influence of religion on our cultural, familial, and personal histories. There was no way to escape religion's pervasive influence in our childhoods and its ongoing influence in our lives today.

In chapter 2, "Reluctance, Anger, and Courage," you will be invited to join a circle of women as they gather their earliest religious memories. In one another's courageous company we will acknowledge the full range of feelings triggered by the journey into our religious past.

Part II: Religious Language and Imagery

In part II we will examine the religious language and imagery of childhood. We had no choice, the God of our childhood was male. Until he is examined, we are not free to name and imagine a God of *our* understanding. Once he has been examined, however, we are free to choose which aspects of the God of our religious past we will weave into our unfolding spirituality. God the father becomes one among many potentially healing images.

In chapter 3, "The God of Our Childhood Understanding," we will examine the power of language and imagination. We will inventory the names and images of God that were imprinted on our childhood imaginations.

In chapter 4, "Our Wounds and Ineffective Behaviors: Exclusion, Inferiority, and Dependency," we will come to a clearer understanding of the relationship between our religious past and the ineffective behaviors that we struggle with today. We will inventory the wounds and ineffective behaviors that result from an immersion in male names and images of the divine.

In chapter 5, "Our Healing: The Changing Face of God," we will develop woman-affirming alternatives to the traditional language of religion. We will name and imagine the God of *our* understanding. We will inventory the healing resources available to us as we honor the changing face of God in our personal experience.

Part III: Religious Myths and Stories

Part III is a journey into the truth of a woman's life, beginning with her birth, traveling through the creation myths and symbols that have shaped her, venturing into her body's unfolding cycles and rhythms, exploring her connections to other women, and confronting the fear of aging that accompanies her throughout life. It includes women's stories found within the Hebrew and Christian traditions, stories that were passed over in the Sunday schools, Hebrew schools, and catechism classes of our childhoods.

The arrangement of the stories is designed to confront specific religious and cultural taboos that surround the unfolding of a woman's life. Familiarity with the particular stories is not essential. You will recognize the themes. They were woven into the teachings you received from family, religion, and society. Inspired by these women's stories, we will move beyond the taboos to reclaim our bodies, to rediscover our spiritual center, and to creatively reinvent the old myths.

In chapter 6, "Fragments of the Forgotten," we will acknowledge the absence of women's stories from the religious history we were taught. I will outline the "Gathering the Fragments" process through which we reclaim women's stories from the margins of religion and history and rewrite the old stories from a woman's perspective.

In chapters 7 and 8, our mythic mothers Eve: The Mother of All Living and Lilith: The Rebellious First Woman, guide our exploration of the creation myths of traditional religion and their crippling effects on generations of women's lives. We are empowered to embrace both our capacity to nurture and to exert, and to create woman-affirming myths and meditations that heal.

In chapter 9, Mary, The Virgin Mother guides our exploration of Christianity's distorted images of womanhood, in which passivity and chastity became the sole ideals of the feminine. We are empowered to reclaim our autonomy and our sexuality, and to move from dependency to self-directedness.

In chapter 10, The Divine Girl-Child guides our exploration of the factors that surround a woman's birth and her reception into a world that prefers men. We are empowered to celebrate our birth and to offer ourselves nurturing self-care.

In chapter 11, The One Who Shed Her Blood guides our exploration of the religious taboos that surround a woman's body and her natural processes. We are empowered to celebrate our beautiful blood and to join with other women in a healing community.

In chapter 12, The Wounded Healers, Tamar and The One Who Was Cut into Pieces, guide us in our exploration of sexual harassment, rape, and incest, and of the religious factors that contribute to sexual violence against women. We are empowered to reclaim our bodies and to shout out the truth.

In chapter 13, The Wise Old Woman guides us in our exploration of the disempowering religious and cultural attitudes surrounding the aging process of women. We are empowered to reclaim our inner wisdom and "to imagine into being" woman-affirming communities.

Part IV: Having Had a Spiritual Awakening

In parts I, II, and III, we explore our immersion in a religion and society that worship a male God. We descend into its language and imagery. We become critical of all that we were taught. We wrestle with old ways of believing and being. We exorcise harmful images. We plant new experiences, images, and stories in the ground of our self-defined spirituality.

Yet our personal transformation is only the beginning of the journey. The ultimate salvation of the world depends upon a coming together of the masculine and feminine, offering their combined strength, wisdom, and compassion in the service of humankind. In part IV we will gather the gifts of our journey through our religious past and bring them into our present relationships.

In chapter 14, "Awakened to Healthy Connections," we will explore the effects of a woman-affirming spirituality on our relationships with our male lovers, colleagues, and friends.

In chapter 15, "Awakened to a Woman-Affirming Spirituality," we will celebrate our awakening to the perspectives of a woman-affirming spirituality.

Entering the Book

Circles of Support

Throughout the book you will be invited to join circles of support in the three ways suggested below. As you read, choose the approach that's most comfortable for you, or create your own.

1. A VICARIOUS JOURNEY: AN EXPLORATION FROM A SAFE DISTANCE

Some of you will want to read through the book from cover to cover without interruption. With this approach imagine that you're reading the book from a safe distance, exploring your religious past vicariously through the experiences of others. The exercises will be optional. Read through them as if they were simply text. If one strikes your fancy, experiment with it.

2. A SUPPORTIVE JOURNEY: STORIES OF EXPERIENCE, STRENGTH, AND HOPE

Imagine that you're at a self-help meeting or a women's support circle. A topic will be introduced and then a circle of women will share their experience, strength, and hope with you. Allow their memories to touch your own forgotten stories. Consider using highlighters to mark those stories or pieces of stories in the text that give voice to your own. You will then be invited to join the circle with the words, "Imagine sitting in a circle with . . ." Add your story to theirs by sharing it with a friend or by writing it in your journal. You will be offered a series of questions to guide your reflection. If the questions are helpful, use them. If they are not, trust your own "Deep Wisdom" to guide the exploration.

3. AN IMAGINATIVE JOURNEY: A SACRED MEETING WITH THE CHILD YOU ONCE WERE

We hold our childhoods within us. Nothing has been lost or forgotten. Many of us try to ignore the past, considering it irrelevant to our adult life. And yet the past makes itself known in troubling physical symptoms, persistent ineffective behaviors, broken relationships, and repetitive difficulties. Some women find it helpful to imagine this repository of childhood memory as a bundle labeled "Childhood." The bundle contains every memory, impression, image, word, event, and formative belief. Through our work together they open the bundle and explore its contents.

Others call the aspect of themselves that remembers the early years The Girl-Child I Once Was. She becomes a healing image that facilitates access to their childhood memories. Women embark on a healing adventure with her. They invite her to tell the stories of childhood.

Some of you may want to use this work as an opportunity to become acquainted with more of the stories of your childhood. As you work through the reflections and explorations of the book, set up an imaginative meeting place with The Child You Once Were. Invite her to meet you in a favorite, safe place you remember from childhood: under the dining-room table, in a special tree, at the beach, or sitting beside a creek or stream. Imagine sitting in this comfortable spot with her. It is here that you will engage in a series of conversations through drawing and writing in your journal. Together you will travel through your "religious past," guided by the "Before Moving On . . ." exercises included at the end of each chapter. If the bundle image is more helpful, imagine a special place in which you sort through the bundle labeled "Religious Past."

Consider writing and drawing with your nondominant hand as you respond to the reflections and exercises. This technique is quite helpful in accessing childhood memories because it helps you bypass the judgment, criticism, and resistance of the adult. Experiment with the technique. Those who do are delighted with the results. The child part of you has much to say. Her voice will become familiar to you over time; you will recognize it as the voice of The Child You Once Were.[1]

Pillows of Support

The week after I began writing this book, I sat at my computer and was unable to work. Rather than berate myself, I listened to the resistant part of me. An anxious voice emerged. Through a written dialogue with "The Anxious One" it became clear that the level of focus and attention required of the writing project was overwhelming me. I asked The Anxious One how I might support her. I began setting up "pillows of support" around my life in order to go the distance with the creative project.

My first commitment was to weekly bodywork. I wrote a check for the first month's sessions to assure the anxious part of me that I was serious about attending to its needs. Each day I checked in with The Anxious One: "Now may I go back to work?" No, was the clear response.

The second pillow of support was a weekly meeting with a group of women writers. We offered each other encouragement and feedback. I checked in again: still not enough support.

My third pillow was to take two full days off every week as a reminder that my life was wider than the writing project. As I assembled this rich assortment of pillows, the anxious part of me eventually relaxed. Three weeks later I returned to my writing tasks without effort.

Inventory the pillows of support that surround your life as you enter into the essential explorations of this book. You deserve support in your life. Joyce's inventory included: regular massage, walks in nature, good food, and weekly self-help meetings. Irene's list included: phone contact with supportive friends, time in her garden, stretching her body, breathing deeply, and music to shift her mood.

There are pillows of support that will make these explorations more comfortable for you. Surround yourself with them. They include:

- A journal-sketchpad
- A special place in which to engage in this work
- A regular time to turn toward the work
- A method for acknowledging any feelings that may surface while you read
- A circle of women to meet with regularly to share the insights and memories that will come up for you

Each of these pillows is described as follows.

A JOURNAL-SKETCHPAD

You will need a journal-sketchpad in which to keep a record of the memories and insights that will be triggered by our work together. Include articles you may read; poems, sermons, or essays you may write; images that may surface; and photographs you may have from your childhood. A First Holy Communion or Bas Mitzvah picture can usually be found in the family archives. If you plan to use this work to get in touch with childhood memories, create a special journal for the writings and drawings of The Girl-Child You Once Were. As you remember her stories, try writing or drawing them with your nondominant hand.

WRITING, DRAWING, DANCING, AND SCULPTING

For some women writing opens the door to memory, feeling, and insight. It empowers them to access and express their own unique voice. Use this book as a meditation. Let it offer you time and space to become quiet enough to hear your inner voice. Write down what you hear. Over time you will become attuned to the voice.

Follow the path that opens through your writing. Perhaps your words will lead you to an image. Try drawing it. This image may lead you to a family album. Spend time with it. And these pictures in turn may lead you to write a letter or create a dance. On and on it goes, an adventure in self-discovery orchestrated by a deep wisdom within you. This is the way writing helps you release old memories and images and gives you the gift of deepening intimacy with yourself.

Words are not the only means of accessing memory, feeling, and insight. For some, drawing, movement/dance, drama, and sculpting facilitate the expression of their inner voice. These expressive arts move us beneath the words. They bypass the barriers we sometimes erect with our words as a defense against feeling and memory. Feel free to engage in the exercises and reflections in whatever way works best for you. Draw your memories. Dance your anger. Sculpt your wounds. Color your healing. Suggestions for creative expression are provided throughout the text.

A SACRED PLACE

As women we have been taught to shape and maintain spaces for others. Here you're invited to create a sacred space for yourself. Susan created a safe and comfortable space in the corner of her home office. She hung her own works of art on the walls. She added comfortable pillows. This is where she retreats to read, to write, and to meditate. Jen's "room of her own" is a transformed garage in which she paints, writes, dances, and meditates. Find your own safe space. Bring along a candle, a pitcher of water, a bowl, and your own unique symbols of your spiritual search into your space. Their purpose will become clear as you move through the book.

A SACRED TIME

As women we have been taught to make time for others. Here you're invited to set aside sacred time for yourself. Susan carved out thirty minutes a day as her sacred time. She allowed nothing short of an emergency to intrude. Her family respected her commitment to herself and learned ways to work out the difficulties they thought only Mommy could handle.

As you journey through this book, surround each reading and meditation experience with silence. Take your time. Plan to spend at least two weeks on each chapter—three weeks if you're working with a group. Read through each chapter at a steady pace the first time. Then go back and enter more fully into the resources that move you.

FEELINGS AS COMPANIONS

Throughout the book I continually invite you to confront old images, to challenge unexamined core beliefs, and to wrestle with the language and images, stories and myths, of your childhood religion. These tasks require gentle attentiveness to all the feelings that may surface. Use the process outlined below with your feelings. Resistance, anxiety, anger, and fear are likely to surface. Instead of resenting these feelings as intruders, embrace them as friends and faithful companions with important information to share with you.

• As a feeling surfaces breathe into it without judgment. Allow your breath to massage the feeling and to help you acknowledge it.

• Imagine the feeling to be a friend. Invite it to have tea with you. Give the feeling a voice through words or images. Dialogue with it in your journal. Listen to its concerns. Ask it, "Anxious One . . . , Fearful One . . . , Resistant One . . . , Angry One . . . , how might I support you?"

• Speak about your feelings with the women in your support group or in a conversation with a friend, sponsor, or therapist. Choose someone who doesn't categorize feelings as good or bad. Ask them to witness your feelings without trying to talk you out of them or make you feel better.

• If you choose to use this work as an opportunity to get acquainted with The Child You Once Were, allow the historic feelings that are unlocked through our work together to be expressed in drawings and writings with your nondominant hand.

A Circle of Women

If possible, invite a group of women to join you in this study. It is in such circles of women that we search for and find a God who looks like us. It is in circles of women that we come to love and accept ourselves as women. It is in circles of women that we are empowered to develop a woman-affirming spirituality. In addition the group offers an ongoing forum within which to share what you learn. It will also encourage you to maintain your commitment to the exploration.

Choose no more than six participants, women you trust and with whom you can be creative, questioning, and open-minded. Choose women who will commit to weekly two-hour meetings for six to nine months. Each member of the group will be invited to incorporate the chapter readings into her daily meditation and reflection time, if possible.

Most women's lives are so full that "homework" between meetings is an unrealistic expectation. Set aside time in each group meeting for reading the appropriate chapter or section of a chapter. It's best to spend at least two weeks on each chapter in parts I, II, and IV, and three weeks on each chapter in part III. Rotate the role of facilitator, whose responsibility it will be to divide the chapter into weekly portions to be read and worked through.

Keep the guidelines simple:

• Attendance: In order for trust to develop, a commitment to regular attendance is essential.
• Confidentiality: What you hear in the group stays in the group.
• Schedule: Make every effort to begin and end each meeting on time.

Keep the format simple:

1. Begin with the Serenity Prayer:

God (*Allow time for each woman to call aloud the name of the God of her understanding: Goddess, Creative Spirit, Inner Voice*) . . . grant me the serenity to accept the things I cannot change, the courage to change the things I can, and the wisdom to know the difference.

2. Follow the prayer with a three-minute check-in. Invite each participant to share whatever she brings to the circle that evening: celebration of a project completed, frustration over an unresolved conflict with a partner or friend, anxiety about an upcoming event. Sharing in this way allows you to acknowledge and then let go of the past and the future. It frees you to be fully present to receive the challenge, support, insight, and healing available to you in this moment (total time: twenty minutes).

3. Read through each section aloud or silently as decided upon by the group (twenty minutes).

4. Allow time for personal writing and/or drawing in response to the reading (twenty minutes).

5. Come together again. Each woman will add her story to those shared in the text. Allow sixty minutes for this sharing. In order for each woman to have the opportunity to share, you'll need a timekeeper. If there are six women in your group, each will have ten minutes to share. You might want to rotate the role of timekeeper.

Allow each woman to share her feelings and stories without interruption. This "no cross-talk" approach supports us as we learn to take responsibility for ourselves and to respect each other's sacred journey. Witness and acknowledge each woman's story in silence. The healing power of respectful listening is astounding. See what comes up for you as you attempt to "just listen" to each other. Eventually, after trust has developed, encourage each woman to ask for specific feedback if she wants it.

6. End with a prayer. Practice the inclusive prayers and meditations as you are introduced to them in the book. Or use a meaningful prayer that emerges from your own individual or group experience.

PART I ❧

Women's Religious Past

CHAPTER ONE 🙠

Religion's Far-Reaching Effects

> Whatever the condition of the Church at this point in
> history, we cannot afford to ignore or dismiss lightly the
> far-reaching effects that centuries of Church power
> continue to have on each of us today, no matter how
> far removed we may be from the actual pulpit or altar.
> —Merlin Stone, *When God Was a Woman*

Religion powerfully affects every aspect of a woman's unfolding life. It's impossible to fully understand our personal past if we don't acknowledge and explore the religious reality that shaped us.

Religion pursues us across the centuries of our cultural history. The God of Abraham, Isaac, and Jacob; the triune God of Christianity; the Hebrew Scriptures and the Christian Bible; and the myths, stories, and rituals of religion are deeply ingrained in every aspect of the American social fabric. Our own personal stories are shaped and directed by the history, culture, and taboos of the world in which we live. It is impossible to extricate our personal story from the wider story of all women's lives.

Religion pursues us across the decades of our family history in the design of our parents' relationship and in the attitudes, lessons, and expectations that surrounded us in childhood. Many of the life patterns, gender attitudes, and family customs that our families took for granted have their roots in the words, stories, and myths of religion. There was no way to escape religion's pervasive influence in our childhoods.

Religion pursues us into the days and moments of our personal history. We carry the language and images of traditional religion with us into adulthood long after we may have discarded a particular set of religious beliefs. Engraved within the wounds and ineffective behaviors that trouble us as adults are the life patterns, gender attitudes, and family customs rooted in our religious past.

Religion's Influence On Our Family of Origin

> It is the rare family that can trace back beyond two or
> three generations and not find that their predecessors were
> deeply immersed in the attitudes and values of one of
> the male-oriented religions. It is for this reason that
> religious pressures are not as far from us as we might prefer
> to think.
>
> —Merlin Stone, *When God Was a Woman*

During the 1940s and 1950s when most of the women I've worked with were children, religion's influence was pervasive and its importance was not questioned. The stories I have gathered—both from those who had religion shouted at them in a church, and from those who were certain religion had no effect on their upbringing—reflect common social customs, family patterns, and gender attitudes clearly rooted in our collective religious past. Through our work together women become conscious of the roots of the customs, patterns, and attitudes that have encircled them from birth. Each of these patterns will be addressed in greater detail later on. Here we will simply acknowledge their presence in our families.[1]

The women whose stories you will read share a common commitment to unearthing childhood memories, attending to childhood wounds and their influence on the present, and learning to make healthy choices based on their deepening commitment to themselves and to their children. Many of the stories included here will echo throughout the book in fuller form.

There were no religious rituals in the churches or synagogues of our childhood that celebrated the birthing powers of women. According to religion's myths, the world was brought into being by a male God, and woman was created from man. In a society that worships a male God, the father's life is more valuable than the mother's. Fathers are superior in every way. Mothers are not to threaten his superiority.

> We kids wanted Mom to get out of the house. She was so bored. We encouraged her to get a job. Her excuse was always the same. "It would hurt your father's ego if I went to work."
>
> —Susan

> Our mother was smarter and stronger than Dad. This was something we were not to acknowledge because everyone knows dads are supposed to be smarter and stronger than moms. We all had to pretend, including Mom. She had to pretend she didn't know what she knew, and that she couldn't do what she could do. No wonder she ate all the time.
>
> —Jen

There were no religious rituals in the churches or synagogues of our childhood that celebrated the birth of the girl-child. According to religion's myths and customs, the birth of the boy-child was honored. The sign of the covenant—circumcision—was for boys only. In a society that worships a male God, sons are more important than daughters. Boys are groomed to administer the world. Girls are groomed to attract and take care of men.

> As a child, I had a keen sense of being on the sidelines. My appropriate place was as a passive observer. I was expected to be ladylike. I was constantly compared to my male cousins who were around my age. They weren't any more accomplished than I was, yet the conversations in our house focused on them. It was their accomplishments that were stressed. My sisters and I were not as important in comparison.
>
> —Liz

> I was groomed to be a man's sexual object, as well as to do his cooking and cleaning. As a mother, I passed this "grooming" on to my daughters. They were expected

> to do the heavy cleaning. My son was taken care of by
> the women in the house. The girls were to pay
> attention to their weight and appearance in a way I
> never expected of him. I encouraged the girls' romantic
> lives by continually asking about boyfriends. I felt they
> should have a man in their life, that to be without
> one was to be incomplete.
>
> —Teresa

There were no religious rituals in the churches or synagogues of our childhood that celebrated the flowing of a woman's blood. According to religion's myths and customs, the blood of sacrificed animals was ceremonialized and the blood of a male savior was honored. In a society that worships a male God, the boy-child looks like God. His resemblance to the divine affords him power and privilege. The girl-child's body and natural processes are "other" than God. She is a "misbegotten male" and the shame of her "otherness" accompanies her throughout life.

> The sense of the world around me was: Let's keep it clean,
> sanitized, and hidden away. The stuff of a woman's life
> isn't acceptable.
>
> —Karen

> Making it through my first period was a great
> accomplishment. No one explained anything to me. My
> mother just said, "Here," and handed me the box of
> Tampax. Becoming a woman was about unpleasant-
> ness and secrecy.
>
> —Emily

Images of strong, self-contained women were exiled from the religious history we were taught. Images of passive women were elevated as the ideals to emulate. In a society that worships a male God, outspoken and independent men are applauded. Outspoken and independent women are called names and ostracized.

> My great aunt never married. She had a mind of her own
> and was considered off her rocker by the rest of the

family. I wasn't allowed to spend too much time with her. They didn't want me to follow in her footsteps. But she was the happiest woman in the family, so why wouldn't I want to be like her?

—Teresa

In my family, and in the Catholic Church, there were powerful prevailing opinions that could never be challenged. These were the opinions of my father and the male God of Catholicism. I remember, even with peers, remaining silent until I could sense the thoughts of others. Only then would I venture forth with an opinion that wouldn't rock the boat. Girls seldom risked an original thought or opinion. We were followers, not originators.

—Sharyn

Traditional religion's elevation of a male God condones men's sexual access to their wives and children. Images of sexually autonomous women were exiled from the religious history we were taught. Images of chaste, submissive women were elevated as the ideals to emulate. In a society that worships a male God, the boy-child's body is subject to uncontrollable sexual urges. The girl-child's body is vulnerable to these urges from birth. "Boys will be boys" even when they grow up and marry. Girls had better be virgins before marriage and faithful to their husbands in marriage.

In adolescence my mother was fearful about the possibility of my "sleeping around." She would drop hints like: "Men like virgins better." I'm sure my brother never heard that. And during the time when my brother was living with a woman, my mother referred to her as a 'slut' because she was sleeping with him 'out of wedlock.' She never referred to my brother in that way. Her standards were not equal. In her eyes, influenced by the Church, a woman's body was subject to much harsher scrutiny and judgment than a man's.

—Annette

> In childhood, when my brother and I drove with my father,
> he made comments about women walking down the street.
> He talked about their bodies, picking them up, and
> how to flirt. These were the lessons he gave my
> brother about relating to women. When I brought it up
> to my mother because I felt it was wrong, she defended
> my father. According to her, it was normal male
> behavior to objectify women as he did. 'Men can't
> help themselves. It's up to us not to arouse them,' she
> told me.
>
> —Mary

There were no religious rituals in the churches or synagogues of our childhood that celebrated the coming of the post-reproductive season of a woman's life. According to religion's myths and customs, it was the old men who presided at the sacred rituals of childhood in the home and in the house of God. In a society that worships a male God, the boy-child looks ahead to increased stature and wealth as he ages. The girl-child will be unprepared to grow old, and she will dread it.

> I fear the isolation and the rejection that seem to go along
> with growing old as a woman. My mother serviced everyone
> around her and yet did not prepare a future for
> herself. She was dismissed and ignored by our family
> and the world as she aged. The opposite was true of our
> dad. He became more influential as he got older.
>
> —Joan

Long after we discard a particular set of religious beliefs, these disempowering customs, patterns, and attitudes linger in our self-concept and contribute to the ineffective behaviors that bring us into a woman's support group, a self-help meeting, or a counselor's office. Whether we considered our family to be religious or not, the pervasive influence of religion in our formative years cannot be ignored. As you read through the book, the connections between your religious past and the wounds and ineffective behaviors that trouble you as an adult will become clear.

Religion's Influence On Our Lives Today

> The reason for the continuing effects of religious symbols
> is that the mind is uncomfortable with a vacuum. Symbol
> systems cannot simply be rejected, they must be replaced.
> Where there is no replacement, the mind will revert
> to familiar structures at times of crisis, bafflement, or defeat.
> —Carol Christ, *Womanspirit Rising*

Many of the women whose stories you will read left the religious institutions and discarded the God of their childhoods long ago. They found their way into the open spaces of spirituality, seeking alternatives to the religion of their childhood. Some explored Eastern religions and experimented with New Age expressions of spirituality. Others joined a Unitarian church, a woman's ritual group, or a Twelve Step meeting. Many of them brought their spiritual questions to a therapist. And yet no matter how far they may have distanced themselves from their history, they carried their religious past onto whatever spiritual path they chose as adults. Nowhere along the way ... in New Age literature, in a woman's support circle, in their therapist's office, or in the recovery community were these women offered the resources to sort through the remnants of their religious past they'd brought with them into adulthood.

New Age Spirituality

Some of the women I work among considered themselves to be New Age seekers who had discarded all remnants of childhood religion. They spent their formative years, however, sitting in Sunday school, catechism class, or Hebrew school. They carry within their lives the indelible imprint of the images and myths of those early religious experiences. And curiously enough the God of their childhood found "his" way into New Age spirituality, bringing with them a confusing blend of the old and the new.

Marianne Williamson's book *A Return to Love* is based on the teachings of "A Course in Miracles," a guide to universal spiritual truths. Many have gravitated to her, looking for an alternative to traditional religion. Along the way they meet once again the Father and the Son they left behind. Consider these passages from her book (italics are mine):

> God created only one begotten Son and *He* loves all of us as one. To *Him*, no one is different or special because no one is separate from any one else.[2]
>
> The issue underlying our need to tell God what to do is our lack of trust. We're afraid to leave things in God's hands because we don't know what *He'll* do with them. We're afraid *He'll* lose our file.[3]

> Whatever spiritual exploration I have engaged in as an adult, I brought the male God of my childhood with me. No matter how clever they may have been to change "his" name to seem more New Agey or inclusive, the image that popped up in my mind's eye was a male God just called by a different name. And some groups didn't even bother to change the name—it was the same old male God reformulated, but still male all the same.
>
> —Teresa

Women's Spirituality

Some of the women I work among have rediscovered an earth-centered spirituality. They used alternative images for the divine in their ritual circles and chants. And yet when they were "on automatic," God remained male to them. The old images had not been exorcised. The male God of their religious past was still as present in their imaginations as he had been in childhood.

Through our work together, however, it became clear to them that the exclusively male image of God had left its imprint on more than their imaginations. Until exorcised, "he" silently affected their lives and relationships, and their presence in the world.

> I claim to have no religious background, and yet when I was asked to fill out a questionnaire about spirituality I kept referring to God as "he." This both surprised

and troubled me. How did "he" get in there? I
considered changing the pronoun to "it" but felt very
uncomfortable with the idea. "He" even shows up
uninvited at my women's circle. The male sense of God
was deeply embedded within me somehow.

—Jane

Psychotherapy

For many women the therapist's office has replaced the confessionals of
childhood. In times of crisis and stress, instead of reaching out to a
minister or rabbi, they call a therapist for an appointment. Once the
initial stress is relieved, their deeper questions often surface. They become aware of a spiritual dimension to life.

Although they sense that religion and spirituality are distinct, they do
not have the words to describe their emerging spirituality apart from
the language of their religious past. They seek the guidance and support
of their therapists to sort through their questions and to develop a personal spirituality.

Many therapists label such questioning as "religious" and steer
women away from their quest. Until beginning this study program,
these women felt lost in the uncharted territory between their religious
past and their present desire for a spiritual connection—with little or
no support from the therapeutic community.

I worked with a counselor for several years who spoke
of God occasionally. She always used "he" to refer to this
God and assumed that this was my understanding as
well. I bristled every time she mentioned "him."

—Susan

The male God of my childhood was a partner in the
dysfunction of my family of origin, and yet when I would
bring "him" up, my counselor would redirect the
discussion away from him. She seemed uncomfortable
with religion. Being a good girl, I never challenged her.

—Jane

The God of the Twelve Step Program

Other women, overwhelmed by their own addiction or caught up in the addiction of another, reached out to the Twelve Step community for assistance. The First Step—"We admitted we were powerless over alcohol and that our lives had become unmanageable,"—was relatively easy for them to acknowledge. It was the unmanageability of their lives that prompted them to seek out a community of support.

The Second Step—"We came to believe that a power greater than ourselves could restore us to sanity"—was harder to accept. Old-time members spoke of "coming to believe" in a God or Higher Power. This "God-talk" triggered their early attitudes, beliefs, and experiences with religion. Images of confessionals and Days of Atonement, pangs of guilt and shame, and the judgmental voices of rabbis and priests welled up within them.

Yet they desperately needed the support of the program, so some of them twisted their God (or absence of God) into the shapes they thought acceptable. They stuffed the religious images of childhood back into the closets of their memory in order to quiet the pangs of guilt and to silence the judgmental voices of old. They mistakenly thought that by ignoring their religious past, they would eventually come to believe in the God espoused by the program. Others left the program unable to "get the God part."

> When I entered Adult Children of Alcoholics and read the Second Step, I was reminded of the early Catholic vision of God, the old father in the clouds with the long white beard and Book of Judgment. This image made me uncomfortable.
>
> —Sharyn

> My response to the "God-talk" of the program was mixed. One part of me was relieved to think I could rely on a power greater than myself. The other part of me was embarrassed to hear members speak of Christianity's God, because it didn't offer me the comfort I yearned for as a child. Its messages were so contradictory.
>
> —Jen

Religion's Influence on Our Original Spirituality

> Some beliefs are like blinders, shutting off the power to
> choose one's own direction. Other beliefs are like gateways
> opening wide vistas for exploration.
> —Sophia Fahs, *It Matters What You Believe*

While at a prayer and meditation retreat I was reminded of a story
about a vibrant child who picked up crayons excitedly on the first day
of school. She filled the paper with flowers of every color. Her drawing
disturbed the teacher, and she asked what the child was doing. "I'm
painting flowers," the child answered. The teacher reprimanded her:
"Flowers are red, and leaves are green. There's no need to see colors any
other way than the way they've always been seen." The child exclaimed,
"Oh, no! There are so many colors in the rainbow . . . so many colors
in the morning sun . . . so many colors in the flowers . . . And I see every one."

The teacher called the child sassy and placed her in the corner with
these words: "There's a way that things should be done. You must draw
flowers in the same colors and shapes that they've always been drawn."
At a time when the child needed encouragement of her vitality, her
voice, and her spirit, she was shamed and ostracized. She was convinced
by her time of isolation that to follow her own impulses is wrong and
that to follow the prescribed formula is right. Frightened and lonely, the
child recanted, parroting the words of her teacher: "Flowers are red, and
leaves are green. There's no need to see flowers any other way than the
way they've always been seen."

Years later the child moved to another school. Her new teacher
said that drawing should be fun, and she began to sing the lyrics from
Harry Chapin's song, "Flowers Are Red": "There are so many colors
in the rainbow, so many colors in the morning sun, so many colors in the flowers. You can use every one!" Unmoved, the child painted
flowers in neat rows of green and red.[4]

In the Very Beginning

In the very beginning of her life the girl-child has direct access to the Spirit of Life. It is as near to her as the breath that fills her. And it connects her to everything. She is not alone. Her spirit is one with the spirit of her beloved grandmother, of her favorite rock, tree, and star. She develops her own special methods for contacting the Spirit in all things.

She climbs a tree and sits in its branches, listening. She loves the woods and listens there too. She has a special friend—a rock. She gives it a name and eats her lunch with it whenever she can. She keeps the window open next to her bed even on the coldest of nights. She loves the fresh air on her face. She pulls the covers tight around her chin and listens to the mysterious night sky. She believes that her grandmother is present even though everyone else says she is dead. Each night she drapes the curtain over her shoulders for privacy, looks out the window near her bed, listens for Grandma, and then says silent prayers to her.

Her imagination is free for a time. She needs no priest or teacher to describe "God" to her. Spirit erupts spontaneously in colorful and unique expressions. God is Grandma; the twinkling evening star; the gentle breeze that washes across her face; the peaceful, quiet darkness after everyone has fallen asleep; and all the colors of the rainbow. And because she is a girl, her experience and expression of spirit are uniquely feminine. They flow from her essence as naturally as the breath. The Spirit of the Universe pulsates through her. She is full of herself and she is very good.

Our Wounding

There are those who are threatened by the girl-child's unique spirituality that cannot be contained in doctrine or creed. Whether well-meaning or abusive, they will attempt to imprison it. They will call her names if she insists on communing with the spirit of a tree, the mysterious night sky, or her grandma. She is told,

Prideful One,
Your grandma is not God; neither is your favorite star or rock.
God has only one name and one face.
> You shall have no gods before him.
God is Father, Son, and Holy Ghost.
> He is found in the Church, in the heavens,
> > in the Holy Book, not in you.
God is the God of Abraham, Isaac, and Jacob.
> He is God of the fathers and sons,
> > the daughters have no say in the matter.
Remember: As it was in the beginning, it is now and ever shall be.
Only boys can run fast, play hard, and climb trees.
> Only boys can be Batman, firemen, and God. No girls allowed.
World without end. Amen.

Eventually she will turn away from the Spirit-Filled One she once was. Her original spirituality will become confined within the acceptable lines of religion. She will be taught the right way to imagine and name God. "He" will be meditated to her through words, images, stories, and myths shaped, written, and spoken by men. In order to survive, she will adopt the God she is given. It is too dangerous to rebel. If she dares to venture out of the lines, she will be labeled heretic or backslider or witch. The fear of abandonment and isolation is so strong that she may never question the God of her early years.

The Spirit-Filled One falls asleep. Occasionally she awakens to remind the girl-child-turned-woman of what she once knew. These periodic reminders are painful. The woman fills her life with distractions so that she will not hear the quiet inner voice, calling her to return home . . . to her own spirituality.

Our Healing

Years later new teachers enter her life: a therapist, a self-help group, a women's support circle, a beloved friend, or perhaps this book. They remind her of what she once knew:

Spirit-Filled One,
Your grandma is God and so are your favorite star and rock.

God has many names and many faces.
God is Mother, Daughter, and Wise Old Crone.
She is found in your mothers, in your daughters, and in you.
God is the God of Sarah and Hagar, of Leah and Rachel.
She is Mother of all Living, and blessed are her daughters.
You are girl-woman made in her Image.
You can run fast, play hard, and climb trees.
You are Batwoman, firewoman, and Goddess.
The Spirit of the Universe pulsates through you.
Be full of yourself. You are good. You are very good.

An Invitation

To deny your religious past is to ignore a significant piece of your history. It is essential to take a careful look at it for the sake of the child you once were, and to bring gifts of awareness, liberation, and truth to your children in the present.

Whether you were directly influenced by religion or indirectly a recipient of its language and images through cultural whisperings, I invite you to enter your religious past to uncover and sort through the early names, images, and beliefs you find there. I invite you to speak out your stories, to awaken your questions, and to acknowledge your feelings. I invite you to let go of old images, allowing them to fall to the ground and die. They will nourish the soil, from which will blossom a spirituality born of your own experience as woman.

Stay true to yourself as you read. Take what you like, incorporating the book's helpful insights into your ongoing journey, and leave the rest. You are the expert. This book is merely a guide along the way, a midwife of whatever is ready to be born. There are no magic remedies offered here. Rather you will be invited to come home to yourself—to the vital, expressive, and Spirit-Filled One you once were.

CHAPTER TWO

Reluctance, Anger, and Courage

> It took courage to enter my religious past. Fear had been
> the source of my reluctance, fear of the unknown and fear
> of dipping into more of my childhood history.
>
> —Erin

Unlocking the doors of our religious past can bring up a variety of feelings and responses. Some of us are reluctant because the exploration means confronting our family history once again. The religion of our early years was an accomplice in the behavior and denial of our parents. Women were told to return to their abusing spouses. Daughters who had the courage to name the sexual sins of their fathers were labeled liars or crazy. And in countless families where the dysfunction was less overt, our religious leaders and institutions colluded in the denial. Regular attendance at religious services was a part of the masquerade that meant the family was intact. The illusion that "fine, upstanding religious families" don't have problems had to be maintained at any price.

In addition the religious institutions of our childhoods offered few resources for dealing with the abuse of power, alcohol, sex, and work by our parents. A workshop participant remembers, "My alcoholic father got his religion for the week at Sunday Mass. Then we'd go home and he would continue his verbal attacks and his abusive power trips in the name of the Church. He felt entitled because he was being a good, authoritarian parent as prescribed by the Church and mirrored by the priests. We, his daughters, were taught by the Church to be 'good girls.' This meant that, along with our mother, we were not to get angry."

It was in those churches that the sins of our fathers went unnamed by the clergy. To have named their sins would have implicated male friends and colleagues, and perhaps even God himself. And most damaging of all, religion cultivated and reinforced the helplessness of our mothers. To have challenged our mothers' helplessness would have meant empowering them to act on their own behalf. Clearly, for many of us, family and religion were intertwined realities.

> Religion was a bone of contention between my parents.
> Mom could never " 'do' it right" enough to suit my dad.
> This was all left unspoken, but we all felt it as
> tension. My alcoholic dad was the self-appointed God
> of the household—the giver and taker of approval and
> disapproval. He shamed my sisters and my mom for not
> behaving in a saintly way in church, for not sitting
> with our legs together or not wearing a hat. My
> mother thought church was boring. She went out of duty
> to my dad.
>   This exploration of my religious past brought up
> the fear of challenging the religion of my father. To
> my surprise simply diving into the exploration diminished
> my fear. My reluctance has gone away in the company
> of other courageous women. It hasn't been as hard as
> I thought it would be. In fact it has been very
> liberating.
>
> —Colleen

> I have a great deal of reluctance to move deeper into my
> religious past. Religion was the focus of my childhood.
> My mother is Lutheran and my father, Serbian
> Orthodox. My parents fought constantly over my
> religious upbringing. Holidays were a nightmare. There
> was an outward veneer that "everything is just fine with
> this family," but under the surface there was always
> this tight-lipped battle going on.
>   As an adult, hundreds of miles away from my family,
> I am afraid they will ostracize me if I continue to explore
> my religious past. I imagine their response to be a
> mixture of anger, pity, and then fervent prayer that I
> repent of my wicked ways. The work I have already done

feels like a giant step toward self-hood. Although I will
not turn back, there is fear.

—Irene

Imagine sitting in a circle with Colleen and Irene. Add your story to theirs.

- Did the religion of your childhood affect your home life? Were religion and home intertwined realities?
- What were your mother's and father's attitudes toward religion? Toward going to services?
- Who were your religious relatives? Did they have an influence on your attitudes toward religion?
- Are you reluctant to enter into your religious past because it will involve a more extensive exploration of your family history? Write of your reluctance and of your courage.

No Advocate in the Heavens

> Man enjoys the great advantage of having a god endorse
> the code he writes; and since man exercises a sovereign
> authority over women it is especially fortunate that
> this authority has been vested in him by the Supreme
> Being.
>
> —Simone de Beauvoir, *The Second Sex*

To unlock the doors of our religious past requires us to acknowledge the deeper woundings in a woman's life and the heavens' participation in them. The truth is that the heavens have not been woman-friendly. Women have had few advocates in the heavens.

For many of us childhood was a time when God the father and his male representatives ruled unchallenged in both family and religion. It was a time when the boys in our youth groups were called to the ministry, while we were groomed to be ministers' wives. It was a time when one out of four of us was being sexually abused by our fathers, religious leaders, and other trusted males who looked like the God of our childhood. And it was a time when our fathers were caught up in the important business of carrying out God's bidding in the world, leaving our mothers to act out their frustrations at home. All the while we were told to love, honor, and obey them no matter how abusive their presence or absence was in our lives.

As long as God is male and his representatives rule on earth, women's concerns will be peripheral. We were appalled by the absence of women in the Senate as we watched Anita Hill being interrogated by rude men. So, too, are we appalled that the heavens are inhabited by a male God who has never known the realities of a woman's life.

Our healing journey is twofold. It includes gathering the fragments of our personal stories from childhood memory, as well as gathering our collective story from the margins of religious and cultural history. The retrieval of our personal stories is not enough. It is critical for us to move beyond our personal stories. It is critical for us to acknowledge our connection to the wider reality of the girl-child born into a society that prefers men and idolizes a male God.

Women are afraid of the anger that may surface as their eyes are opened to the wider reality of a woman's life. They have been taught to be nice, not angry. At some deep level women know that to explore their religious past is to touch a deep rage within them—the accumulated rage of generations of women who were taught to resign themselves to the pain and suffering inherent in a woman's life. Underneath it all they also fear that the level of awareness and anger triggered by this exploration will make it impossible for them to relate to men again.

Reclaiming their courage and power, women are opening their eyes and confronting the truth. They are using their anger to fuel the search for a God who looks like them. And to their surprise they discover that all of their relationships are enhanced as a result of the discoveries they make along the way. The women who share their fear and reluctance in this chapter will return in chapter 14 to celebrate the transformation of their relationships with male friends, lovers, and colleagues as a result of their discovery of a woman-affirming spirituality.

I am reluctant to explore women's religious past because it brings up my feelings of hopelessness. Why bother? Nothing is going to change. I spent years with no intervention from Church or family to stop my father's sexual abuse. And when I entered a self-help program, I found very little support for my need to relate to issues of spirituality from a woman's perspective. Now I am searching for the feminine face of God, another area for which there isn't much support.

And then there's the big question: If I pursue this exploration, will I ever be able to relate to a man again? In my experience they really don't want to look at these issues. Why should they? They have their God! And he looks like them. But I don't seem to have much choice. I cannot continue my healing journey in a spiritual vacuum. This is the first time in my life that I have ever even felt a spiritual connection with the God of Anyone's Understanding.

—Ferrel

I am reluctant to explore my religious past because it reminds me of how women were degraded, ignored, and minimized in the Catholic church of my childhood. I am reminded of the pain of not having any positive role models or affirming images of women; of adopting the male image of God as a part of me; and of abandoning myself to fit into the expectation that all women were to emulate the Blessed Virgin Mary.

It takes courage to develop a spirituality that is woman-affirming, because to do so means that I choose to stand apart from the mainstream. Specifically it is a choice to stand apart from my family. This is a lonely path at times because my family thinks I'm sinful. Yet I know I'm on the right path for me. And this gives me the strength and courage I need to move on with the exploration of my religious past.

—Robin

Imagine sitting in a circle with Ferrel and Robin. Add your story to theirs.

• How did you respond to these statements: "The truth is that the heavens have not been woman-friendly. Women have had few advocates in the heavens."

• How might your relationships with men be altered through our explorations?

• Are you willing to have your eyes opened to the deeper wounding of all women's lives? Write of your reluctance, your courage, and your anger.

Silenced Voices

> How dare I explore my religious past? In the same way that I felt honor-bound to keep my family's secrets, I also feel that I must not question anything in the heavens. That it's best to keep that door shut and leave well enough alone.
>
> —Jen

Many of us are reluctant to explore our religious past because we were taught not to question either our parents or God. Our families employed a variety of techniques to quiet us as children. There were certain things we were not to talk about—usually the things that affected us the most: our parents' alcoholism and arguments; the acts of verbal or sexual harassment within the family; our discomfort with the behavior of an abusive relative.

So, too, the Church has used effective means to silence women and others who dare to question the inequities of the heavens. Whenever Irene questioned something that didn't make sense about religion, the answer she received from church-school teachers and parents was, "God works in mysterious ways. He is beyond human understanding." The words used to quiet Jane by her pious and battered mother were, "God's ways are not our ways, my dear. We live by faith, not understanding."

Within the Church the phrase "God is faithful. God is good. God is love," convinced most of us that God was not to be questioned and that we were to accept and submit to his goodness however it was expressed. This refrain is not a new one. It has been spoken throughout the centuries to silence anyone who asks the wrong questions . . . suspicious questions. We learn to be good girls. We become reluctant to question anything. The Church continued the lessons we learned in our homes: Don't question. Don't feel.

My questions were continually silenced within the homes, institutions, and churches of childhood and adolescence. Whenever I questioned the alcoholism, abuse, and abandonment of those early years, I was told, "All things work together for good for those who love God." Whenever I questioned the inequities that I observed around me, I heard the words "God is good." My questions were muzzled by traditional religion's familiar refrain, "God is faithful. God is good. God is love."

As a child, I asked,

"Why does Daddy hurt Mommy? Why do we have to hide from Daddy again?"

"Why does he come into our bedroom late at night? I'm afraid of his shadow."

"Why do the nuns wear habits and eat with us in the cafeteria while the priest wears whatever he wants and is served steak and lobster in his own apartment?"

The Catholic church answered, "Father God is faithful."

As a teenager I asked,

"Why are only the boys in our youth group called to the ministry, while the girls are called to be ministers' wives?"

"Why is it called a 'sermon' when one of the boys preaches and a 'concluding testimony' when the girls do?"

The Protestant church answered, "Father God is good."

And as an adult I asked,

"Why is it that only four Princeton Seminary women have received calls to serve in churches while most of the men, though not as articulate, creative, or wise, received calls months ago?"

The Protestant church answered, "Father God is love."

My feelings were not welcomed in the Church. I learned to deny their existence. When I felt lonely, I was told, "Christians are never alone." When afraid, I was told, "Thou shalt not fear." When angry, "Sin not." When needy, "Know the fullness of Christ." To feel my own feelings was to deny God's all-sufficiency. I learned to swallow my loneliness, anger, and fear. They were imprisoned within my belly.

PAUSE AND REFLECT

• Have you ever dared to question the inequities of the heavens? What happened?

• Did you ever hear the phrases "God works in mysterious ways. He is beyond human understanding." Or "God's ways are not our ways. We live by faith, not understanding." Or "God is good. God is faithful. God is love."

• Were you taught not to question either your parents or God? What techniques were used to quiet you as a child?

• Imagine your "reluctance to challenge the heavens" as a friend. Invite it to have tea with you. Give it a voice through word or image. Dialogue with it in your journal. Listen to its concerns. Ask it, "Reluctant One, how might I support you as I begin the exploration of my religious past?"

A Collage of Memories

> At first I didn't think my old beliefs were relevant. But since I am trying to develop a spirituality that works for me, perhaps a look into the past will shed some light on why it is so hard for me to have faith of any kind today.
>
> —Ferrel

Having acknowledged both our reluctance and our courage, we are ready to begin gathering the fragments of religious memory from the far corners of our lives. Our reflection will become more focused in subsequent chapters. At this point we will simply gather our earliest religious memories.

Listen to the stories of women who were certain they had no religious memory, and others who believed that their religious past was of no consequence in their present life. The memories that follow surfaced during early workshop sessions. As you explore with us in this book, you will witness each woman's process deepen as layer upon layer of memory is peeled away. You will witness her pain. You will celebrate her healing. These women invite you to join them in their circle of support and healing.

Allow the memories of each woman to touch your own forgotten stories. Perhaps you will remember the church or synagogue you attended regularly as a child; a sermon or Sunday school lesson; a verse from the Bible or a song from vacation Bible school; a funeral or Bas Mitzvah; your First Holy Communion or a prayer you memorized. Allow each memory to take shape in words and drawings. Then step beyond the text and pursue your memories. Follow this adventure of self-discovery that is being orchestrated by the Deep Wisdom within you.

> We only went to church once a year, which was unacceptable to the church people, so I felt left out and judged when we did go. The people "got happy," ran up and down the aisles, and made lots of noise. I was terrified of the noise, and no one explained to me what was happening. I was afraid that the minister was going to die in front of me because he got so excited while he preached. I remember breathing for him. I would look and listen and then leave feeling angry and empty. Nothing sounded right.
>
> —Erin

> Church was boring, so I always found a way to sit on the aisle and look at people's shoes. Deciding which shoes I liked and didn't like was the most interesting thing to do at church. I also made up reasons why God didn't show up. One day I figured it out as I looked at a book about a genie who flew over Baghdad. God is exactly like that genie, I thought, except God can fly without the carpet. And the reason he didn't come to church was that he was busy feeding the poor people in India. My father traveled a lot to earn money for the family; God traveled to care for the poor.
>
> —Annette

> I remember feeling the exclusion of being Jewish. The Protestant and Catholic churches seemed elegant and exclusive. I wondered whether I'd be thrown out without explanation if I went in, as if I could be

identified with some strange accuracy as being Jewish.
Obviously there were feelings of anxiety, guilt, and
persecution there.

My mother was agnostic and rebelled against her
Orthodox Jewish parents. There was poverty in her
choice, but also a freedom and joy in letting go of
orthodoxy. One vow she did make to her parents was to
have us go to Hebrew school briefly. The Hebrew alphabet
was intriguing to me, yet it was the one area of
academics that I could not master.

—Laura

I thought I had no background in religion. What comes
up for me now is that my early ideas of religion have
everything to do with my father's stories of his
mother, whose first name I was given. She was a very
religious person, a Holy Roller. She belonged to the Church
of the First Assembly of God. Throughout my childhood
my father would tell me stories about how she was a
crazy fanatic who wouldn't allow her children to go
to the movies, to dance, or to date. He said religious people
were like my grandmother—stupid, and gullible. We only
went to church when she visited from Kansas. My
whole idea of religion was being nervous when she
came to visit because there was alcohol around our house
and we wore makeup.

—Ferrel

*Imagine sitting in a circle with Erin, Annette, Laura, and Ferrel. Add your
story to theirs as you reflect on your earliest religious memory.*

• Experiment with writing or drawing with your nondominant hand to give
The Girl-Child You Once Were an opportunity to bring her earliest religious
memory into the light.

• If the bundle image is more helpful, imagine opening the bundle of
childhood memories labeled "First Religious Memory." Write or draw whatever
you discover in the bundle.

• From whom did you first hear about *religion*: parents, teachers, religious leaders, playmates?

• What was your childhood sense of religion?

PART II &

Religious Language and Imagery

CHAPTER THREE

The God of Our Childhood Understanding

> Words, words, words. I discount their power because I
> see the events of my past as a blur. The exploration of
> my religious past has brought the reality of my
> wounding as a woman into focus by pulling the
> words out of my history to be examined.
>
> —Colleen

Religious language is very powerful and exerts a lasting influence on our lives. The language of traditional religion permeates our society. By the time we reached grade school, we had already developed a sense of what religion was all about. Most of us heard "religious" conversations on the playground: our friends talked about their First Holy Communion, their new church dress, their big brother's Bar Mitzvah. Joan's parents were nonpracticing Jews. She learned everything she knew about God from her Catholic girlfriends at school. By the time she finished elementary school, she was praying to God the father and the Virgin Mary. She had little understanding of the God of Abraham, Isaac, and Jacob. The schoolyard served as her religious training ground.

Others faced discrimination in their neighborhoods for being Protestant, Catholic, or Jewish. Joyce grew up in a Catholic neighborhood in Chicago, where "religious wars" were common. She was harassed by the Catholic kids in the neighborhood because she was Protestant. She remembers, "One day the kids on the block said to me, 'Go to hell and fuck the devil.' I didn't even know what those words meant. I felt confused. Religion just didn't make sense."

At holiday times we were all inundated with the images of Christian religion whether our families believed in them or not. Christmas carols blared from speakers at shopping malls and in doctors' offices. Words rehearsing the birth, death, and resurrection of Jesus permeated the atmosphere along with images that linger within our childhood memories: the manger scene, the cross, and the empty tomb.

And at some point during our childhood there was the death of a relative or family friend that required even the most irreligious of families to pay their respects. A study-group participant wrote, "My earliest religious memory is of going to my great-grandfather's funeral when I was five. My mother thought it would be a good experience for me. I remember a huge Catholic church. The statues were impressive. I knew I wasn't supposed to cry. I felt so much fear and confusion about the whole thing. It is a painful memory."

By the time we reached grade school, God had been given a gender. The God who was spoken of on the playground, in the neighborhood, and at holiday times was "he." And even if our family was not religious, the God they railed against had a name and a gender. While I was working on this manuscript, a friend asked me the title of my book. I told him that the working title was "The Feminine Face of God." He responded, "I don't believe in God, so *his* face is of no consequence to me." I replied, "It's interesting to me that the faceless God you don't believe in has a gender." Imagine this man as a father—what words would his children have heard as he let them know of his nonbelief. The face of the God he didn't believe in would linger within their memory, and that God was male.

We had no choice, the God of our religious past was male. And yet within the religious institutions of our childhood, whether Catholic, Protestant, or Jewish, we were taught that God does not possess a body and can be neither male nor female. Our teachers told us that God is a spirit. This was a confusing message when you consider that in the Catholic Mass we were confronted with at least fifty pronouns and images referring to God as male. And from the Hebrew Scripture and Protestant Bible, read regularly in church or synagogue, we heard verses such as (italics are mine):

"God rested from all *his* work which *he* had done in creation." (Genesis 2:3, *Revised Standard Version*)

"The Lord is my strength . . . and *he* has become my salvation; this is my father's God and I will exalt *him*." (Exodus 15:2, *New Revised Standard Version*)

"For God so loved the world that *he* gave *his* only begotten son that whosoever believeth in *him* shall not perish but shall have everlasting life." (John 3:16, *King James Version*)

We were taught that God was greater than all of our attempts to enclose "him" within a language. And yet there it is again, that male pronoun. Rather than employ a variety of names to more effectively illustrate the mystery of God, the teachers and preachers of our childhood always used the male pronoun. Their words contradicted the lessons they taught us. Religion had given God a man's name while claiming that God was beyond naming, that "he" was a mystery.

God was not a mystery to the women among whom I work, and "he" certainly had a name! When I ask women to name the God of their childhoods, without exception they name a male God. Here is a sampling of the childhood names of God that appear most frequently in women's writings: Jehovah; Master; Sovereign; Ruler; Yahweh; Lord, God Almighty; King; All-Powerful and Ever-Living God; Our Father; Heavenly Creator; God the Son; The Holy Spirit; Elohim; Jesus Christ; Holy Ghost; Hashem; God of Heaven; Master of the Universe; King of Heaven; Adonai; Prince of Peace; The Good Shepherd; The God of Abraham, Isaac, Jacob.

> Although my mother was a Jewish agnostic, she did refer to Jehovah. He was stern and judging, she told me. He was a harsh God, harsher than Christ. He evoked fear and judgment.
>
> —Laura

> God was a man; there was no doubt about that in my childhood. In prayer, we said "Our Father." Jesus was the only Son of God. And I could never figure out who or what the Holy Spirit was. I imagined it as a

magical person, male of course. There was nothing female about the God of my childhood.

—Jane

God is a man like my father. He is distant. He is God the father. He is strict. He does not laugh. He has no meaning in my life. He is somewhere else. Christ was good. He was a man too. He suffered to show his faith. Jesus the man: what a life he lived. He denied his body; this is holy to do. He was serious. It's no fun being religious. You are poor and suffering. You do not enjoy life. The Holy Spirit was a bird with light. I don't understand it.

—Sandi, with nondominant hand

Imagine sitting in a circle with Laura, Jane, and Sandi. Add your story to theirs.

• From whom did you first hear about *God*: from parents, teachers, ministers, rabbis, playmates?

• What names were used for God in your childhood? List as many names as you can remember.

• How was God addressed in the prayers you heard or recited in school, church, synagogue, or home?

• Record the memories, thoughts, and reactions that are triggered as you reread the sampling of childhood names of God that appear most frequently in women's writings. Were they familiar?

The Image of God

Ain't no way to read the bible and not think God white, she say. Then she sigh. When I found out God was white, and a man, I lost interest.

—Alice Walker, *The Color Purple*

The use of masculine pronouns and names for God has been accompanied by an impressive array of masculine images. As children and adolescents, whether sitting in Sunday school, catechism class, or He-brew school, we were told that both man and woman were created in the image of God. Yet every picture, painting, and sculpture we saw of God in the Christian church depicted "him" as a man. And although the God of Abraham, Isaac, and Jacob was not captured in an image within the synagogues of their childhoods, Jewish women are clear that the face not to be imagined was the face of a male God. Every priest, minister, and rabbi—the representatives of God who presided at the sacred ceremonies of our childhoods—was male as well.

The official teachings of both Judaism and Christianity acknowledge that God can never be fully known, named, or imagined. The visions of God excavated from our religious past, however, remind us that the images of childhood burrowed far more deeply in our hearts and minds than did the teachings we received. When I ask women to draw the God of their childhood using their nondominant hand, it is the face of a male God that they draw most often.

Robert Coles in his book *The Spiritual Life of Children* has accumu-lated 293 pictures of God. Of these 255 are of God's face. He writes, " 'I'LL DRAW HIS FACE'—that is a refrain I've heard spoken in many languages by children of Christian denominations, and by those who deny any religious persuasion."[1] We leave childhood with the face of a male God permanently imprinted on our memory.

Women make a distinction in their writings and drawings between Jesus and God. Their pictures of Jesus are filled with either his kindness toward animals and children or bloody depictions of his death. And sadly the face of God the father, the "big guy in the sky," is most often drawn as distant and angry.

Confession was the weekly reminder of the punitive face of God for Catholic girls. We imagined God as mad at us. And as we genuflected before the crucifix, we secretly wondered about the gruesomeness of a God who would sacrifice his own son on the cross. The catechism that each Catholic girl memorized as a prerequisite to First Holy Commu-nion etched upon her imagination the severe penalties of sin. It ex-presses more clearly than any theological discourse on the subject the images of a punitive God that were planted in our hearts and lives by the religion of our early years.

From Lesson 8 of the Catechism of Christian Doctrine, The Redemption:

What is meant by the Redemption? By the Redemption is meant that Jesus Christ, as the Redeemer of the whole human race, offered His sufferings and death to God as a fitting sacrifice in satisfaction for the sins of men, and regained for them the right to be children of God and heirs to heaven.

What do we learn from the sufferings and death of Christ? From the sufferings and death of Christ we learn God's love for man and the evil of sin, for which God, who is all-just, demands such great satisfaction.[2]

Both Judaism and Christianity revere a savior God whose task it is to rescue humankind from evil, injustice, or oppression. There are no girl-children honored within these traditions as the bearers of salvation. According to classical Christian theologians, it was not some arbitrary occurrence based on the dance of X and Y chromosomes that Christ was male, it was of absolute necessity.[3] God certainly would not have "sent his only begotten daughter that whosoever believeth in her shall not perish but have everlasting life."

The expected Jewish Messiah was male as well. His coming promised deliverance from oppression and the liberation of the Hebrew nation from its enemies. In the words of a Jewish workshop participant, "There was no doubt in my mind that the coming Messiah would be male. The God of Abraham, Isaac, and Jacob always sent one of his own kind to do the important tasks in our Hebrew history." Whatever their task, the saviors, messiahs, and rescuers were always male in fairy tales, in the movies, and in the Bible.

Whether comforting or frightening, the images of God excavated from our religious past are male. And these images pursue us into adulthood.

> God was a man in a long white gown with long hair and
> a beard. He was handsome. God the father rules the earth
> and watches over us. There was a big painting of Jesus
> at the altar. He was standing on the ocean, reaching
> out his hand to a man who was drowning.
>
> —Jane, with nondominant hand

> My association with the God of my religious past was
> tenuous because it wasn't informed. My family didn't
> practice Judaism much, and it wasn't necessary or

desirable to educate a girl in religious ways. Going to synagogue for a couple of days a year and hearing gobbledygook in a foreign tongue didn't give me any face of God to hang my spirituality on.

—Hallie

The image that comes is of God looking down at me from a big chair. He is very judgmental. If I didn't go to church, he would get me and punish me. I imagined him as the Big Zapper in the sky. The images of Jesus are different. I remember visiting my uncle's house as a child and being frightened by the picture of Jesus with thorns and blood running down his head. I couldn't avoid the picture. We saw it every time we climbed the stairs.

—Karen H.

The savior of my Catholic girlhood was Jesus. Not only were there no female saviors in my childhood religion, even the process one had to go through to become a savior was incredibly macho: physical violence of the most extreme sort in crucifixion. It seemed clear that the characteristics most often associated with women, such as nurturance, compassion, and creativity, were not capable of bringing about salvation.

Even the female saints I knew of in my childhood, Joan of Arc, Katherine, Barbara, seemed to have been chosen for sainthood primarily because of their ability to withstand violence and pain "like men." Living a decent, *human* life brought no recognition or glory, but dying a gruesome death at the hands of torturers was portrayed as the ultimate heroism.

—Karen S.

Imagine sitting in a circle with Jane, Hallie, Karen H., and Karen S. Add your story to theirs.

• Think back to the churches you visited or attended regularly as a child. Were there paintings, pictures, sculptures of God? Describe the images of God that come to mind.

• If you attended synagogue or temple, were there images of famous forefathers—rabbis, philosophers, and other important godlike figures?

• Describe the saviors, messiahs, and rescuers in the fairy tales, movies, and Bible of your childhood and adolescence. Were they male? Whom did they save? From what?

• Were there any saviors portrayed in the Church or synagogue who looked like you?

Dangerous Questioning

> Man corrupt everything, say Shug. He on your box of
> grits, in your head, and all over the radio. He try to make
> you think he everywhere. Soon as you think he
> everywhere, you think he God. But he ain't.
> —Alice Walker, *The Color Purple*

I realize that I'm treading on dangerous ground when I call into question the exclusively male language and imagery for the divine that permeate our religious and cultural life. For many the male God of traditional religion has been a rich and meaningful concept. And the roots of these God-words reach deep into the Hebrew and Christian traditions.

However, these traditions also teach that God is beyond human naming and imagination. Thus I carry out this questioning not as a heretic but in compatibility with the original teachings of traditional religion. It is my work among women that gives me the courage to call for an examination of the images and words for God that we heard in our childhoods and continue to hear today. It is these words and images that have shaped our sense of ourselves. Women have been excluded from the divine.

Before moving on, linger awhile with chapter 3:

৺ THE POWER OF LANGUAGE

• Be aware of the use of language as you read magazines, newspapers, and books this week. With a red pen, circle the male names and pronouns used to represent God.

• Take the exercises and questions of chapter 3 into your workplace, your home, your therapist's office, and your place of worship. Engage your lover, parents, therapist, and religious leader in this exploration. Ask them to recall their earliest religious memory and to describe the God of their own childhoods in words and images.

• If you attend self-help Twelve Step meetings, pay attention to the memories and feelings that are triggered for you as God is mentioned, as the Twelve Steps are read, and as the Our Father is prayed. What images of God rise from your childhood memory? As you read through program literature this week, highlight male language and imagery.

৺ WORDS THAT HURT, WORDS THAT HEAL

Set aside time each day this week to converse with The Girl-Child You Once Were. Imagine sitting with her in your meeting place. Draw and write with your nondominant hand in response to the following questions:

DAY 1. *Words Hurt, Words Heal*

• What names were you called on the playground, in the classroom, or at home by your sisters and brothers, parents, teachers, and friends?

• What words felt good to hear? What words hurt you?

• What words shut you out? What words invited you in?

• What words made you feel bad about yourself? What words made you feel good about yourself?

DAY 2. *Church Words*

• Draw a picture of each childhood house of God that you visited or attended.

• Draw the ministers, priests, and rabbis you remember. Where did they stand or sit in the church? What words did you hear from them? Pretend that your picture is a cartoon; write the words you remember in a bubble above their heads.

DAY 3. *Family Words About Religion*

• Draw the dinner table in your childhood home. Draw each person who is sitting at the table. The topic of religion is brought up: Your brother asks about hell, your father criticizes the priest's sermon, your mother complains about not enough volunteers to help in the church. Reconstruct a conversation that might have been heard one evening in your home. Who says what and in what tone of voice?

DAY 4. *Names of God*

• Do you remember the following prayers?

"Glory be to the Father, and to the Son, and to the Holy Spirit. As it was in the beginning, is now, and ever shall be, world without end. Amen."

"God is great. God is good. And we thank him for our food. Amen."

"Hear, O Israel: The Lord our God, the Lord is one. Praised be his name whose glorious kingdom is forever and ever."

• Recite other prayers you remember from childhood. How was God addressed in each of them?

DAY 5. *Images of God*

• Were there pictures of God or Jesus in your church or home? What did God look like in the church? Draw a picture of God. Draw a picture of Jesus.
• Who was God in your home?

DAY 6. *Moods of God*

• What mood was the God of your childhood in most of the time? Did God make you happy? Sad? Scared?
• When you did something wrong, what did you think God would do?

DAY 7. *Who Will Save Me?*

• Who were the rescuers in the fairy tales of your childhood? Draw them. Whom did they save?

• Who saves the world from evil? Who will rescue you from evil? Can a girl be a savior? Can a girl be saved?

CHAPTER FOUR

Our Wounds and Ineffective Behavior

Exclusion, Inferiority, and Dependency

> I have come to believe that my ineffective behaviors stem
> from the deep wounding that took place in my childhood
> over which I had no control. This belief turns religion
> on its head, reaffirms me as a woman, and frames my
> ongoing healing process in a woman-affirming perspective.
> —Christine

All of us were wounded in one way or another in childhood. It may
have been a result of the piercing taunts of classmates, the betrayal of
our trust by a beloved teacher, humiliation at the hands of our siblings,
or the severe criticism of a parent. There is no way to escape childhood
without a scrape or two, no matter how loving our family. Those of us
who grew up in dysfunctional families were more seriously injured.

Our awareness of these wounds no matter their intensity comes to us
through the troubling and ineffective behaviors we bring into adulthood. These may include troublesome relationships; overeating; chronic
debt; or addiction to substances, sex, or work. At some point we realize
that these behaviors do not support the quality of life we desire as
adults, and we reach out for help in dealing with them.

If overeating is the behavior that disturbs us as adults, we go to
Weight Watchers or Diet Club, pay our money and drink our formulas.
Or we go to Overeaters Anonymous and commit to countless food

plans of one sort or another. They work for a while, and then the weight reappears.

If our ineffective behavior shows up in troublesome work relationships, we read an article on effective interactions with co-workers, visit a therapist, go to a communications workshop, and for a while we're able to interact in a healthier way with those around us. Eventually, though, the same old patterns reappear.

If we are repeatedly drawn to alcoholic partners, this may be the frustrating, and at times life-threatening, ineffective behavior that brings us to a support group or to a therapist. We leave the relationship, thinking that once the alcoholic is out of our lives, we will never again be "stupid" enough to be drawn to such a person. Many of us find, however, that without our consent, we are drawn again into a dysfunctional relationship.

It becomes clear to us after years of therapy appointments, religious services, Twelve Step meetings, or women's support groups that there are extremely deep wounds beneath the behaviors we talk about each week. These injuries do not respond to psychological theory, no matter how skillfully employed by our therapist; or to elaborate theologies, no matter how carefully articulated by our minister; or to the rhetoric of recovery, no matter how informative and interesting the spokesperson.

Trying to deal with our ineffective behaviors without acknowledging their roots in the wounds of childhood will always prove fruitless. These behaviors are the voices of our deep injuries. Some injuries require very little attention—given time and a basically supportive environment, they heal. There are other wounds, however, that reach more deeply and require tender care and special attention.

Although women choose a variety of spiritual paths, our wounds are similar based on our birth into a society that worships a male God and prefers men. Whether the face of our childhood God was comforting or frightening, punitive or kind, the exclusive imagining of God as male has deeply wounded women. Our immersion in these images convinced us that we are excluded from the divine, that we are inferior to men, that we are in need of a male savior, and that to name and imagine God in any other way than *he* has always been known is blasphemy. The religious images of childhood burrowed away in the girl-child's heart and mind. They limited her dreams and the expression of her gifts to the world.

Until this deep wounding is acknowledged and healed, we hope and pray, we make resolutions, we commit to countless diet plans, and we try the advice of one expert after another, but our efforts to change bring only momentary relief. Our ineffective behaviors are the indirect way these injuries seek to get our attention. They are our clues to look beneath them. To become entirely ready to have the behaviors removed is to plunge into the woundedness of our lives. In this chapter we will begin our descent.

> I rejected the punitive male God of Christianity thirteen years ago. My logical self told me that I had tossed aside this image as useless baggage. Yet I have come to believe that the shame I experience of "not being enough" was inflicted by that early religious image and fuels my work addiction today. My hope now is for the healing of childhood wounds.
>
> —Karen H.

> There was a time when I could not see beneath my obsessions; they seemed absolute. Gradually I have turned my energy away from them and have slowed down enough to look at the underlying wounds. Where did it all begin—in the womb, in the incubator, after my father died, in my adolescence, living with the violent alcoholic-addict? Was it the loss of snugness and safety, of warmth and relaxation, of self-respect? I pause to recognize and acknowledge that I am injured. Moving inward toward my injuries and away from the obsessive symptoms that express them, I begin to regain my power.
>
> —Laura

Exclusion: No Girls Allowed

> Mankind is everyone supposedly, but when I say the word,
> all I see are men.
>
> —Ann

As a result of our immersion in male names and images of God, we have been excluded from the divine. God and humankind ("*man*kind") have been imagined as male. Therefore men have been considered representative of a full and complete humanity. They are divine and their experience is normative. We are not divine and our experience is considered peripheral. Thus we have been barred from full participation in family, world, and church.

During adolescence I read the biographies of several Christian men in an attempt to discover the common denominator of their greatness. In typically adolescent fashion I wanted to accomplish great things in God's name. I wanted to be a woman of God. If only I could find their secret. My exploration disappointed me. I was not able to find a detailed prescription for Christian greatness.

Singing the hymn "Rise Up, O Men of God" one Sunday, however, their secret dawned on me: They were men and so was God. Men were called on to do great things for God; girls were groomed to be ministers' wives. Boys could be God, girls could not. The images of childhood burrowed away in my heart and mind, limiting my dreams and the expression of my gifts in the world.

Sadly the girl-child of today is as thoroughly convinced that she is other than God and excluded from the divine as I was in the 1950s. Recently a friend told me of concerned parents in her parish. They were deeply disturbed that their daughter had been chosen to play the part of God in a church-school play. Although she was excited by the prospect, one can only speculate about her parents' thoughts and feelings: Would it be blasphemy for a girl to play God? Would God be angry? Would he rant and rave in the heavens? They had been taught to "color" God within the prescribed lines of religion—a certain sex and color.

These parents probably have noble expectations of this daughter, and yet they place severe limitations on what she can do and be. Her brother could be God in the school play; she could not. So, too, her parents could probably imagine their son as a doctor, lawyer, or president. Their aspirations for their daughter are that she marry a powerful and influential man. The image of God that was implanted within us in the early years—whether shouted at us in fundamentalism or whispered to us in our culture—has a deep impact on our lives as women. It affects our treatment and expectations of our daughters and of ourselves. It *does* matter what we believe. The girl-child has been excluded from the divine.

> A girl cannot be God because God made only man in his image. Woman was an afterthought and a product of man, not God. I was raised with this story. And in the Lutheran church it was played out every day. The ministers, ushers, elders, and people in power were all male. Women taught Sunday school and carried out the charity work in the church and community. They cooked and served at holiday gatherings. I was envious of the Catholics because at least the nuns seemed to have some status and power.
>
> —Irene

> I have two very dear Irish-American male friends. Their love for the Church is hard for me to accept. They feel at home. They like the rituals. They have a confidence and self-esteem that I have never experienced in the Church. I constantly remind them of their identification with the male God and the affirmation they have received from that heritage.
>
> As a young person I believed the Church when they said that *Man* included me and that we were all created and loved equally by God. Then, around puberty, the horrible reality began to seep in: that I was inferior along with Mary, Eve, and the rest of the women who surrounded God; that I was seen as sexual, not as a person; and that I was evil. The rules had changed, and I felt betrayed by God and the Church.
>
> —Robin

Imagine sitting in a circle with Irene and Robin. Add your story to theirs.

• Reflect on the memories, thoughts, and reactions that are triggered by the following words and phrases. Do you feel excluded by them?

One man, one vote
All men are created equal
Mankind
Congressman, spokesman,
  chairman

Rise up, O men of God.
The God of Abraham, Isaac, Jacob
Brotherhood

• Now reflect on the thoughts and reactions that are triggered by the following series of words and phrases. Is it easier for you to feel the possibility of men's exclusion than to feel the actuality of your own?

One woman, one vote
All women are created equal
Womankind
Congresswoman, spokeswoman,
  chairwoman

Rise up, O women of God
The God of Sarah, Rachel, and Leah
Sisterhood

• Imagine singing the hymn "Rise Up, O Men of God" in your childhood church. Imagine singing it today.

Rise up, O men of God! His kingdom tarries long;
Bring in the day of brotherhood and end the night of wrong.
Rise up, O men of God! Tread where his feet have trod;
As brothers of the Son of Man, Rise up, O men of God![1]

• Reflect on the ways that the images and words of the male God limited your dreams and curtailed the expression of your gifts in the world.

Inferiority: Girls Are Second-Rate

> For the little girl in me there is nothing female about God. As a result, I grew up hating almost everything female, including my mother.
>
> —Jen

As a result of our immersion in male names and images of God, the girl-child becomes convinced that masculine qualities are more valuable than feminine ones. She develops a deep sense of inferiority and will grow up denigrating all things feminine. I asked the young man who is a cashier at my favorite restaurant, "Is God a man or a woman?" Without a moment's hesitation he said, "A man of course." "How can you be so sure?" I asked. "Well, God is big and strong, and powerful enough to be in control of everything. He couldn't be a girl. They're weak and not as smart as men."

The young woman working with him behind the counter was listening to our exchange and she became outraged. In a moment she got it: Girls are second-rate! It didn't matter that she was a cook with expanding possibilities at the restaurant and he a mere fill-in cashier. He could be God—this gave him built-in status despite the reality of his inferiority to her. Sadly her outrage was directed toward the fact that she is a "girl," not toward the assumption that God is male. She didn't question that. Her final comment to me was, "I wish I were a boy."

While studying at Princeton Seminary I was encouraged to read the book *Man Becoming* by Gregory Baum, a Catholic theologian. I was struck by the following passage:

> To believe that God is Father is to become aware of oneself not as stranger, not as an outsider or an alienated person, but as *a son* who belongs or a person appointed to a marvelous destiny, which he shares with the whole community. To believe that God is Father means to be able to say "we" in regard to all *men*.[2]

I put down the book. It was clear that the author, although I am certain he would claim otherwise, was writing to men, about men's experience of God. I rewrote the passage in my journal:

> In my experience as a woman . . . To believe that God is only father is to become aware of myself as a stranger, an outsider, as alienated person, as a daughter who does not belong, who is not appointed to the marvelous destiny offered to the sons of the father. To believe that God is only father says that "I am other" in regard to all men and in regard to the divine.

I am reminded of the threefold thanksgiving prayer of the rabbis: "Blessed art Thou, O Lord, our God, King of the Universe, who has not made me a heathen . . . a bondsman . . . a woman . . ."[3] We wonder: The gentile man could become a Jew, and the bondsman could become free, but how do we undo our womanness? This has been the riddle of most women's lives. The use of exclusively male imagery convinces women that they are other than God, and therefore deficient, inferior, and never quite good enough.

> The priests were men and they had female housekeepers.
> The nuns taught in school, but the priest came in for the
> really important things. I couldn't be an altar boy
> because I was a girl. If God is male, I am other than
> God, limited and second-rate.
>
> —Sharyn

> According to my father, religion was associated with
> gullibility and weakness—in other words with girls and
> women. I felt so much shame about being female that
> for many years I have actively resisted identifying with
> the feminine side of me or life. I turned away from the
> feminine to please my dad. He was judgmental, and
> although I tried, I was incapable of pleasing him.
>
> —Joyce

Imagine sitting in a circle with Sharyn and Joyce. Add your story to theirs.

• What feelings were triggered as you read the quote from Gregory Baum's book and the threefold thanksgiving of the rabbis? Rewrite them from your perspective as a woman.

• Continue your reflection on the ways that the images and words of the male God limited your dreams and curtailed the expression of your gifts in the world.

Dependency: Images of Saviors Linger

> I expected men to save me from loneliness, social
> disapproval, boredom, failure, and mechanical breakdowns.
> I have treated men as godlike. This never seemed

wrong to me, since I've been surrounded by women
who go to extremes to please their men at all stages
of life.

—Liz

As a result of our immersion in male names and images of God and in
the images of saviors that linger in our memories from fairy tales and
Bible stories, the girl-child becomes convinced of her inability to save
herself and of her need of a male savior. Our lives remain on hold as
we wait for the Deliverer to come. We long for human saviors: "If only"
I had a new husband or partner, a job change, an exciting happening,
a new apartment, a knight in shining armor. And we long for divine
saviors: "If only" I had a vision from heaven, a definite word from God
through my therapist or guru—a miracle. From childhood women are
taught to look outside themselves for legitimacy, direction, and salvation.

We look to men to legitimize us. Historically, a child was considered
"illegitimate" unless it bore the name of the father. It is not enough to
be born of woman. And once born, we were to be legitimized by a series of men, beginning with our fathers and later by boyfriends and
husbands. The fear of illegitimacy is so deeply embedded within us that
even in contemporary relationships in which the woman chooses to
keep her name, the children invariably bear the name of the father.

We look outside ourselves for direction. We are taught to defer to
men. They are the actors in the drama of our lives. We are the observers
and the supporting cast. Joyce explores the ineffective behaviors that result from her deep sense of inferiority: "I am an observer in work situations that involve men. My brain stops functioning around them. My
awareness goes out the window and I defer to male logic. I know intellectually that their logic is not superior, but I'm not able to push
through my strong feelings of inferiority, so I defer."

We look to men for our salvation. Our mothers, whether in healthy
or abusive relationships, passed on to us the myth of the necessity of a
male savior in our lives. As a result some of us stay in abusive relationships because to be without a man is to be "unsaved." A workshop participant acknowledged, "I was taught that men would save me from
financial insecurity and the shame of not being 'chosen.' They were to
give me companionship and respectability. When I found myself in an

abusive relationship, I was unable to leave because that would prove my unworthiness and reinforce my deep inferiority."

Surrendering our lives to a male God, a guru, a boyfriend or husband, a New Age philosophy, or a Higher Power continues our disempowering dependence on powers outside of ourselves to legitimize, direct, and save us. In the process we become alienated from our own inner resources. Reflect with Joyce, Sharyn, and Susan on the saviors, messiahs, and rescuers you have looked to for legitimacy, direction, and salvation.

As a child I was preoccupied with feeling accepted by my parents, especially my father. In a sense the acceptance I sought was a desire to be saved from worry, continual self-evaluation, and fear. I carry this process with me today in seeking the acceptance of men, whether bosses, co-workers, lovers, or dance partners.

When I moved to California, my saviors became workshops, New Age books, and friends who were well versed in New Age thought. I still succumb to these saviors and look to them to save me from my flawed thought processes and to fix whatever is wrong with me.

Focusing outside myself for salvation and validation has caused me to stay in three therapeutic relationships and several love relationships long after they became harmful. I thought I needed the permission of the other person before I could leave.

—Joyce

I was taught by my parents and society that my life would be complete if I had a husband. For years I remained in a miserable relationship because I was "more" as half of a couple than I would be single. This saved me from the responsibility of making my own decisions, leading my own life, and creating myself. I blamed my deep unhappiness on my partner and his shortcomings, not on my own lack of definition.

—Sharyn

The Higher Power of recovery seemed to be the male God
of my childhood past, just called by another name. My
life was unmanageable in many ways when I showed
up at my first meeting. As a sex and love addict I
found it really easy to believe that a Higher Power would
deliver me from the mess I was in. Men have always been
my fix. It's strange that my recovery sponsors didn't
get it. They were asking me to replace my addiction
to men with a surrender to a Higher Power who would
rescue me. I wonder, is there a difference?

—Susan

*Imagine sitting in a circle with Joyce, Sharyn, and Susan. Add your story
to theirs.*

• What saviors were you taught to look to for salvation, legitimacy, and
direction? List them for each period of your life. What did you expect them to
deliver you from? Were they effective saviors? Were there any women among
them?

• Reflect on the following statement from your own experience: "A shame-
based religion, therapeutic process, or recovery emphasizes our inability to
function in our own lives without dependence on outside forces and encourages us as women to project our power onto men and gods."

• Who are you turning your life and will over to currently? A boyfriend? A
therapist? A guru? A Higher Power? A New Age philosophy?

• Which response comes to mind when you are faced with a difficult
situation: "Who will save me?" or "What resources do I have to face this
challenge?"

Imprisoned Imaginations

How dare I question God the father? Even bringing up
the discussion of the God of my past is frightening. If
my father found out about these exercises, he would
damn me to hell.

—Colleen

It was necessary for us to adopt the God of the institutions by which our lives were bound as children and adolescents. It was too dangerous to rebel, and for many of us the fear of abandonment was so strong that it took most of us many years before we were ready to question the God of our early years. Fear comes with good reason. We feel as if we are committing a mortal sin to imagine God as anything or anyone other than God the father. We were told that there was no need to see God in any other way than as "he" had always been seen. Frightened, we put aside our original sense of the many colors of the rainbow with which to "color" God. We joined in the prayers and the imaginings of home, Church, and society. Whether the image of God is comforting or frightening, whether his face is kind or punitive, he has imprisoned our imaginations.

Several years ago I read a feature article in *Life* magazine entitled "Who Is God?"[4] *Life* asked this question of a variety of women and men. It was not surprising that all but two of those interviewed imagined God as exclusively male. They, too, had been told how to name, imagine, and "color" the God of their early understanding. However, it was the editors' introduction that was the most disturbing. In it they assign the Supreme Being a gender through the use of that ever-present male pronoun, along with their choice of a picture of God as an old white man with a beard. Their assumption that God is male is further evidence that our personal and societal imaginations have been imprisoned.

It takes very little imagination to envision God as male. This image has dominated the imaginations and self-concepts of men and women for centuries. Our imaginations have been held hostage by God the father. The "grandest of human imagination" will most certainly come up with a plurality of faces to inhabit the heavens, and with names that move us beyond the limitations of an exclusively male God.

Years ago as I sat in a Sunday school class of adults, we listed the words and images we each employed for God in our adolescence. The list was full of diversity, reflecting the variety of people in the class: father, answerer, boundary setter, friend, judge. As I looked at the list, I experienced a dual response. On the one hand I shivered at the thought that God is created from our own need. We create our own gods! A person needing stability and control created a Father God with those qualities. Someone else full of questions during that turbulent period created a "God Who Answers." On and on, down the list I went, shocked and impressed at our ability to imagine gods and then to move on to new ones as our needs changed. On the other hand I realized that our imaginations were free within a very limited arena—every God on our list was imagined as male. And due to the imprisonment of my imagination, I did not even consider alternatives. The feminine face of God had been off-limits to me.

As a result of the imprisonment of our imaginations, women cannot imagine a God who looks like them. I have asked hundreds of women over the years—workshop participants, friends, colleagues, salespeople, and waitresses of all colors, creeds, and walks of life—"Is God a man or a woman?" The answer was unanimous: "God is male. A woman cannot be God." I then invited them to conjure up an image of God as woman. For most this seemed a ludicrous suggestion based on the effectiveness of their childhood religious training. Others attempted the assignment until the image of an angry male God shouted from the depths of them: "Thou shalt have no gods before me."

Clearly our imaginations have been held hostage by God the father. "He" has been an undisturbed idol for too long. His image has been used to convince us that we are excluded from the divine, that we are inferior to men, that we are in need of a male savior, and that to name and imagine God in any other way than "he" has always been known is blasphemy. A woman's inability to imagine a God who looks, bleeds, feels, thinks, and experiences life as she does is an indication of how deeply injured she has been by her religious past.

Imagine sitting with a group of women friends. Consider the following questions:

- Is God a man or a woman?
- Close your eyes for a moment. Imagine God as a woman. What image rises from your imagination? Draw it or describe it in writing.
- What feelings surface as you attempt the assignment?
- Is there fear in the face of an angry male God shouting, "Thou shalt have no gods before me"?
- Do you visualize a God who looks like you with freedom and pride?

• Did you ever see a picture of a God who looked like you or your mother in childhood?

• Reflect on the following statement: "A woman's inability to imagine a God who looks, bleeds, feels, thinks, and experiences life as she does is an indication of how deeply injured she has been by her religious past."

Before moving on, linger awhile with chapter 4:

✑ AN INTERVIEW: CAN A GIRL BE GOD?

Interview your lover, friends, co-workers, therapist, and clergy person.

• Ask them, "Who is God?" "Is God a man or a woman?" "Can a girl be God?"

• Invite them to imagine God as a woman. Invite them to draw the image or to write about it.

• Explore with them the feelings that surface as they attempt the assignment.

✑ AN INVENTORY: IF GOD IS MALE, THEN . . .

Inventory the wounds and ineffective behaviors that were the result of growing up immersed in male names and images of the divine. Begin by adding to the following list of "If . . . then . . ." statements gathered from the writings of workshop participants. Invite a group of women friends to expand the inventory with you. Personalize it. The statements explore the connection between our religious injuries and the ineffective behaviors we bring with us into adulthood:

If God is male . . .

Then men are active participants in life and I am an onlooker.
Then masculine qualities are more valuable than feminine ones.
Then I am incapable of choosing my own direction or path in life without his assistance. I wait for men to clue me in on what's right for me. They have the natural abilities that I lack.
Then men were made in God's image—body and all—and I was not.

My body is "other" and defective. It is never enough. I compulsively eat and then compulsively exercise. My body bears the brunt of my self-hatred. I never saw a God who looks like me . . . with breasts and the roundness of a woman. The sex goddesses like Marilyn Monroe were created by men and do not look like me at all.

If God is male, then men are gods and . . .

I defer to men in work situations. I back down in any argument with a man. I get quiet in mixed groups, allowing men to dominate the discussions.

I diminish my life and quiet my intelligence so that male co-workers, lovers, and even professors won't be threatened by me.

A relationship with a man is to be highly desired. He becomes a God. His needs are more important than my children's, my friends', and my own.

I set aside my own life in order to pursue men and then consider it my duty to meet all of their needs—sexual, emotional, and physical—just as my mother dedicated her life to my father's needs. He was the God of our family.

Men's interests are much more important than mine, and their conversations, careers, and decisions carry more weight than mine. I enlarge my life to learn and grow as a result of their interests. I have learned to like football, to go fly-fishing, to read *Sports Illustrated,* and to cook their favorite meals. These gods have seldom shown any interest in any idea, project, or curiosity of mine.

They are superior and I am inferior. I have never had a healthy and mutual relationship with a man. I think it is impossible.

The men in my life have always been taller, smarter, and wealthier than I. I become dependent due to my inferiority, and eventually I begin to believe that I am incapable of taking care of myself. It seems that the only possible relationship is one in which the man is dominant and I am subordinate.

❧ NO GIRLS ALLOWED

Set aside time each day this week to converse with The Girl-Child You Once Were. Imagine sitting with her in your meeting place. Draw and write with your nondominant hand in response to the following questions:

DAY 1. *No Girls Allowed*

• With your nondominant hand write a story with pictures to illustrate a time you felt excluded or left out because you were a girl.

DAY 2. *Boys Can Be God, Girls Can't*

• Draw a picture of the things a girl can do on the left side of the page.

• Draw a picture of the things a girl can't do on the right side of the page.

• What were the areas of life that were off-limits to you as a girl?

• Can a girl play the part of God in a Sunday-school play? Would God be angry?

• Can a girl be a bishop, a minister, a pope? Can a girl be God?

DAY 3. *Girls Are Second-Rate*

• With your nondominant hand, write a story with pictures to illustrate a time you felt inferior or less than because you were a girl.

DAY 4. *Boys Are More Important Than Girls*

• Who is more important: a boy or a girl . . . a priest or a nun . . . a mother or a father . . . a nurse or a doctor?

• Whose life is more fun: your mother's or your father's?

DAY 5. *Girls Need Boys to Save Them*

• With your nondominant hand write a story with pictures to illustrate a time you felt dependent or in need of a boy because you were a girl.

• Who will take care of you when you grow up?

• Can a girl save people?

DAY 6. *I Wish I Were a Boy*

• With your nondominant hand write a story with illustrations to detail all the reasons why you wish you were a boy.

DAY 7. *A God Like Me*

• Did you ever see a picture of a God who looked like you or your mother in childhood?

• Who looks more like God: your mother or your father?

• What would a woman God look like? Draw her.

Our Healing

The Changing Face of God

> My first step from the old white man was trees. Then air.
> Then birds. Then other people.
> —Alice Walker, *The Color Purple*

From my experience and that of the women among whom I work, I am convinced that our healing and empowerment deepen when the face of God reflects our own; when we imagine God in our own image and likeness. The evolution of the face of God occurs over time. It is an essential journey toward self-love, self-trust, and the indwelling of our power as women.

The journey toward a feminine face of God involves the exorcising of the old names and images, and the embracing of woman-affirming alternatives. These new images are the bearers of healing. As we immerse ourselves within them, healing reaches down into the depths of our self-hatred.

It is very difficult and sometimes impossible for psychological theory, elaborate theologies, and the rhetoric of recovery to penetrate to those depths. Without consciously embarking on our own spiritual journey, these approaches by themselves are powerless to heal the wounds and to untangle the patterns of ineffective behavior that have controlled us for years. Our deepest injuries are reached by a God who looks like us.

I invite you to reflect on your experience of the changing face of God as you read through the following four sections. Although you may identify with my story, don't compare it to your own. I've included it to trigger your personal memories, not to prescribe your responses. Consider writing a prayer, letter, poetic expression, or reflection to the face of God presented in the reading or to the images of the divine that surface from your own experience.

God, The Father: A Controller Above It All

Memories of my early years are filled with fear. The devastation of alcoholism filled my life with violence, inadequate financial resources, and changing caretakers, schools, and homes. My external world was in chaos. These experiences created in me a deep longing for order and control. From an early age I related to God as father. I looked to him to bring security and freedom from chaos. This image helped me construct a rigidly controlled inner world in which I did everything to please God the father. I scrutinized all my thoughts and impulses in light of this relationship.

This image also provided a rigidly controlled outer world as well. All my actions and interactions were shaped in response to it. My adolescent need for an ideology to follow led me to devote my life to God, and that devotion insulated me from both the chaos and the joys of life. In his company I lived above it all. No painful memories or feelings could reach the pedestal upon which we sat. My journals reflect the intensity of this all-consuming relationship. I wrote to him each day all through high school and college.

At fourteen I wrote,

Father God, I desire an inner beauty that makes you happy. Please work on me today so that my only concern is maintaining this inner beauty and guarding against anything that mars it, like vanity and pride. Holiness is beauty. Lord, make me holy. May your life be made more and more manifest in me.

At sixteen I wrote,

Father God, I am selfish in many ways. Let me live every minute thinking of others and how you want me to serve them. Pour out your blessings through me. I have nothing to say apart from you; nothing to pray apart from you. I am nothing without you. Let me keep my eyes on you and walk each minute with you.

God, The Son: A Compassionate Presence

The ending of my marriage set off a series of tremors in my life that threatened this "safe" pedestal upon which I sat with God the father. The tremors intensified into a genuine earthquake, and I experienced a "breakdown" in graduate school that demolished the pedestal. As I lay in the medical clinic at Princeton, I called out to Jesus. Father God seemed far away, and I wasn't sure he would be able to accompany me into the feelings and memories of the first twelve years of my life. They had accumulated such force that they were no longer able to be contained.

It was the image of Jesus as a Compassionate Presence that accompanied me into the frightening forest of emotions and memories in which I now found myself. As Father God receded, the image of Christ drew me inward. I descended into my humanness and set out on the road to self-understanding. The journals of this period remind me of this deepening relationship.

It is most difficult for me to stand in the midst of existence. I am petrified of its winds, of its darkness, of its intensity, passion, and anger. I want to climb back onto my pedestal above it all with God the father . . . to figure things out, to confine life's contradictions within a category, to control life with contrived explanations. I want desperately to move out of this present moment.

In recent days I have longed for your presence, O Christ. No longer avoiding life with walls of protection and tentacles of control, I am facing the awesomeness of "what is," trusting in your presence. You embrace the contradictions that frighten me. You call me to face the vulnerability and the responsibility of this moment.

God, The Holy Spirit: A Refreshing Presence Within

The traditional images of Father and Son were so specific that I had no freedom for my own imaginings. Because there was no masculine imagery associated with the Holy Spirit, I imagined it as an energy that pervaded all of life, connecting me with every living thing. There were treasured moments in which I would experience the Spirit filling me with the joy of being alive.

Years later I discovered that *spiritus* meant breath, and I imagined the windows of my life opening wide and the Holy Breath blowing through my existence, reaching back into the old suffocating rooms of my childhood. I prayed, "Come, Holy Breath, come. Blow into the dusty rooms of old. Refresh and make new." In those moments I was unafraid, and I allowed the Spirit of Life to surprise me.

The image of a Refreshing Spirit Within escorted me unerringly toward my own life. My journals reflect this movement. No longer are the prayers to a God far from me. They are directed to my feelings and dreams, and to The Child I Once Was. My spirituality began to emerge from the depths of me as I recognized the presence of the Divine Spirit within my own personal experience. It was no longer imposed by a male God from outside of my life.

I called on my feelings:

Feelings of a lifetime, I hear your clamor. Your containment has been self-destructive. Please rise slowly from the depths of me. Rise, so I may listen to you and come to know you. Now I am ready.

I invoked my dreams:

Dreams, push through my reluctance to hear you. There is a part of me that longs to listen to your rich messages. You remind me to trust my inner life, to discern its intricate design, and to listen to its healing truth.

I invited the Spirit resident within my childhood, imagined as The Child I Once Was, to tell me her stories:

Little girl, why have you been so petrified? Why do you so powerfully hold on to life, controlling its every moment? How skillful you are at sensing love's approach. How quickly you take the offensive so you will never have to allow love to seep into that deep hiding place behind your locked door. When did you go behind that door from which you intricately maneuver the details of life to suit you? What is your master plan? What is its motivation?

A God Who Looks Like Me

Twelve years ago I wrote these words:

> My God, You are a Spirit, neither male nor female. You have been my Father for so many years, today I ask to know you as Mother. You are too vast to fit into only one compartment. How foolish of us to confine you to one image. It feels uncomfortable to call you Mother. They have spoken of you as Father for centuries. Yet I have always wondered how there could be a father without a mother. How is it that the feminine face of God has been obscured for so long? They tell me now that there is a God who looks like me. It's hard to take it all in.

On that day I was surprised by Mother God. I wondered how the writers and editors of religion's sacred books had been able to obscure the divine feminine so completely that there hadn't been a trace of her in my religious training, except in the outrage of the prophets at the "false gods." Sadly I realized that all the while I was learning to worship the one true God and to have no other gods before him, many of the "false" gods referred to were goddesses who looked like me: the Queen of Heaven, Asherah, Baalat, Astarte, and Anath. As an adolescent I had applauded the zeal of the prophets in ferreting out these "false gods." I had cheered as her followers were destroyed and her sacred groves were burned down. I conspired in the denigration of a God who looked like me.

On this day I realized that I had not been told the whole truth in my religious past. In my search for the truth I began to explore the historical and archaeological evidence supporting the fact that the most ancient image of the divine was female and that this image reached back 25,000 years.[1] There was a time when God was imagined, known, and worshiped as a woman. She has been called by many names. In the prophet Jeremiah's time she was worshiped as the Queen of Heaven. The "cakes" that she was offered by her followers are thought to have been in the shape of a woman's body.[2] Jehovah's words to Jeremiah, however, convinced me as an adolescent that there was only one true God and that there would be grave consequences if I worshiped false gods such as the Queen of Heaven:

> Offer up no prayer, Jeremiah, for this people, raise no plea on their behalf, and do not intercede with me; for I will not listen to you. Do you not see what is going on in the cities of Judah and in the streets of Jerusalem? The children gather wood and the fathers kindle the fire, and the women knead the dough to make cakes in honor of the queen of heaven; and drink-offerings are poured out to other gods than me—all to provoke and hurt me. (Jeremiah 7:17–18)

I discovered that biblical translators and scholars made language choices that obscured the fragments of the feminine face of God that did find their way into the sacred texts of traditional Judaism and Christianity. El Shaddai, for example, is a name of God used in the Hebrew Scriptures. One of the original meanings of *shaddai* is "breast." The translators chose to use its alternate meaning, which is "high places."[3] Thus what might have been an affirming image for those of us with breasts, "A God with Breasts," was altered to further entrench the male imagery of the divine, "The God of the High Places."

Each discovery I made intensified my suspicion of God the father. Suspicion gave me the courage to examine all that I had been taught in his name. And it fueled a search for the Woman God who had been ignored in my background, the one who had been eradicated from religion's stories and myths. I have invited hundreds of women to join me in this search over the years. Part III of this book chronicles our journey and the discoveries we made along the way.

Throughout childhood and adolescence, like many women, I had been told that there was a God-shaped space within my soul and that I would not be satisfied until it was filled with the male God of my childhood. Yet as hard as I tried, the male God would not fit. I felt that this was my problem, that there was something flawed about me. So I twisted myself out of shape and he still didn't fit. It wasn't until I encountered the feminine face of God that I realized that there was nothing wrong with me. As I descended into the wealth of my own life, I discovered that she had been there all the time. Her presence restored me to a loving relationship with myself.

PAUSE AND REFLECT

• Reread your writings on the God of your childhood from previous chapters. Was there a sense of security in your childhood image of God as father? Did he offer you the qualities you longed for in your human father?

Continue to reflect on the changing images of God in your own experience.

• Were there accessible images of God that revealed themselves to you during your life? What images come to mind?

• Have you known God as companion and friend?

• Reflect on these images of God: Compassionate One, Companion, Friend, Presence, Gentle Guide.

• Was there a time when God moved inside your life? Was this movement accompanied by greater self-awareness?

• Reflect on these following images: Breath of Life, *Ruach*, Sacred Breath, Universal Spirit, Spirit of Life, Surprise Presence, Refreshing Spirit Within, Spirit Resident Within My Body, Spirit Resident Within My Breath, Spirit Resident Within My Experience.

• Has the face of God changed in your experience? What were the stepping-stones to the God of your current understanding? As an adult, have you ever imagined a God who looks like you?

• Reflect on the following images: Mother God, Mother of All Living, Source of My Life, A God with Breasts Like Mine, One Who Wipes Away Tears, Womb of Compassion, Fertile Womb of All, Womb Center.

Obstacles Along the Way: No Gods Before Me

> I am reluctant to imagine Woman God because the words from childhood flash into my head: You shall have no gods before me. Pagan, go to hell.
>
> —Karen H.

As women consider the possibility of naming and imagining a God who looks like them, they face formidable obstacles. One of the first is the negative treatment and portrayal of women through word, image, and story in the churches and synagogues of our childhoods. As women explore their religious pasts, Mary is the most prominent feminine image that surfaces—Mary as she was presented to us through the eyes of men.

In part III we will ask Mary to break out of the confines of traditional religious interpretation and we will ask several other women from our religious past to tell us their stories. Here we simply acknowledge Mary's presence in our religious memory. Joyce remembers, "Mary was weakness, passivity, and powerlessness. People gave token appreciation to her. But the main role players were God the father and the son." And Sharyn adds, "I thought Mary was a wimp. The nuns made a point of telling us that Mary was not God. She was the mother of God. She was just a woman."

As a result of these childhood images of the feminine, most women cannot imagine God as a woman. Jane wrote, "Women aren't powerful enough. They cannot possibly be God. They are weak and need to be taken care of by a man." And Colleen refused to write a prayer to the image of a Mother God, saying, "I can't write this prayer. I feel deeply divided about this. I'm uncomfortable. If I do, I would be saying to my father, 'Damn your truth.' Anyway, woman is innately the follower of God, not God. She's humble and gentle. I attribute the angry authority of my father to God, so he is closer to God in my mind. Mother is lesser."

There are only fleeting references to the Goddess in women's writings. The child learned well to have "no other God before him." Until very recently, to most of us the Goddess was "sinful," a pagan abomination of some sort. In the words of one participant, "We never talked about the Goddess. There was only one God, world without end. That was written in stone. There is no other way. Amen." And from the depths of the child within her, a survivor of sexual violence wrote these words with her nondominant hand: "Men hate the Goddess. I must hide that I love her for fear they will hurt me like they have hurt her. The little girl in me is in terror. It is not all right to choose another God besides the male God."

And finally, to name the world is to own the world and its gods. Beginning in the Garden of Eden when Adam named the animals and the woman, "owning" has been the prerogative of men. We have not been encouraged to name ourselves—or to own our lives. Clearly the naming of God has been off-limits to us. Thus to name our own gods is to venture into uncharted waters, and this accentuates our fear. To name the God of our understanding as "Goddess," or "Woman God," or "God the mother" and to speak it aloud at our support-group meetings, in our churches and homes, is a monumental task for most of us. It means that we are taking responsibility for our lives, that we accept our own empowerment, and that we are ready to step into our rightful and legitimate place *beside* the man. Our challenge is to find enough courage and self-love to carry out this task.

PAUSE AND REFLECT

- Who are the women in your religious memory?
- What feelings, images, words, memories come up for you when you read the word *Goddess*?
- Sketch yourself in relationship to a male God. What terms come to mind for the relationship? Sketch yourself in relationship to a Woman God. What terms come to mind for the relationship? Compare the terms for both images. How do you feel about your body . . . your parents . . . men in relationship to each image?
- Write a prayer or letter to Mother God. What feelings come up for you as you address God as woman—discomfort, fear, delight?
- Consider the following statement: "For a woman to name her own gods means that she is taking responsibility for her life, that she accepts her own empowerment, and that she is ready to step into her rightful and legitimate place *beside* the man. Her challenge is to find enough courage and self-love to carry out this task."

Religion's Original Lessons

God ain't he or she, but a it . . . don't look like anything. It ain't something you can look at apart from anything else, including you. I believe God is everything. Everything that is or ever was or ever will be. And when you can feel that, and be happy to feel that, you've found it.

—Alice Walker, *The Color Purple*

In the very beginning of our lives, our imaginations were free. We did not need a teacher or priest to describe "God" to us. Spirit erupted spontaneously in personal and unique expressions. God was our grandmother, the gentle breeze that washed across our face, the peaceful quiet darkness after everyone had fallen asleep, and God was present in all the colors of the rainbow. I trust that the following four insights will remind you of what you once knew in the very beginning of your life and encourage you to explore a wide range of names and images for the divine. Each insight is rooted within the deepest and most basic lessons of religion.

1. The Ultimate Truth, Wisdom, and Power of the Universe is far deeper, higher, wider, and richer than any name or image we use to refer to it. Every name and image has limitations and must be held loosely. Whatever or whoever God is cannot be confined within a language.

• Locate a copy of Alice Walker's novel, *The Color Purple*. Read through the conversation about God on pages 164–168 with a friend. Notice your reactions. Read through it twice, each of you taking a turn being Celie and Shug.

2. The elevation of one image of the divine is idolatry and limits the vast potential of our imaginations. The wounding of women as a result of the dominance of male God language must be acknowledged. Until we are freed to name and imagine the God of our own understanding, God the father will lurk in our minds and hearts, whether we realize it or not. At some point along the way to the God of our present understanding, we will glimpse a God who looks like us. And as our healing deepens, we are free to choose which aspects of the God of our religious past we will weave into our unfolding spirituality. God the father becomes one among many potentially healing images.

• If God the father continues to be a rich and meaningful companion in your spirituality, write him a letter. Tell him that you will be exploring other images, that you are going on a search for the feminine face of God. Arrange to check in with him regularly through prayer and journaling. If he is a loving guide, father, and friend, he will support your search. If he rants and raves, if he threatens "lightning, floods, and earthquakes" and fills you with fear, you may want to reflect on the effect such an angry and shaming image has had on your life as a woman.

3. Each religious tradition holds within it a dual message. At certain times in the Hebrew tradition, female images for God were used. The image of God as father proved too limiting to express the variety of qualities the Jewish people experienced in their relationship to God. When expressing God's compassion and mercy, for example, the early writers occasionally employed womb imagery for God. In Hebrew the root word for both God's compassion and womb is *rechem*. Women are reclaiming the feminine face of God from religion's sacred texts. Although greatly obscured, we catch glimpses of her in the text.

• You might want to incorporate the following scriptural readings in your daily devotions:

Exodus 19:4	God as a Mother Eagle
Isaiah 42:14	God as a woman in labor
Isaiah 49:15	God as an attentive mother
Hosea 13:8	God as a mother bear committed to her cubs
Matthew 23:37	Jesus as a hen gathering her chicks
Luke 15:8–10	God as a woman searching for what is lost

4. The Universal Spirit reaches out to us in our individuality, enters into our personal histories, and fleshes out its presence in terms of our need. There may come a time when a particular image is no longer useful. As we open ourselves to the Universal Spirit resident within our lives, new images will emerge. The face of God will change. We honor the changing face of God in our life.

• Experiment with using feminine imagery in prayer. Begin with the images listed below. You might want to create a prayer-litany in which you follow each name with the requests "Nurture me, support me, empower me."

Midwife	Faithful Mother	Comforting Mother
Divine Feminine	Goddess	Sophia
Womb of Compassion	Shekhinah	Queen of Heaven
Nurturer	Healer	Counselor
Seeker of the Lost	Helper	Welcoming Friend
Source of All Life	Shelter from the Storm	The Still Presence
Burning Love	Soaring Mother Eagle	Laboring One
Ferocious Mother Bear	Tender Nursing Mother	Gathering Mother Hen

Women have been entering the ministry in record numbers since many of us have left the churches of our childhood. These courageous women have been confronting the idolatry of God the father and unearthing woman-affirming resources from within the Hebrew and Christian traditions. We applaud their efforts. They have become the feminine face of God to those among us who remain loyal to the religion of our early years.

Clearly, God the father has not always been faithful to women. It is a miracle of trust that women have remained within traditional religion. Our suspicion is the gift we offer to the Church today. Perhaps as we shout out our questions, we give voice to the One whose face has been obscured and whose ways have been distorted. As did the prophets of old, we call the religious community to confront its idolatry of God the Father. We call on religion to remember its original lessons.

Before moving on, linger awhile with Chapter 5:

THE CHANGING FACE OF GOD

• Incorporate the alternative images of the divine from this chapter into your prayer and meditation practice this week. Write a prayer, compose a poem or a song, or create a dance in response to them.

Christ images:

Compassionate One, Companion, Friend, Presence, Gentle Guide.

Spirit images:

Breath of Life, Sacred Breath, *Ruach*, Universal Spirit, Spirit of Life, Surprise Presence, Refreshing Spirit Within, Spirit Resident Within My Body, Spirit Resident Within My Breath, Spirit Resident Within My Experience.

Feminine images:

Mother God, Mother of All Living, Source of My Life, Heart of My Life, One Who Wipes Away Tears, Womb of Compassion, Fertile Womb of All, Womb Center, A God with Breasts Like Mine, Midwife, Faithful Mother, Comforting Mother, Divine Feminine, Goddess, Sophia, Womb of Compassion, Shekhinah, Queen of Heaven, Nurturer, Healer, Counselor, Seeker of the Lost, Helper, Welcoming Friend,

Source of All Life, Shelter from the Storm, The Still Presence, Burning Love, The Divine Womb of Darkness, Laboring One, Ferocious Mother Bear, Soaring Mother Eagle, Tender Nursing Mother, Gathering Mother Hen.

• In every prayer you recite, express, or read this week, use a feminine image of the divine. Pay attention to the feelings and reactions that surface as you practice naming your own gods.

• Gather alternative names and images of the divine into a special journal. Consider arranging them in categories such as: Feminine images, Masculine images, Childhood images, Images from the natural world, Images beyond gender. Add to your lists the names and images you discover in this book and in discussions with your friends, and those that rise from your own imagination.

• Gather the names of women rabbis, priests, and ministers in your area. Plan to visit their churches or synagogues while reading this book.

✑ IN THE VERY BEGINNING

Set aside time each day this week to converse with The Girl-Child You Once Were. Imagine sitting with her in your meeting place. Draw and write with your nondominant hand in response to the following questions:

DAY 1. *In the Very Beginning*

• Reread the story entitled "All the Colors of the Rainbow," page 33.
• Describe the Spirit-Filled One you once were.
• What special methods did you develop for contacting the Spirit in all things?

DAY 2. *Spirit in Prison*

• For how long were all the colors of *your* rainbow tolerated?
• How did others imprison your spirit? How was God to be "colored"?

DAY 3. *New Teachers*

• What new teachers have entered your life—a therapist, a women's support circle, a beloved friend, or perhaps this book—to remind you of what you once knew?

• What words and images served to awaken the Spirit-Filled One you once were?

DAY 4. *Healing Words*

• Imagine hearing these words as a child: "Spirit-Filled One, your grandma is God and so are your favorite star and rock. God has many names and many faces. God is Mother, Daughter, and Wise Old Crone. She is found in your mothers, in your daughters, and in you. God is the God of Sarah and Hagar, of Leah and Rachel; She is Mother of All Living, and blessed are her daughters. You are girl-woman made in her image. You can run fast, play hard, and climb trees. You are Batwoman, firewoman, and Goddess. The Spirit of the Universe pulsates through you. Be full of yourself. You are good. You are very good."

• Personalize the preceding words into an affirmation of your original spirituality. ("I am Spirit-Filled One . . . ; My grandma is God . . . ; I am girl-child created in her image . . . ; I can run fast.")

DAY 5. *The Natural World*

• Reach back and gather the abundant resources of the child's connection to nature. Where in the natural world did she go to find spirit?

• What was her connection to the shining bright stars, the flowing brook, the majestic mountains, the puffy clouds, the fine morning dew, the spider's web? Draw her favorite tree, her favorite pool or stream. Draw her hiding places in the natural world.

• What gifts did she receive from the natural world?

DAY 6. *All the Colors*

• Reach back and gather the abundant resources of the girl-child's colorful imagination. How did she "color" spirit? What were her names for God?

• Draw a picture for each of these images. Are any of them familiar to you? Starry Night Sky; The Wind in the Trees; The Quiet of the Dark Night; Strong Tree; Branches That Reach to the Heavens; All the Colors of the Rainbow.

DAY 7. *Support Today*

• How might the Spirit-Filled One support you to reclaim your original spirituality today?

• Write her a letter and ask, "Where are you within me?"

✑ HIGHER POWER FROM A WOMAN'S PERSPECTIVE

If you have chosen to use the Twelve Steps as your spiritual guide or you have discarded them as irrelevant to your life as a woman, set aside time each day this week to reflect on the Steps from a woman's perspective.

DAY 1. *The Original Intentions of Alcoholics Anonymous*

Central to the practice of the Twelve Step program is the importance of choosing one's own concept of a "Higher Power." Both AA and Al-Anon give us the permission to name the God of our understanding in whatever way is helpful to us.

Reflect on the following passages. Ask yourself the following questions as you read: What is my conception of God? Who is the God of my understanding?

"Much to our relief we discovered we did not need to consider another's conception of God . . . our own was sufficient to effect contact."[4]

"It was left entirely up to us what the name of God meant to us personally. We might have imagined him to be a ruler or judge, or the God of our understanding might have been the quality of Universal Love, revealing itself in our lives. To some it might have been a personal God powerful but separate from us, while to others, God might have been thought of as an essential part of all creativity."[5]

DAY 2. *God as We Understand Him*

Although "Higher Power" was chosen as a more inclusive concept than God by the founders of AA, the recovery literature reflects the times in which it was formulated. The male God of the culture found his way into the program by way of the male pronouns and the use of the Our Father as the closing prayer said at most meetings.

Visualize the Higher Power you found in recovery rooms. What images come to your mind's eye? What names for God come up at meetings? Are they familiar childhood names? Is there anyone in your meetings who uses his or her own imagery of God? Mother God? Creative Intelligence? Buddha-nature? What are your reactions to names other than the traditional God-talk?

DAY 3. *A Search*

There has always been a voice in the recovery community that affirms a universal spirituality and a wisdom beyond gender. A search through *The Big Book* of AA uncovered the following inclusive images. Respond to each image through writing or drawing; incorporate one or more into your prayer and meditation today.

Universal Mind (page 12)   Spirit of Nature (page 12)
Spirit of the Universe (page 12) All-Powerful, Guiding, and
                                    Creative Intelligence
                                    (page 49)

Great Reality Deep Down   Presence of Infinite Power and
   Within Us (page 55)   Love (page 56)
The Mighty Purpose and
   Rhythm That Underlies All
   (page 55)

DAY 4. *A Meditation*

Below you will find Bill Wilson's (one of the founders of AA) description of his spiritual awakening. Although his experience was eventually reduced to Christian constructs, its original expression contained no traditional religious language. Reflect on the images he used: Light, Spirit, Wind, and Presence. Hold these freeing images in the stillness of your heart and respond to them through writing or drawing today.

The room lit up with a great white light. I was caught into an ecstasy which there are no words to describe. It seemed to me . . . that I was on a mountain and a wind not of air but of spirit was blowing. And then it burst on me that I was a free man. Slowly the ecstasy subsided. For a time I was in another world, a new world of consciousness. All about me and through me was a wonderful feeling of Presence.[6]

DAY 5. *Coming to Believe*

As the face of God changes in our experience, we bring our own images of the divine to the steps. I encourage recovering women to substitute the names and images of the God of their understanding for Higher Power. And then I challenge them to personalize Step 2 based on their beliefs. Reflect on the following reworkings of Step 2. Notice your reactions to them. Do they please you or trouble you? Do you consider them blasphemous and heretical or healing?

> I have come to believe that there is a Sister God who
> stands beside me, offering support and gentle guidance.
> She is a peer rather than a Power distant or apart
> from me. She holds my hand as I make the choices
> that shape my life. She restores me to clarity and serenity.
> —Sharyn

> I imagine "Higher Power" as the power at work in me
> and in everyone throughout the universe. I can let go into
> this source of empowerment. In doing so, I am not
> surrendering; rather I am choosing life.
> —Emily

> I have come to believe in myself. I know that the voices
> within me of negativity, derision, and self-mocking are not
> my own but are the voices of my family. I believe
> that at the very depth of me is the truth of my life.
> I am being restored to a quietness in which my truth makes
> itself known to me.
> —Susan

DAY 6. *Personalizing the Second Step*

Practice personalizing the Second Step. It will give you an excellent opportunity to give voice and form to what you believe. Use the formula below or creatively rework the Step inspired by Sharyn, Emily, and Susan.

• Describe the God of your understanding. Substitute for *Higher Power* the names that are meaningful to you: I have come to believe

_____.

• Describe what "sanity" would look like in your particular situation, and personalize the last part of the step based on your description: I will be restored to _____.

DAY 7. *The Courage to Change the Things We Can*

Make a proposal at your group's next business meeting to use a more inclusive closing prayer than the Our Father. Suggest the Serenity Prayer. Or introduce your group to "I Put My Hand in Yours" which is being used in areas of the country where inclusivity is valued:

I put my hand in yours and together we can do what we could never do alone. No longer is there a sense of hopelessness. No longer must we each depend upon our unsteady willpower. We are all together now reaching out our hands for a power and strength greater than our own. And as we join hands, we find love and understanding beyond our wildest dreams.

PART III &

Religious Myths
and Stories

CHAPTER SIX

Fragments of the Forgotten

> Glory be to the Father, and to the Son, and to the Holy
> Spirit. As it was in the beginning, is now, and ever shall
> be, world without end. Amen.
> —The Catholic Daily Missal

Religious stories hold within them tremendous power. The stories of Adam and Eve, David and Solomon, Moses and Pharaoh, and Jesus, Mary, and Joseph would rank high on a Bible recognition quiz. These stories permeate Western society. Whether shouted at us from the pulpit, or whispered to us in the culture, they exert a powerful influence on our lives. They seek to convince us of the customary way to view our lives and our relationship to the divine.

Centuries ago it was men who wrote down and then gathered together into sacred books the stories that were circulating by word of mouth throughout the Hebrew and early Christian communities. These storytellers, writers, and then translators were all rooted in a culture and society that worshiped God the father and thus preferred men. Their choice of what was meaningful and to be preserved carried this dominant male perspective.

In both the Hebrew and the Christian Scriptures, men's stories took center stage. In the unfolding process from telling to writing to translation, women's stories were lost or included only as they related to the more important stories of the men. In the process, women were dismissed and relegated to the margins of history and religion.

The Hebrew Scriptures are a record of the establishment of Israel as a nation and as a religious community. The families within this community were male-dominated and their Scriptures supported the superiority of men on the national and religious levels. The New Testament is a record of the life and teachings of Jesus Christ. In this record we catch glimpses of the centrality of women in Jesus' ministry. After his death, however, the early Christian church adapted itself to the male-dominated structures of the surrounding culture. It excluded women from leadership functions and relegated them to subordinate roles.[1]

When we were growing up, the preachers, rabbis, and priests were men. The specific stories they chose to include in their teaching and preaching from the Christian Bible or the Hebrew Scriptures were influenced by the fact that they were men. As a result we were not told the whole story in the formative years of our childhood and adolescence. The stories we did hear convinced us that women's lives and stories were not as important as men's.

> I do not remember being told any stories about women
> in the church of my childhood. Religion was about men.
> The women were on the sidelines except for the
> Virgin Mary. The absence of women from religion
> mirrored my home. My mother was considered inferior.
> My father was the authority figure, and our lives revolved
> around him. As a result there was a complete denial
> of any feelings labeled feminine, because in church
> and home the feminine was looked down upon.
>
> —Emily

> In my religious training women were at best an aside, and
> their worth centered around their passivity and submission.
> This has contributed to my feelings of powerlessness
> and to the belief that my life is inconsequential. The
> big deal about the virgin birth was always disturbing. It
> implied that women's bodies and natural processes were
> impure and unclean. As a result I have carried shame
> about my body into my adult life.
>
> —Joyce

God, Jesus, Mary, and Adam and Eve were the religious people in my childhood awareness. Although Mary wasn't a savior, I saw her height as a statue and figured she was up there with God and Jesus, above it all. I related even more to Eve. She was human and made a big mistake. As a result I have spent a lot of my life making up for her sin. I get a deep satisfaction from pain and suffering, somewhere, deep down in the wounded part of me.

—Erin

In Search of Women's Stories

When I hear the constant refrain of "The God of Abraham, Isaac, and Jacob," I want to shout aloud, "What about Miriam, Rachel, Sarah, and ME?"

—Hallie

As the face of God changed in my experience, I searched for the stories of women in my religious past. It became apparent to me that healing into the present meant retrieving both our personal stories from their hiding places within the family memory as well as the collective story of women from the margins of history and religion. As I gathered the fragments of women's stories from religious history, I discovered several types of stories.

I read again the familiar Bible stories that were told over and over in our childhoods. As I read them through the lens of my experience, strength, and hope as a woman, I became aware of the ways these stories had been distorted. Eve (chapter 7), Mary (chapter 9), and The Wise Old Woman (chapter 13) had each been imprisoned within men's interpretation of their experiences.

I discovered that some of the familiar stories were read, studied, and told only because of the importance of the man around whom the woman's story revolved. The women are given no voice in these stories. The Divine Girl-Child (chapter 10) and The One Who Shed Her Blood (chapter 11) are unnamed and included only as props for the important man's story.

I also discovered unfamiliar stories in the Bible that were seldom read in the churches and synagogues of our childhoods. These are graphic and brutal stories of violence against women. The stories of Tamar and The One Who Was Cut into Pieces (chapter 12) were quickly passed over as the stories of their fathers, brothers, and violators were read. And no one—neither in the Bible texts nor in the pulpit—expressed outrage at the treatment of women in these tragic stories.

I became aware of unknown stories that had been excluded from the Bible for a variety of reasons, depending on the particular viewpoint of the rabbis or church fathers who gathered together the "orthodox" texts. And yet some of these stories have been particularly stubborn and have continued to survive on the margins of religious history. The story of Lilith (chapter 8) is being reclaimed by women today.

Throughout my explorations I kept hearing rumors of an unknown story that shadows the whole Bible and its development. There was a time when God looked like us. Tragically around five thousand years ago the worship of Mother God—the Goddess—began to be systematically annihilated. Her temples were destroyed or confiscated. Her writings were burned. Her symbols were denigrated. Her followers were persecuted and killed. This is the story that reaches back before the Hebrew and Christian Scriptures were written. However, in the churches of our childhood we were told, "As it was in the beginning, it is now and ever shall be, world without end. Amen." And "the beginning" was defined by men. Through my exploration I became aware of the woman-affirming stories from the very beginning![2]

As I read and reread the women's stories from the Bible, I became angry at God the father. I wanted to leave the Church. And then I heard the women of old whisper across the centuries in the fragments of their forgotten stories,

> Do not leave until you tell our stories,
>   for in the telling, you will hear your own stories
>   and those of your mothers and grandmothers.
>
> Do not leave until you free us from men's interpretations.
> Our stories reach back in time before we were imprisoned
>   within Hebrew and Christian myths.
> In our freedom, you will discover your own.
>
> Do not leave until you recover our former glory.
> Free our voices to shout out the truth and courage of a lifetime.

Gathering the Fragments

> *We listen carefully to the stories. We hear the women whisper.*
> *They whisper in the fragments of the forgotten.*

Embracing the challenge of the women of old, I asked them to visit my dreams, to whisper their names across the centuries, and to become the feminine face of God for me. I developed the Gathering the Fragments process through which we reclaim women's stories from the margins of religion and history. This process has its roots in Hebrew history. The rabbis reinterpreted the ancient stories to make them relevant for present circumstances. They saw themselves as a bridge between these stories and the contemporary world. Women are now using similar techniques to rewrite the old stories from a woman's perspective.[3]

The Story: As It Was in the Beginning

We gather the fragments of women's stories from our religious memory and from the margins of religion and history. We spotlight their story even if it is only a few lines long. We remember our childhood associations with these stories. We draw pictures and write with our nondominant hand about the women of old. We invite them to visit our dreams, to tell us their names.

The Culture: It Is Now and Ever Shall Be

We study the culture in which each of these women lived and its attitudes toward women. Our stories have always been deeply affected by the history, culture, and taboos of the world in which we live. We cannot extricate our personal stories from the wider story of all women's lives. We imagine the details of the life of the woman we are studying. We imagine her feelings as she goes about her daily affairs. We imagine and expand the story as we place ourselves in her story.

Our Wounds: A World That Prefers Men

We swallow her story into our own lives. We read her story through the lens of our experiences today. How do our stories intersect? What do we know of shame, isolation, violation? We descend into each woman's injuries. As we encounter damaging images, we bring them to the surface. We dance, draw, and write our wounds.

Our Healing: In the Very Beginning

We are reminded of a time when God looked like us. We reach back to when her temples were extravagant; her writings, honored; her symbols, revered; and her stories, celebrated. We reclaim the story that reaches back before the Hebrew and Christian Scriptures were written, before "the beginning" defined by men. We reclaim woman's history from the very beginning! We gather the fragments of the Goddess's forgotten story into our stories, into our bodies, and into our lives. As we encounter healing images, we bring them to our stories. We dance, draw, and write our healing.

A Retelling: A Time That Once Was

Now we retell the story incorporating the healing images of this woman-affirming time. In the retelling we enter the story by means of our own experience, strength, and hope as women. In the retelling we reclaim the fragments of her forgotten story and of our own. Our retelling is a radical act: We extricate women's stories from the all-encompassing stories of men. In this part of *A God Who Looks Like Me*, we will read through the old stories, both as they were told to us and as we transform them by swallowing them into our own.

Ritual: The Community Remembers

The ritual movements of priests and rabbis, the religious images on walls and windows, the sacred dramas of seder or Mass, the meditative silences and chants, and the repetitive litanies and prayers captured our childhood imaginations and linger in our memories. These events were all designed and facilitated by men. Thus the religious beliefs and convictions we were to affirm through these rituals were not based on women's experiences and stories.

As we gather the fragments of women's stories from the margins of religious history and imagination, we breathe life into them in many ways. We give them a voice in our spirits through prayer. In our imaginations through images and symbols. In our bodies through movement. In our breath through silence and meditation. And in our community life through healing touch and creative response.

With creativity and compassion we weave together our movements, prayers, images and symbols, silences and meditations, touch and creative response into a ritual of remembrance. Each ritual shouts across the centuries, "Sisters, we remember you." Each ritual whispers into the depths of our woundedness, "Sister, you are good. You are strong. You are sacred. You are wise. You are whole."

Entering the Fragments

> *Come, enter into the fragments of the forgotten.*
> *They will be unto you healing and life.*

The stories of women will continue to play a prominent role in our explorations. We extend our circle to include the sisters of old. If their stories are known to you, you will be invited to remember childhood associations with the story. For those of you unfamiliar with the Bible, I have chosen stories to illustrate the truth of a woman's life. Familiarity with the particular story is not essential.

Each of the following chapters is a rich tapestry of poetry, ritual, story, meditation, and history. Each chapter is a self-contained experience based on a weekend or week-long retreat. Take your time. Linger with the stories. Allow each woman to accompany you for at least two weeks, preferably a month. As you read through part III, imagine these women of old being invited to your women's spirituality group, to a recovery meeting, or into your home to tell their stories.

Enter into the Courage of Their Stories

We are encouraged by myths, fairy tales, the Bible, movies, and TV to revolve around men—our energy depleted, our attention distracted, and our lives and experiences entangled in theirs. As these women of old extricate their stories from the all-encompassing story of the male God, we will gather more of the fragments of our own stories.

Beginning with our birth as girl-children we will travel through the creation myths and symbols that have shaped us. Then we will venture into our body's unfolding cycles and rhythms. We will explore our vulnerability to rape and incest. At the end of our journey we will embrace the beauty and wisdom of our old age. As we travel together, we will be transformed. We will move out of our isolation and shame. We will move out of our silence and denial.

Along the way we will confront the societal and religious myths that have shaped our reality and our understanding of ourselves:

- The myth of Original Sin that convinced us women are bad
- The myth of the necessity of a male savior that convinced us women are dependent
- The myth of an exclusively male God that convinced us of women's inherent inferiority

These myths were tightly woven into the religious literature, instruction, and rituals of our childhoods. They have been passed on from one generation of women to another. With the support of courageous women we will free ourselves from the crippling effects of these myths. We will recover our former glory, our Original Goodness, power, and divinity.

Enter into the Wounds of the Women of Old

As we allow ourselves to feel what they felt, we will uncover our own wounds. We will see how profoundly we have been affected by the religious stories and myths that have gripped our imaginations. In these stories women's bodies and natural processes were denigrated through powerful religious and cultural taboos. Long after we may have discarded a particular set of religious myths and beliefs, we remain silently poisoned by these taboos. They encircle our natural functions: menstruation, childbirth, and menopause.

The absence of women from the religious history we were taught, and the denigration of our natural processes, have made it impossible for us to imagine our mothers as God, our daughters as savior, or our grandmothers presiding over sacred rituals. This is our deepest wound: We cannot imagine a God who looks, acts, bleeds, or ages as we do. The ineffective behaviors that bring us into the counselor's office, a women's support group, or the recovery community spring from this wound. We want a quick fix, yet our ineffective behaviors keep recurring because the roots of our self-loathing remain untouched.

The healing of these depths takes time and tender patience. To become entirely ready means to plunge into the woundedness of our lives. Only there will we find the God of our understanding. In part II we began our descent. In part III we need to plunge even deeper, since these religious myths and taboos have penetrated into our bodies and our very essence as women.

Enter into the Healing of the Women of Old

No longer imprisoned by men's interpretations, finally speaking in their own voices, these women become the feminine face of God to us. As we glimpse her face, we will find that we are no longer excluded from the image of God. We will no longer believe that we are inferior and flawed. We will no longer need to look to others for validation, legitimacy, and salvation. Instead we will turn toward the rich resources within us. We will move beyond the crippling taboos to claim and honor our bodies, to rediscover our spiritual center, to explore woman-affirming images, and to creatively reinvent old myths.

A Prayer

May you meet Woman God in these pages. May you see her
face in the images. May you bless her body in the meditations.
May you celebrate her life in the stories. With courage confront
the obstacles that may keep you from her.

Face her without shrinking. She is lovely to behold. Face her
without cringing. She is not your judge. Face her without
drawing away. She offers you abundant life.

With assurance and determination turn toward her. She will
inspire you to act on your own behalf in your personal
life and with compassion in the world.

CHAPTER SEVEN

Eve
The Mother of All Living

The Story

As the face of God changes in our experience, we search for the Mother, the Source of All Life. Although intellectually the creation myths of Genesis may seem outdated and irrelevant, they continue to influence each of us. According to Genesis, the book of beginnings, there was no mother present at the creation of the world. The girl-child hears of a motherless beginning. It was the male God who brought the world into being through a series of verbal commands.

The religion of my early years considered the creation myth of Genesis to be the literal truth. It would have been blasphemy even to suggest that the story was a myth woven from the imaginings of our Hebrew ancestors. Because of the literal nature of the teachings I received, the image of a male God ordering the world into being was firmly imprinted on my imagination. I did not even notice the absence of the mother.

A Motherless Creation

> I do not permit a woman to be a teacher, nor must she domineer over man; she should be quiet. For Adam was created first, and Eve afterwards; and it was not Adam who was deceived; it was the woman who fell into sin.
>
> —I Timothy 2:14, *The New English Bible*

Whether it was considered a fanciful myth transmitted to us through the artwork, literature, and drama of our culture, or whether it was considered a literal description of creation pounded into us from the pulpit, the message of Genesis was clear: The God of the heavens was male, and by the words of his mouth the world came into being. The strength of the mother as nurturer and giver of life was effectively eradicated from the account of creation given in Genesis. Just as it was necessary for us to acknowledge the idolatry of God the father, so now we must acknowledge the absence of God the mother. Her invisibility is one of the obstacles we face as we search for a God who looks like us.

Not only was the Mother absent during the creation of the world, the biological process of birthing was reversed so that it was out of man's rib that Eve was born. The tale of Adam, Eve, the rib, the apple, and the Fall is the most fully described story in women's writings. We know this story. It was engraved on the canvases, storybook pages, and memories of our childhoods. The information about Eve that women pick up in their childhoods is simple and very clear.

In my workshops each woman writes a story from childhood remembrances with her nondominant hand. This story is typical:

> Eve was Adam's wife. She was created from his rib. God told them not to eat fruit. The snake tricked Eve and she ate the apple. Then she seduced Adam and he ate it too. They were naked and put clothes on. Eve was bad and God punished her.

It is apparent from women's writings that this story effectively convinced us of our "proper place" as women, of the qualities that define the essence of womanhood, and of the pain and suffering that is the lot of a woman's life. We will explore the three segments of this composite story and the particular ways it has affected the lives of women, whether it was shouted at them as the literal truth in fundamentalism or subtly enforced in the family as they watched it imitated in their parents' lives and relationships.

1. *Eve was Adam's wife. She was created from his rib.*

The image imprinted on women's imaginations is clear: A male God created Adam in his image. Eve was merely an afterthought. She was to keep the man company, to service him sexually, and to keep the garden neat and clean while Adam and God carried on the important business of running the world.

> I was convinced of the inherent inferiority of women. The myth of Adam and Eve firmly embedded this in my consciousness. Woman was given to man as property. This is how I defined "a helper fit for him." My sole purpose was to help and serve men.
>
> —Ann

> The story of Adam and Eve was acted out on a daily basis at my house. From early on I was conscious that my mother was training me to be a housewife and mother. She gave me "helpful hints" about cleaning house, baking, and ironing my father's clothes. I grew up feeling that I was less than my brothers. I learned my role from watching Mom. I was to take care of men and to be available to meet each and every need of other people. My time, energy, and life were not my own. They were to be used in service of others. I was being prepared to meet my Adam and carry on the noble tradition.
>
> —Susan

2. *God told them not to eat the fruit. The snake tricked Eve and she ate it anyway. Then she seduced Adam and he ate it too. They were naked and put on clothes.*

Eve was morally weak and more susceptible to the wiles of the devil than the man was. She was the first to surrender to temptation. She violated God's law and then seduced the man. It was her sexuality that caused the downfall of all humankind.

> I was convinced that Eve was imperfect. She was fatally flawed in some way that made her "fall" inevitable. Her behavior proves the natural inferiority and fickleness of woman.
>
> —Jen

> Eve was bad. She did something wrong. She symbolized that women held a deep-seated corruption within them. Women were corrupters and manipulative temptresses.

> Eve was so evil that she persuaded the most righteous
> man to sin. She used her sexuality as a weapon to seduce
> and destroy him. Her body and beauty were tempting and
> negative.
>
> —Irene

3. *Eve was bad and God punished her.*

Pain and suffering are the lot of a woman's life. We continue to bear the brunt of Eve's act of defiance and her twofold punishment: We are to be submissive to men and we experience pain and suffering in childbirth. Thus Eve's shame and guilt are passed on to all women.

> I was convinced that a woman's punishment extends to
> all of life. She was to be ruled by the man. And from
> all I saw around me, this relationship was painful
> from beginning to end for the woman.
>
> —Jen

> Every time I experienced pain in labor and delivery, I
> cursed Eve for her sin. On a primal level beyond any
> churchy kind of memories, I believed she was the
> cause of my pain. I was being punished as her
> daughter. The pain and pressure of childbirth was to
> remind all of us that we are the daughters of Eve.
>
> —Susan

> As a child I was sure Eve's sin had something to do with
> being curious. Women were curious. It killed the cat.
> Curious women who wanted to know about things
> got cast out of paradise. They got turned into pillars
> of salt by angry male gods. They got sentenced to lives
> of pain and hard labor—in the fields and in childbirth.
> It was all supposed to hurt because Eve was curious.
>
> —Irene

Imagine sitting in a circle with Jen, Ann, Susan, and Irene. Add your story to theirs.

* Had you noticed the absence of the Mother in the creation account?
* Reflect on the relationship between your mother and father. Does it bear any resemblance to the myth? Are they Adam and Eve?
* Do your relationships with men, whether brother, father, lover, spouse, boss, co-worker, or religious leader, bear any resemblance to the myth?
* Use the following as starter statements and reflect on what you were convinced of as a result of this myth:

"Eve was Adam's wife. She was created from his rib."
"God told them not to eat the fruit. The snake tricked Eve and she ate it anyway. Then she seduced Adam and he ate it too. They were naked and put on clothes."
"Eve was bad and God punished her."

Our Wounds

Our first step toward healing is to give voice to the experiences of our personal and religious past that convinced us of the mother's unimportance in the scheme of things, and of our original sinfulness. In the company of courageous women we will acknowledge the wounds of the girl-child who was born into a world that prefers men and worships a male God.

The Exile of the Mother

> My friends were all boys because they were smart and did important things. Women didn't do things that were valuable.
>
> —Hallie

Just as the Mother was exiled from the story of the birthing of the world, so many of us have exiled our own mothers. In a father-centered world separation from the mother is valued. Home is denigrated and eventually left behind. Our mothers had been trained to be expert care-takers and "help-mates" for their men. We watched them ignore their own creativity and vocational interests, set aside their own projects and dreams, and postpone completing their own degrees in order to finance the dreams of others with their blood, sweat, and tears. As we observed our mother's life, we went to any lengths to exile her. Some of us left home, following our father. Creating a home and bearing and nurturing a child were not considered compelling tasks. Making our mark in the father's world was.

I am reminded of a cartoon showing a young girl standing next to her mother at the washing machine. In a moment of enlightenment, she says, "You mean you don't get paid for this!" Daddy gets paid. Mommy doesn't. Many of us who grew up in the sixties and seventies became determined that we would get paid for whatever we did. We postponed or eliminated family as an option. We pursued our careers and wouldn't allow anything to stop us. Our choices seemed to make great sense. The father in Genesis exhibited great power. He com-manded the world into being. He was the initiator of life. The image of Mother God was absent. And the one mother present in the story—Eve—was not valued. She brought sin and death into the world.

Many of us have also exiled the feminine from within us. In order to make it in a man's world, we have felt it necessary to ignore our dreams, intuition, feelings, and tenderness. We considered our feminine qualities an obstacle to our success, so we worked hard to eradicate them. We adopted male characteristics. Now we find ourselves compet-ing with men at their game and adapting to their standards and values.

One woman proudly wrote, "I took a test that was being passed around the office. It had been published in a male-oriented magazine and purported to score one's maleness, machismo, and aggressiveness. 'Just how big are YOUR balls?' it asked. All the guys in the office were taking it, and some smart aleck gave it to me. You can guess the results. I got the highest score in the office. I had the most 'balls.' I've always been very proud of that." At what cost to herself, one wonders, did she achieve that score?

The exile of the Mother has led us to devalue our female sensibilities and gifts. In essence we have exiled ourselves from ourselves. This is why so many of us are now finding that our lives have become unman-ageable. We are plagued by ineffective behaviors that do not support the quality of life we desire. It is the inability to live with these behaviors that has led women into counseling, the recovery community, and supportive women's circles. Are any of the ineffective behaviors listed below familiar to you?

We are relentless in our pursuit of perfection. We have become doers and overachievers. We are driven. We are always on the move.

We deny ourselves close relationships for fear intimacy will distract us from our chosen path. As a result we have become divided within ourselves.

We are unable to ask for what we need. Asking for help is motherly. Going it alone is fatherly. In order not to appear needy like our mothers, we go it alone.

We view other women as competitors not to be trusted.

We keep extra weight on our bodies or wear masculine clothes so as not to be identified as ornamental, frivolous women.

Across the distance we glance back at our mothers imprisoned in societal myths, continuing to limit their lives and eradicate their dreams, and we feel judgment and anger. As they look at our lives across the same distance, they feel resentment and jealousy of our apparent freedom. We can't find our way back home.

Sitting in a circle, the women share the truth of their lives. One by one they speak out of the silence of a lifetime:

> My mother's shame about herself was directly deposited inside of me, so that I now feel her shame. She never seemed to love, respect, or feel proud of herself. She spent all her time giving to and helping others. This infuriated me. Why didn't she just help herself? My anger about this keeps me from being like her. It also keeps me from feeling at peace.
>
> —Sandi

> Being born into a world that prefers boys heightened my sense of perfectionism. For years my primary goal in life was to compete successfully against men. I was driven to prove that I was "as good as" a man. Only work and career achievement were valuable to me. I wanted to be

unlike my mother, the primary alcoholic in my
family. She was a housewife, so if I were a successful
professional, then perhaps I wouldn't become like her. I
ignored my own voice and sense of what would make
me happy. I wanted to be taken seriously, so I played
by the rules that men set.

—Karen S.

The focus of the early political acts of the feminist
movement was on denying and erasing our bodily role
as the creators of life. We wanted to be the same as
men. If we acknowledged the essential biological
differences between the sexes, we would have been
politically incorrect. I think that the language of choice
surrounding pregnancy and motherhood was a not-so-
subtle admonition to choose not to be pregnant, and
if somehow one got pregnant, to choose abortion.
Menstruation was to be suffered through with as little fuss
as possible so as not to pander to the notion that
women were somehow less capable and more
emotionally and physically incapacitated than men.

—Hallie

*Imagine sitting in a circle with Sandi, Karen, and Hallie. Add your story
to theirs.*

• Did the conversations in your home revolve around the activities of your
mother or your father? In mixed groups, whose interests dominated? To whom
were questions directed?

• What sacrifices did your mother make to fulfill her role as mother, nurturer, and housekeeper?

• Can you recall an incident, a moment of enlightenment, when you
became aware that your mother's value in the world was less than your
father's?

• As you observed your mother's life and work, what were your feelings
about your own future life and work?

• Describe your relationship to your mother. Did you emulate your mother or
rebel against her choices?

• Have you exiled the nurturing mother from within you? What ineffective behaviors has this led to?

Original Sin

> In iniquity I was brought to birth and my mother
> conceived me in sin.
>
> —Psalm 51:7

As we have discovered, religious language, imagery, and stories are powerful and exert a long-lasting influence on our lives. Through its words and stories religion deposited shame and guilt within us. According to one interpretation of the Genesis story, God created the world in perfection. Then our original parents committed an act of disobedience— instigated by Eve—and paradise was lost. The children of Adam and Eve, you and I, are born with Original Sin. We are irrevocably flawed, without having taken any willful or conscious action, merely by reason of being born. No matter how hard we try to do what is right, it's an impossible task. We are sinful to our very core, and in need of a savior.

Although Original Sin is a shaming idea for all children, male and female, it carries an extra stigma for the girl-child, since we were taught that it was definitely Eve and not Adam who took the first bite of the forbidden apple. Eve shows up again and again in women's writings. She reminds us that we are responsible for humankind's sin. Erin describes this awesome sense of responsibility: "I feel punished. Yet my only crime was being born. As a child I felt my sin, so I rejected myself. I didn't like the feel of my skin. I didn't like being inside my body. The image of Eve biting the apple left me with a lot of shame. As a girl-child I felt responsible for anything negative, and that it was up to me to make it right."

The early church fathers would be proud of us. We learned their lessons well. Tertullian was a powerful influence in the second-century Church. In his essay "On the Apparel of Women" he addressed women with these words:

And do you not know that you are [each] an Eve. The sentence of God [on this sex of yours] lives in this age: the guilt must of necessity live too. You are the devil's gateway; you are the unsealer of that forbidden tree; you are the first deserter of divine law; you are she who persuaded him who the devil was not valiant enough to attack. You destroyed so easily God's image, man. On account of your desert—that is, death— even the son of God had to die.[1]

Eve was exiled from the garden and shamed throughout religious history as a result of her "sinful" deed. And from a tender age her daughters are taught that what flows naturally and spontaneously from within them is evil, wrong, and punishable. We grow up asking, "What's wrong with me?" This question regularly punctuates our lives as we search far and wide for someone to give us an answer, for someone to offer us a magical insight, treatment, or cure. We have learned a shame-based way of perceiving ourselves and relating to the world. As a result our natural tendency is to feel inadequate, that we're never quite good enough no matter what we do.

In time we internalize those shaming voices of childhood. We place ourselves in a corner as our teachers did. We exile ourselves from the garden of life, as God did. We develop our own self-shaming answers to the question "What's wrong with me?" Each answer becomes another thread in the veil of shame that separates us from the human community. We watch life from a distance, fearful of being found out, of being exposed.

The concept of Original Sin is absent from the Jewish understanding of the Genesis myth.[2] Its shaming implications, however, are whispered loudly enough in the culture and in Jewish legends and folklore to be heard by Jewish women.[3] Embedded within all women is a deep sense that we are flawed and that we are to atone for Eve's sin.

As you read the following stories, reflect on the images, words, and myths used by traditional religion that convinced you of your original flaw and deposited shame within your heart. Although you may have discarded religion's concept of Original Sin as outdated and irrelevant, these women's stories will make you aware of how deeply this sense of sin has affected you.

Sitting in a circle, the women share the truth of their lives. One by one they speak out of the shame of a lifetime:

> The Catholic God of my childhood was condemning, always disappointed in me, and incredibly remote. God

was my father. He was domineering, critical, rigid,
lecturing, angry, and tense. He was drunk, sentimental,
embarrassing, and weak. He was also loving, so it was
confusing. We were imprisoned by his anger. I was a
little clown at his table trying to quell his simmering rage.
The face of God that I internalized was of an angry and
disappointed father whom I could never cheer up or
please.

—Colleen

The "Day of Atonement" as practiced by my family of
origin provided the childhood images and words I associated
with shame and guilt. I never understood what sins
we were to atone for except for the most serious one
of all, breaking the commandment, "Honor thy father and
thy mother." As a preteenager my anger or frustration at
my parents would threaten to erupt, but I kept it in
for fear of breaking that commandment. Every child
must be guilty of that one.

—Hallie

Every time I went to confession, I couldn't remember if
I'd sinned in the past week, so I invented sins and then
multiplied them in the confessional just in case I
missed any. Confession made me feel that there was
something intrinsically wrong with me. As an adult, when
I think of my life and personal growth, I tend to think
of my imperfections and where I need to improve. I
feel unredeemed. A lot of my insecurities are rooted
in the childhood belief in my need for redemption from
Original Sin.

—Annette

When I was seven, a Protestant Sunday school teacher
asked, "Who in this class prays?" Everyone raised their
hand but me. I thought honesty was very important
as a little girl, and because I did not pray, I didn't
raise my hand. I didn't pray because I didn't believe. I
wanted to believe. I tried very hard to understand it all.
But I just couldn't get it. I wondered how everyone

else seemed to get it so easily. Well, the teacher said,
"Let's pray for Joyce's black heart." I felt so embarrassed,
so shamed. I couldn't figure out at that young age how
I could have a black heart. So I began monitoring
myself all the time. I would ask, "Is this going to
cause my heart to be black? Does it get black all at once
or does it darken in patches?" These were the questions
I carried in my heart as a little girl.

—Joyce

*Imagine sitting in a circle with Colleen, Hallie, Annette, and Joyce. Add
your story to theirs.*

• A shame-based religion is one that stresses our wrongs, our defects, and
our insufficiencies. Was this your experience in the church of your childhood?
How did this shame-based perspective affect your attitude toward yourself?

• A shame-based existence is one in which our natural tendency is to feel
inadequate, that we're never quite good enough no matter what we do. Is this
your experience as an adult? How does this shame-based perspective affect
your life on a daily basis?

• As an adult, which question is easier to answer: "What's wrong/bad about
me?" or "What's right/good about me?" Which would be an easier list to
compose: a list of your flaws and character defects or a list of the life-affirming
behaviors that flow from your life?

• Describe your search to find out what's wrong with you. What books have
you read? List the therapists, gurus, and experts you have consulted. What
answers were you given to your question? What insights, treatments, and cures
have you tried? Tally the time and money you have spent on this search.

Our Healing: The Feminine Face of God

Our first step toward healing has been to give voice to the childhood
experiences that convinced us of the mother's unimportance and of our
Original Sinfulness. Now, with courage, we will reclaim the woman-
affirming images and stories of the very beginning, when God was a
woman. We will creatively reinvent old myths and develop new medi-

tations and rituals. As we immerse ourselves in these transformational resources, we will reclaim the Mother of All Living. In her presence we will recover our Original Goodness.

Reclaiming the Original Mother

> As long as we have all male Gods in heaven, we shall have all male rulers on the earth. But when the heavenly mother is revealed, and is sought unto as free and confidingly as the Heavenly Father, then will woman find her proper sphere of action.
>
> —Antoinette Doolittle, 1872[4]

Every people and culture has created stories to make sense of their beginnings. Although in one sense myths are narratives that lie outside of historical time, they are influenced by the values of the community that invents them. The values of the early male-dominated Hebrew community profoundly influenced the myths that were imaginatively created to answer their questions about the origins of life. There is evidence, however, that the Genesis creation myths were not a benign attempt to answer these questions but rather an intentional reversal of older female-oriented creation myths.[5]

In the creation stories that have come down to us from our earliest ancestors, the cosmos and its inhabitants, both human and divine, were birthed by the Great Mother. All gestated within her body and emerged in the fullness of time.[6] The Hebrew mythmakers twisted these stories, in which the Mother had been very much present at the birthing of the world, into a creation "out of nothing." They replaced her with a male God who brought the world into being by a series of verbal commands. Not only was creation motherless but when fragments of the feminine birthing imagery of these earlier myths found their way into the creation stories of Genesis, they were often mistranslated to eliminate all connection to women.

In ancient Mesopotamia it was believed that the Goddess made humankind out of clay and infused it with her own menstrual blood, the fluid of life. In the verse "Then the Lord God formed a man from the dust of the ground," we catch glimpses of this earlier time. Yet the later religious writers chose to translate *ground* as "red clay" rather than its more accurate feminine interpretation, "bloody clay." In this inaccurate translation lies a deep denial of woman and her intimate involvement in the origins of life.[7]

In the Assyrian scriptures the Goddess was referred to as Mother Womb and the Creatress of Destiny. She created male and female in pairs. There are hints of this story in Genesis 1, but the writers changed *she* to *he*. *He* replaced the Goddess. This shift of pronouns indicates a shift of power and a rejection of the feminine.

From the Assyrian scriptures:	*From Genesis 1:27:*
"The Mother-Womb, the Creatress of destiny, In pairs *she* completed them. In pairs *she* completed before her."[8]	"So God created man in his own image; in the image of God *he* created him; male and female *he* created them."

In Deuteronomy 32:18 Moses speaks these words to Israel: "You forsook the Rock that begot you and have forgotten the God that formed thee." The Hebrew word for *begat* refers to the laboring action of a birthing woman, which is an exclusively female image. In certain translations this verse is accurately translated, "You neglected the Rock that begot you. And forgot the God who gave you birth" (The New English Bible). In others the verse reads: ". . . And forgot the God who fathered you" (The Jerusalem Bible). This choice is inaccurate and obscures the feminine qualities attributed to the divine.[9]

✎ AN ENCOUNTER WITH EVE: THE ORIGINAL MOTHER[10]

We reclaim the Mother of All Living by telling the truth of another time, a time when God looked like us. We reach back to when her temples were extravagant; her writings, honored; and her symbols, revered. We reclaim our woman-history from the *very* beginning!

Imagine for a moment that it didn't happen the way they told you in Sunday school, catechism class, or Hebrew school. Imagine that Eve is walking among us. In the depths of your imagination listen as she tells her story, as she reclaims her former glory:

I am Eve, the Mother of All Living, culmination of creation.
I hold and nurture life within me.
In the fullness of time I thrust and push life from me.
And all that I have given birth to is good, it is very good.
  Honor all that has been demeaned.
  Receive all that has been cast aside.

I was once known throughout the world as the Mother of All Living. The wisest among you have always honored me in your myths of beginnings. I have been called by many names, Fertile One Who Births All Things, The Great Mother, Law-Giving Mother, The Bearing One, She Who Gives Birth to the Gods, Queen of Heaven, True Sovereign, Mother of the World, Queen of the Stars. I was called Inanna in Ur; Ishtar in Babylon; Astarte in Phoenicia; Isis in Egypt; Womb Mother in Assyria, and Cerridwen among the Celts.

I was worshiped for many centuries before the God of the Hebrews was imagined into being. As men became threatened by my power and by my intimate involvement in the origins of all life, they swallowed my stories into their unfolding mythologies and twisted my truth. My original power and glory are hardly recognizable in the stories you heard about me in the churches, synagogues, and homes of your childhood. The image of a Father God ordering the world into being was firmly imprinted on your imaginations. Did you even notice the absence of the Mother?

According to the Genesis myth, I was born of the man, from his rib, they say. I am outraged at this twisting of the truth. Who among you was not nurtured in my womb? Who among you has forgotten the source of your life? Jehovah was ignorant of his Mother. In his foolishness he said, "I am God. There is none beside me." His arrogance has always troubled me.

As the Mother of All Living I exist before all things. From my body all that is proceeds. Every mother who bears a child is the embodiment of me. In her pregnancy she holds and nurtures life within her. In her labor she thrusts life from her. She is woman, strong and powerful. She is the Mother of All Living. I am outraged that woman's good, strong body, containing all things necessary for life, and the body of Mother

Earth, which receives back all good things to herself, are objects of disgust and fear, to be controlled and dominated in the Genesis story.

In the very beginning was the Mother.

On the first day, I gave birth to light and darkness. They danced together.

On the second day, I gave birth to land and water. They touched.

On the third day, I gave birth to the plants. They rooted and took a deep breath.

On the fourth day, I gave birth to land, sea, and air creatures. They walked, swam, and flew.

On the fifth day, my creation learned balance and cooperation.

On the sixth day, I celebrated the creativity of all living things.

On the seventh day, I left space for the unknown.

Honor all that has been demeaned.
Receive all that has been cast aside.
The Mother is good. She is very good.

Allow your acquaintance with me to transform your vision of your mother. It is her silence that became your voice; her fear, your courage; her sleep, your awakening; her imprisonment, your freedom. She is your savior. Her silent groanings to be free of confining myths rise up within you and empower you to choose freedom. Together you speak the pain and healing of a lifetime.

Many of your mothers walked and prayed and worked within the Church for years, and their wounds were never touched. Oh, yes, they were prayed for and preached at, but their pain of a lifetime was never touched. How could the words of a male God reach their pain? Of what comfort was a male God who taught your mother to love, honor, and obey her man no matter how abusive his presence or absence? Of what help was a male God who swallowed your mother's anger and imprisoned her protests within her own belly?

I walk among your mothers. I say to them,

Be angry! The prisoners of your bellies are freed.
Shout out your stories. I give you voice.
No more shame. No more fear. No more silence.
Fill the space with your power and your stories.

The wise ones among you walk in solidarity with your mothers, even if at a distance. Speak to her of your commitment across the distance born of anger and of love:

Mother, I will free your voice to shout out the pain of a lifetime.
Your silence is mine. My voice is yours.
Your pain is mine. My healing is yours.
Together we will speak and heal the pain of a lifetime.

*The Mother of All Living has been exiled from the myths of old, from within
us and from among us. For the salvation of the world, may she return. Reclaim her stories from the very beginning. Embrace her within you. Honor
her among you. Embody Her in your life.*

Sitting in a circle, the women reclaim the original Mother:

We reclaim her stories from the very beginning:

> I have discovered early civilizations that honored the Great
> Mother and that held sacred a woman's body. These people
> were connected to the Mother Earth. I yearn for a nurturing,
> loving mother—the mother I never had growing up.
> Perhaps the Great Mother will heal the wounds inflicted
> on the Earth as well as the wounds deep within me.
> Perhaps she will fulfill my deepest needs, needs I
> didn't acknowledge in my journey into the Father's
> world, needs that were neglected in my quest for
> accomplishment in the world.
>
> —Karen H.

We embrace the Mother within us:

> While working to be acknowledged by the outside world,
> I was blinded to the feminine needs to create and nurture,
> and to experience intimacy in my interactions with
> people. I am deeply saddened by my complicity in purging
> the feminine from my life. My family and society
> were highly effective in persuading me to ignore
> essential parts of myself. It was not until I had been in
> recovery two years that I even considered having children
> someday.
>
> —Karen S.

*We remember the times when our Mother reached for the apple, the mo-
ments when she remembered her former glory and refused to obey. We honor
the Mother among us:*

In praise of *my* mother, who allowed me freedom from the Church. She didn't have a spirituality of her own, but she did have a basically woman-affirming perspective on life. This led her to be deeply suspicious of the Church and its priests. She was openly resentful of the Church's view on marriage and child rearing. She rejected the feminine stereotypes that were forced on her. She was a deeply sensual person, and she felt oppressed by the social rigidity of the Church.

Her independence of the Church's influence allowed me to take all of it—Mass, catechism, priests, nuns, my father in his religious persona, and God *him*self, with a grain of salt. Even though we went through the motions in order to avoid incurring my father's wrath, it was clear that she did not swallow what the Church was handing out and that I didn't have to either. Thank you, Mom, for this.

—Colleen

Imagine sitting in a circle with Karen H., Karen S., and Colleen. Add your story to theirs.

• What were your reactions to the reworking of the Genesis story? Were you pleased? Were you troubled? Did you consider the reworking to be blasphemous and heretical, or healing?

• How did your mother's silence become your voice; her fear, your courage; her sleep, your awakening; her imprisonment, your freedom? How did her silent groanings to be free of confining myths rise up within you and empower you to choose freedom?

• Although imprisoned within the Hebrew myth, Eve remembered her former glory as she reached for the apple. Recall the times when your mother reached for the apple, the moments when she remembered her former glory and refused to obey. Imagine your mother breaking out of the myths that have held sway in her heart and life. What might she have done in her life?

• In every tradition there have been alternative creation myths that support a woman-affirming vision. There are stories of a simultaneous creation of man and woman, myths of male and female creators, and myths of the interconnectedness of all living things. Create a series of stories in pictures or in words to explain the beginning of all things. Reflect on the impact each would have on the unfolding of women's lives. Experiment with various Creators: The Great Mother, Mother-Father God, a single male Creator, a single female Creatress, a Cosmic Womb.

Reclaiming Our Original Goodness

> The Mother of All Living saw all that she had given birth to and it was very good.
>
> —"An Encounter with Eve"

As we immerse ourselves in mother-centered myths, we recover the ancient woman-affirming beliefs. They affirm that all of creation is good; that we are originally blessed, not cursed; and that there is strength, goodness, and creativity within each of us. These birthrights are considered the gifts of life. This rich heritage is found within every religious tradition and is rooted in a time when God was imagined as woman. We align ourselves with each tradition that affirms the Original Goodness and sanctity of all life.

We reclaim our Original Goodness by making known the unknown story that shadows the Bible and its development. We reclaim the life-affirming images of the very beginning. Listen as The Mother of All Living continues her story, as she breaks out of traditional religious interpretation.

AN ENCOUNTER WITH EVE: OUR ORIGINAL GOODNESS[11]

I am Eve, the Mother of All Living, culmination of creation.
I hold and nurture life within me.
In the fullness of time I thrust and push life from me.
And all that I have given birth to is good. It is very good.

I refuse to carry the shame of man within my body.
I refuse to carry the helplessness of woman atop my life.
No more!

I was given a pivotal role in men's developing mythology. They say that out of feminine weakness I ate the fruit and then seduced Adam. That

I set in motion a series of events that resulted in our expulsion from the Garden and the release of misery and death into the world.

They say I am guilty and that evil is grounded in my very existence and nature. I have been called the Devil's Gateway, the unsealer of the forbidden tree, the first deserter of divine law, and the destroyer of God's image. Of me was written, "From a woman was the beginning of sin and because of her we all die." For thirty centuries of Jewish and Christian history I have carried the burden of humankind's guilt and shame. No more!

Honor all that has been demeaned.
Receive all that has been cast aside.
I am good. I am very good.

The snake is my wise adviser, counselor, and the interpreter of dreams. Symbol of Sophia, of wisdom, the snake is the bearer of immortality. Life is renewed in the shedding of its skin. Worn on my forehead, held in my hands, and coiled around my body, the serpent has always been my special companion and the symbol of my life-renewing powers.

The mythmakers recognized the importance of the serpent to me. My trusted adviser was no longer to be trusted. Our special connection was demeaned. Instead of trust they placed enmity between the snake and the woman. And the interpreters of Scripture renamed the snake "devil," to be feared and eventually crushed.

Honor all that has been demeaned.
Receive all that has been cast aside.
The snake is good. It is very good.

In the very beginning the sacred grove was the birthplace of all things. Its trees of knowledge and life were intimately connected to my worship. They were not my private property, nor did I wish to control humankind's access to their wisdom. We honored the trees of the grove. We cared for them and caressed them. They held within them the secrets of life, the wisdom of the earth and her seasons, and the awareness of sexuality.

Many Hebrews worshiped in my sacred groves. Hebrew women followed me. Some, in the secret of their hearts. Others boldly rejected Jehovah and convinced their husbands to follow me. When King Solomon grew old, his wives turned his heart toward the Goddess. He did not remain loyal to Jehovah as his father, David, had done. He built hill-shrines in my honor. The mythmakers twisted the truth to serve as a warning to the Hebrew people not to visit my sacred groves nor to eat of the fruit of its trees. And the most zealous of Jehovah's prophets cut down my groves and burned the bones of my priestesses.

To eat of the tree's fruit was to eat of my flesh and to drink of my life-giving fluid. In the woman Eve you catch glimpses of my former glory. She was intelligent, curious, eager, and strong. She ate of the fruit and received the wise secrets of life and the awareness of sexuality. For some this may be the forbidden fruit. For those of us who are Wisdom's daughters, it is a fruit of rare beauty and goodness.

Honor that which has been demeaned.
Receive all that has been cast aside.
The tree and its fruit are good. They are very good.

As the Mother of all All Living, I pick the fruit of life. It is good and satisfies hunger. It is pleasant to the eye and offers pleasure. It is wise and opens the way to self-discovery and understanding.

Those among you who are curious, who lust for life in all its fluidity, dare with me: Bite into life, eat of the fullness of its possibility. Take, eat of the fruit, the good fruit of life. Open to the depths of goodness within you. Believe in your goodness. Celebrate your goodness. Live out of the abundance of who you are as a Child of Life. Affirm the Original Goodness of your children and your children's children until the stories of old hold no power in their hearts.

I am Eve, the Mother of All Living, culmination of creation.
I hold and nurture life within me.
In the fullness of time I thrust and push life from me.
And all that I have given birth to is good. It is very good.

SELF-CELEBRATION

Inspired by the Mother of All Living, we look at the question of "sin" through the lens of our own experience as women. We come to realize that pride, the willful pursuit of power, and the desire to be like God have not been our sins. Godlikeness has never been an option for us. The earth has been ruled by men, and we have had no access to the heavens. Both power and divinity have been denied us. Our place has been clearly secondary and supportive. Our sin has not been pride, it has been self-denigration. And this is not the result of moral defectiveness, but rather it is the result of a profound injury inflicted by a society that worships a male God and prefers men.

If man's sin is pride, then ego-deflation may be an appropriate remedy. Woman's sin has been self-hatred and self-denigration, therefore self-acceptance and self-celebration are more appropriate remedies. Instead of looking outside of our lives toward a male God or Higher Power, we look deep within. We reach beneath our obsession with "bad" behaviors, beneath the accomplishments that mask our sense of unworthiness, beneath years of alienation from ourselves, toward the goodness at our center. We discover that the good is deeply embedded within us and that it is broad and generous enough to include our wounds. As we embrace our Original Goodness, our inner spaces, once cluttered with shame and guilt, are cleared out and reclaimed as our own. We find rest within our lives and accept all of ourselves as worthy.

I invite women to include self-celebration in their daily spiritual practice. Initially this task is overwhelming. We are much more comfortable listing our flaws. Hallie exclaimed in honest exasperation when asked to describe her goodness, "I'm not healed enough for this yet!" And most of us do not even have the words at our disposal for expressing goodness. We begin with a series of affirmations that counter the shame-filled words and images of our childhoods. They offer us a vocabulary for self-celebration. The following affirming words become our Inner Advocates, capable of healing our deepest wounds:

> *I am good, not bad. I am not defective. I was wounded by a society, religion, and family of origin that prefer men and worship a male God. I was taught ineffective behaviors that do not support the quality of life I desire. As I heal, I am opening to the depths of goodness within me. From my goodness life-affirming behaviors flow.*
>
> *I (include your name here) believe in my goodness.*
> *I (include your name here) celebrate the life-affirming behaviors flowing from my life.*

We continue to prepare for self-celebration with a simple meditation that we weave into our daily prayer and meditation. Imagine the Divine Mother approaching you, bearing a multicolored jewel in her hands. She carries it into the darkness of your heart of hearts. The jewel illuminates the many facets of your stunning goodness and giftedness as a Child of Life. Imagine her saying to you, *"Open to the depths of goodness within you. You are good. Celebrate your goodness. You are very good. Live out of the abundance of who you are as a Child of Life. You have everything you need."* Pause for a few moments and acknowledge the goodness and giftedness she illuminates.

Sitting in a circle, the women describe the goodness illuminated by the Mother. One by one, they heal of the shame of a lifetime:

> I have truly descended into my own life over the past five years. At first I only saw darkness. But little by little I am able to discern the faint glimmers of long-neglected or never-acknowledged parts of myself. My therapist has been a beckoning candle on this journey. Instead of finding monsters in my descent, I have found the truth of my childhood. I was never allowed to be just me; I always had to perform.
>
> In searching for a wholeness to my life that, despite outward success, was not there, I am choosing life not death. I now think of my breakdown with its despair and thoughts of suicide as my most life-affirming behavior. By refusing the safe, accustomed mode I had been in, I voided the spiritual death that comes from fragmentation of the soul. And while the abyss I fell into was terrifying, I now see it as the necessary prelude to the fullness I'm stepping into. I'm discovering the treasure of my own spirituality, my need for community, and my essential feminine nature.
>
> —Hallie

> I am no longer ashamed to celebrate myself and the goodness of my life. I am very strong, capable, and coherent. I am actively making wise choices. I am a good mother. I am aware of my boundaries, and I respect those of others. I am nurturing myself by redesigning my life to be simpler, by reevaluating my priorities, and by appreciating what is before me in each moment. I am taking care of my body. I am letting go of any restraints that have kept me from living my life with gusto! I am in touch with my spirituality, defining it according to my truth without any

interference from others, past or present. I am good. I am very good!

Life-affirming behaviors flow from my goodness. To my work, which is hairstyling, I bring creativity. I express my inner beauty through my hands. I touch others and bring beauty and self-love to my women friends. It warms me to know my gift, to grow in my gift, and then to give it away. To my relationships I bring a willingness to finish unfinished business. I choose to be fully present and not to abandon difficult relationships. I love being completely open and not disappearing.

—Erin

Imagine sitting in a circle with Hallie and Erin. Add your self-celebration to theirs.

• Imagine the Mother's jewel illuminating the many facets of your stunning goodness and giftedness as a Child of Life. Describe what you see.

Practice with the following forms of self-celebration. Experiment with one a day for a week.

DAY 1. *Affirmations*

Personalize these affirmations in your own words in your journal and display them in a prominent place in your home or office. Say them throughout the day.

I am good, not bad. I am not defective. I was wounded by a society, religion, and family of origin that prefer men and worship a male God. I was taught ineffective behaviors that do not support the quality of life I desire. As I heal, I am opening to the depths of goodness within me. From my goodness, life-affirming behaviors flow.

I (include your name here) believe in my goodness.

I (include your name here) celebrate the life-affirming behaviors flowing from my life.

DAY 2. *Goodness Illuminated*

Tape your own voice reading the Divine Mother meditation on page 123. Enter into it. Write or draw a description of the stunning goodness and giftedness that the Divine Mother illuminates.

DAY 3. *Discovering Treasure*

Imagine descending beneath your obsession with "bad" behaviors, beneath the accomplishments that mask your sense of unworthiness, beneath years of alienation from yourself, toward the goodness at your center. Describe your descent and the treasures of goodness you discover in words or images.

DAY 4. *Goodness and Life-Affirming Behaviors*

Reflect on the goodness that resides within you and on the life-affirming behaviors that flow from it. List the goodness you bring to your life, your work, and your relationships.

DAY 5. *What's Right About Me?*

Answer this question: "What's right with me?" Spend time with each area of your life, elaborating on all that is right and good: in your work, relationships, choices, body, thoughts, and feelings. Share what's right about your life with a friend today.

DAY 6. *Eat the Good Fruit*

Bring apples into your sacred space. Imagine Eve walking into your space. As she looks into your eyes, she hands you an apple. Hear her say, "Take, eat of the fruit, the good fruit of life. Open to the depths of goodness within you. Believe in your goodness. Celebrate your goodness. Live out of the abundance of who you are as a Child of Life. Affirm the Original Goodness of your children and your children's children until the stories of old hold no power in their hearts."

• As you eat the apple, write a creation story that celebrates your Original Goodness. Read it often to The Girl-Child You Once Were and to the children in your life today.

DAY 7. *Transformation*

At the end of the week reflect: How does the concept of Original Goodness challenge your self-concept? How might daily self-celebration transform your life, your relationships, and your choices?

Before moving on, linger awhile with chapter 7:

❧ REVISITING GENESIS

Set aside time each day this week to converse with The Girl-Child You Once Were. Imagine sitting with her in your meeting place. Converse with her as you would with a daughter or a niece. Draw and write with your nondominant hand in response to the following questions:

DAY 1. *Adam and Eve*

• With your nondominant hand draw a picture of the creation of the world, of Adam and Eve, and of the snake and the apple. Then write a story from each picture.

• With a group of friends pool the fragments of your memory and create a collage of childhood remembrances of the beginning of the world and of humankind.

DAY 2. *Mothers and Fathers*

• Draw a picture of all the things that your mother does in her life. Draw a picture of all the things that your father does in his life.

• Whose life looked like more fun—Mom's or Dad's?

• Did you want your life to look like your mother's or your father's when you grew up?

DAY 3. *Shameful Words and Images*

• Draw the *images* that were imprinted on the imagination of your childhood, the images that shamed and accused you.

• List the *words* used by traditional religion and your family of origin that deposited shame within your Little Girl's heart.

DAY 4. *A Black Heart*

• Reread Joyce's story (page 120) and reflect on how, as a seven-year-old African-American girl, you would have felt about yourself and God to hear your Sunday school teacher say, "Let's pray for ＿＿＿'s black heart."

• Was the color black used to refer to evil or sin and the color white used for purity and goodness? Did this accentuate your sense of sinfulness?

DAY 5. *What's Wrong with Me?*

• Imagine yourself at five, ten, and fifteen. For each age write a list of what's wrong with you. For each age write a list of what's right with you. Which list is longer?

• As a child would it have been easier to answer "What's wrong/bad about me?" or "What's right/good about me?"

DAY 6. *In the Very Beginning*

Create a series of stories in pictures or in words with your non-dominant hand to explain the beginning of all things. Allow the child's imagination to fill you. Experiment with a range of Creators (see the list below). Would their worlds look different?

• The Great Mother
• Mother-Father God
• A Single Female Creatress
• The Cosmic Womb
• A Big Egg

DAY 7. *Be Full of Yourself*

Encourage The Girl-Child You Once Were to write a brag list of all the things she's been proud of in her life. As a good parent, support her to be full of herself.

✑ EGO-DEFLATION FROM A WOMAN'S PERSPECTIVE

If you have chosen to use the Twelve Steps as your spiritual guide, set aside time each day this week to reflect on the Steps from a woman's perspective.

DAY 1. *Ego-Deflation*

The Twelve Step program was influenced by the founders' experiences as men and by traditional religion's sense of Original Sinfulness. Grandiosity, "self will run riot," and pride were considered to be an alcoholic's sins. Ego-deflation was to be the alcoholic's salvation.

• Reflect on these words from AA's Twelve Steps and Twelve Traditions: "All of AA's Twelve Steps ask us to go contrary to our natural desires . . . they all deflate our egos." How does it make you feel that each of the Steps was constructed to deflate the egos of proud and willful alcoholics?

• List the answers each Step gives to the question "What's wrong with me?" For example: Step 1: "I am powerless." Step 2: "I am insane." Step 3: "I am willful." Continue through Step 10.

DAY 2. *No Goodness Apart from Him*

A shame-based expression of recovery stresses our wrongs, our defects, and our insufficiencies. The language of recovery carries on the shame-filled legacy we bring with us from our childhoods.

Reflect on your feelings and reactions to the italicized words. How have you understood these words? Did they trigger early images of shame and guilt?

Step 4: Made a searching and fearless *moral inventory* of ourselves.

Step 5: Admitted to God, ourselves, and another human being the exact nature of *our wrongs*.

Step 6: Were entirely ready to have God remove all these *defects of character*.

Step 7: Humbly asked him to remove *our shortcomings*.

DAY 3. *A Focus on Flaws*

Reflect on whether you would find it easier to list your flaws or to acknowledge your goodness as you read Joyce's words: "I have become very good at focusing on my own wrongdoings and insufficiencies as a result of years of practice. And not surprisingly this has not brought me happiness and purity, but more of the same self-flagellation and introspection."

DAY 4. *Hiding Flaws*

Join the women in our spirituality group and add the "flaws" you are ashamed of to the list below:

I try to hide my judgmental ways.
I hide my strong need to project perfect pictures.
I hide the times when I feel nothing, when I'm numb and hollow.
I hide the fact that I've never been married.
I hide my food binges.
I hide my anger from my family.
I hide the flaw of being needy and human.
I hide the fact that I once chose an abusive man and became a battered
  woman.

DAY 5. *A New Language*

Inspired by the concept of Original Goodness, we look at our ineffective behaviors not as evidence of our fundamental sinfulness but as a consequence of our woundedness. This does not excuse us. We are responsible for our choices. And yet we no longer batter ourselves. Joyce reflects on her changed attitude toward her "flaws": "I believe that it is important to be accountable for my behavior. However, I no longer believe that this occurs by constantly monitoring myself. Instead I am finding that the person I have wanted to be resides deep within me. Healing has involved the gradual uncovering of this person from beneath layers of shame and guilt."

• How might the following word shifts alter your sense of yourself? From *sinfulness* to *woundedness*. From *flaws* to *ineffective behaviors*. From *constant monitoring of ourselves* to *a gradual shedding of layers of shame and guilt*. From *ego-deflation* to *self-celebration*.

DAY 6. *Self-Celebration*

• How might the following words transform your recovery and life? "If man's sin is pride, then ego-deflation may be an appropriate remedy. Woman's sin has been self-hatred and self-denigration, therefore self-acceptance and self-celebration are more appropriate remedies."

• Incorporate the self-celebration exercises on pages 132–134 into your prayer and meditation practice.

• Practice viewing yourself through the lens of Original Goodness today. Each time you are tempted to denigrate yourself or to label yourself as flawed, be reminded of the Mother's words: "You are good. You are very good. There is no blemish."

• Imagine sharing with the Mother of All Living the list of flaws that you wrote on Day 4. Together practice transforming your vision of each flaw based on the concept of Original Goodness and the reality of your deep woundedness.

• Share what's right about your life this week at meetings.

DAY 7. *Transforming the Steps*

Imagine that the development of the Twelve Steps was based on the belief in our Original Goodness. Imagine that each Step answered the question "What's good and right about me?" Rewrite the Steps from this woman-affirming perspective. For example, "Step 1: I do not have all the resources I need to deal with my alcoholism. I have reached out for help to AA. This was a brave action on my own behalf. I celebrate my courage today." "Steps 8 and 9: I will make a list of all those I have hurt in my life and of all those I have helped. I will take responsibility for my ineffective behaviors that have hurt others. I will celebrate my life-affirming behaviors that have helped others even in the most overwhelming moments of my addiction."

CHAPTER EIGHT

Lilith
The Rebellious First Woman

The Story

As the face of God changed in my experience, I searched for images of strong women. My search led me to a remarkable publication. In 1898 *The Woman's Bible* was published by a group of women who were outraged at the inaccurate interpretations of the Bible used to support women's inferior position in home, Church, and society. Written by Elizabeth Cady Stanton and her Revising Committee, *The Woman's Bible* is composed of a series of commentaries and essays dealing with portions of the Bible that had the most impact on the lives of women, either in its degraded portrayal of them or in the glaring absence of their stories and concerns.

The creation and publication of *The Woman's Bible* was a courageous act. In it Stanton and her committee challenged the powers that be: divine authority in the heavens, centuries of male biblical interpretation, and ingrained Church custom. Their look at the Bible from a woman's perspective in 1898 offers us empowering insights as we, in 1995, search through its pages for glimpses of a God who looks like us.

In the Beginning: Two Stories

> A woman must be a learner, listening quietly and with
> due submission ... For Adam was created first, and Eve
> afterwards ...
>
> —I Timothy 2:11–13

Did you know that there are actually two accounts of the creation of
woman and man recorded in Genesis? Which one did you hear in
childhood? (italics added)

A Simultaneous Creation: Genesis 1:26–28

26 And God said, Let us make man in our image, after our likeness: and
let them have dominion over the fish of the sea, and over the fowl of the
air, and over the cattle, and over all the earth, and over every creeping
thing that creepeth upon the earth. 27 So God created man in his own
image, in the image of God created he them; *male and female* created he
them. 28 And God blessed them, and God said unto them, Be fruitful,
and multiply, and replenish the earth, and subdue it; and have dominion
over the fish of the sea, and over the fowl of the air, and over every living
thing that moveth upon the earth.

Woman from the Man's Rib: Genesis 2:18, 20–23

18 Then the Lord God said, "It is not good for the man to be alone. I
will provide a partner for him." [God then created the animals and birds
and gave the man the task of naming them.] 20 But for the man no
partner had yet been found. 21 And the Lord God caused a deep sleep
to fall upon Adam, and he slept; and he took one of his ribs, and closed
up the flesh thereof. 22 And the rib which the Lord God had taken from
man, made he a woman, and brought her unto the man. 23 And Adam
said, This is bone of my bone, flesh of my flesh: she shall be called
woman because she was taken out of man.

In the first account man and woman were created simultaneously,
and both were to have dominion over the earth. In the second, woman
was created from the man and named by him. Elizabeth Cady Stanton

comments on them: "The first account dignifies woman as an important factor in creation, equal in power and glory with man. The second makes her a mere afterthought. The world in good running order without her. The only reason for her advent being the solitude of man."[1]

The second account has been favored throughout Hebrew and Christian history. Its dominance reflects centuries of male control of the teaching, preaching, and interpretive tasks in the Church. From the male perspective its preference may make perfect sense. From a woman's perspective it was a tragic choice, a myth passed on from one generation to another in song, story, and image, convincing generation after generation of girl-children of their inferiority and limiting their dreams and the expression of their gifts in the world. This myth has shaped our sense of ourselves and has provided the blueprint for our interactions with each other.[2]

Although in the churches of our childhood there was no acknowledgment of the contradictions inherent in the two stories in Genesis, there have been many attempts to make sense of them by scholars, who could not ignore the glaring discrepancies. Rabbis who studied and interpreted the Scripture to make its insights relevant to each succeeding generation assumed that God made several attempts to fashion a suitable mate for Adam.[3] Genesis 1, according to these rabbinical commentators, records God's first attempt, which proved unsuccessful and required a second try, which is recorded in Genesis 2. According to the rabbis' legend, a rebellious woman named Lilith was Adam's first wife. She was eventually replaced by Eve, a more docile substitute.[4]

The rabbis borrowed material from the oral traditions, stories, legends, sayings, and folktales of surrounding cultures. They reworked this material and wove it into their commentaries. Because the Goddess was worshiped in the surrounding culture, remnants of her stories found their way into Hebrew myths and interpretations. And because the rabbis were immersed in a male-dominated worldview, their use of Goddess imagery was distorted, and negative images of women abound.

Originally Lilith was a Sumerian goddess called the Divine Lady. Her roots reach into ancient Mesopotamia, dating back to 2300 B.C.E.[5] She was honored as the assertive and sexually self-possessed wild spirit of the night. By the time she found her way into the rabbinical legend as Adam's first wife in the tenth century C.E., her story had been twisted out of shape. She had been stripped of her divinity and had become a demonic image to be cast out. Lilith was greatly feared well into the Middle Ages, and many names and stories have followed her and her daughters, "the Lilim," throughout history.[6]

In the brave tradition of *The Woman's Bible*, we ask Lilith, the legendary first woman, to break out of the confines of traditional religious interpretation. We creatively retell her story from a woman's perspective, incorporating the healing images of the very beginning . . . when God was woman.

PAUSE AND REFLECT

• Which creation story did you hear either in whispers or in shouts as you were growing up: the simultaneous creation of woman and man, or woman created from man's rib?

• Did anyone acknowledge the discrepancies in the stories? Did you notice them yourself?

• How might your life have been different if the first account had been the dominant myth in the religious institutions of your childhood? Which account would you want your daughters to hear?

• Did you ever hear the story of Lilith?

✒︎§ AN ENCOUNTER WITH LILITH: IN THE VERY BEGINNING[7]

I am Lilith. My story is unknown to most of you.
It was excluded from the Scripture.
Yet it is a stubborn story,
    surviving on the margins of religious history.
I am Lilith, the rebellious first woman.
I will tell my own story.
I will reclaim my former glory.

In the very beginning,
    There was Darkness. It flamed forth in power. It asserted itself and I was created. In the image of the Moon was I brought forth. I reach toward the Depths.
    There was Light. It flamed forth in radiance. It asserted itself, and the Sun was created. It reached toward the Heights.

Darkness and Light were equal in dignity. Moon and Sun shone equal in splendor. Depth and Height were held equal in respect.

In the beginning,
There was a dispute. The Light feared the Darkness and its power. The Sun feared the Moon and its night. The Heights feared the Depths and their unknown.

The Light swallowed the Darkness. The Sun swallowed the Moon. The Heights swallowed the Depths. The old ways were almost forgotten. New stories were written.

According to the rabbis, the Breath of Life and the Dust of Earth formed me and Adam. We were created from the same source, so I expected full equality with him. He did not agree with me on that and other matters. He demanded that I serve him and that I lie beneath him when we made love. I was outraged. With the help of "The Name That Is Not to Be Spoken," I flew away. I vanished into thin air and settled at the Red Sea. Adam complained to God, who sent three angels after me. Their attempts to capture me were fruitless. I preferred living alone to life with the man.

My story is very simple. Remembering my former glory before I was swallowed into the rabbis' commentary, I refused to be mistreated by man or God. I did what any self-respecting woman would have done. I said, "Enough is enough," and I left! But you should hear the names they have called me and the stories they have told about me over the centuries. Here are a few:

They call me Spinster because I live alone and am perfectly content. I refuse to allow men to hold me in check. This they cannot understand, so I am called spinster.

They call me Night Hag, not to be confused with ugly, mind you. Some thought my daughters and me so beautiful and so expert at lovemaking that after an experience with us, a man was never again satisfied with mortal women.

They call me Whore, Harlot, and Seducer. Celibate monks tried to keep me away by sleeping with their hands over their genitals, clutching a crucifix. Men say I distract them from their progress toward personal salvation. Eve is the wife, the faithful woman. I am a seducer.

They call me Tormentor of Men. Although my story disappeared from the Bible, my daughters, the Lilim, are said to have haunted men for thousands of years. Well into the Middle Ages Jewish men were manufacturing magic charms to keep away the Lilim. We supposedly appear at night and exert magical powers over young men. They said we caused them nocturnal emissions.

Woven into my reputation are men's deepest fears of impotence and weakness. All that I represent threatens them, so they call me names. They call my refusal to be submissive and subordinate ... rebelliousness. They call my assertiveness in taking care of myself ... bitchiness. They call my independence of men ... unfeminine. They call my sexuality, unconnected to a husband ... unnatural. I am tired of their names!

Woman, is it any wonder you, too, have feared me? They have convinced you that all that I represent is evil, unnatural, and unfeminine. Is it any wonder that you exile me from within you?

Our Wounds

It is essential that we give voice to the experiences of childhood that convinced us that our power, courage, and independence are unfeminine and unnatural. In the company of women we will take our first steps toward healing as we acknowledge these experiences and the societal and religious realities that have shaped them.

The Exile of Lilith

> For over a century, the edge of adolescence has been identified as a time of heightened psychological risk for girls. Girls at this time have been observed to lose their vitality, their resilience, their immunity to depression, their sense of themselves and their character.
> —Gilligan and Brown, *Meeting at the Crossroads*

Although men and women alike are encouraged and rewarded for conforming to the norms of the society in which we live, for women these norms are particularly restrictive and limiting. The girl-child's sense of her life and destiny will be narrowly defined according to a traditional view of femininity. She will not be allowed the fullness of her vitality, expression, power, courage, or independence. In fact she will be taught to denigrate anything that emerges from the depths of her own life.

Born into a world that prefers men, she learns early to twist herself into the acceptable shapes of Church, family, and culture. She will exile her Lilith-like qualities, rejecting her original power, courage, and self-possession. She will feel more comfortable with delicacy, passivity, and dependency.

There was a time, however, in the very beginning of her life, when the girl-child was acquainted with the Lilith within her. At the age of nine a majority of the girls in a survey of three thousand were confident and assertive and felt positive about themselves. Sadly this season of a girl-child's life is short-lived. By the time she reaches high school, she will have forgotten her Lilith-like qualities. She will emerge from adolescence with a poor self-image, relatively low expectations from life, and much less confidence in herself and her abilities than boys have.[8]

OUR ORIGINAL POWER

In the very beginning the girl-child is acquainted with the powerful Lilith within her. She is capable of carrying out any task that confronts her. She has everything she needs within the grasp of her mind and her imagination. She accomplishes great things—in the neighborhood, in her room, and in her mind. The power of the universe pulsates through her. She is full of herself.

There are those who are threatened by the girl-child's Lilith-power. Whether well-meaning or abusive, they will attempt to squash it. They call her names if she insists on owning her power. She is told, "Proud and Uppity One, don't get too big for your britches. Pretend you can't do it so the boys will help you. You'll never be a doctor. The world's a big and scary place for Little Red Riding Hood. Eve's daughters are small, weak, and powerless."

Eventually the Powerful One falls asleep. Occasionally she awakens to remind the woman of what she once knew. These periodic reminders are painful. The woman fills her life with distractions so that she will not hear the quiet inner voice calling her to return home . . . to her own power.

I am a large woman and the world sees this as negative
and threatening. It is not natural for a woman to be
big and strong. At times I have used my size to protect
myself. I can exude an energy that says, "Stay back!" If
I do stand up for my rights, I am considered a bitch.
If I do things my father doesn't understand, he
dismisses me as a lesbian along with any woman who is
strong and powerful.

—Erin

I have a tremendous fear of being better than men, so I
have squashed my strength and deferred to men. As a
woman I have been taught that it is more important
for people to like me than it is for me to express my
full self in the world. I would much rather say, "If you
don't like me, tough. I will not squash myself so that you
will feel better." But I have never said that. Instead I
continue to squash myself, and when I do, I get
depressed, lose all of my energy, stay home, and watch
television.

—Sandi

Imagine sitting with Erin and Sandi. Add your story to theirs.

• Did you ever hear the phrase *the fragile male ego*? Was it ever used to
remind you not to threaten men by displaying your intelligence, your ability to
take care of yourself, and your capacity to carry out complicated tasks without
a man's assistance?

• As an adult have you ever pretended that you don't know what you know,
or that you can't do what you can do, when in the company of men? In what
ways have you "squashed" your power?

• What lessons have you passed on to your daughters regarding a man's
ego and a woman's power?

OUR ORIGINAL COURAGE

In the very beginning the girl-child is acquainted with the courageous
Lilith within her. She is a warrior. Whatever the difficulty, she knows
there is a way to face it. It takes no effort for her to summon up her
courage, to arouse her spirit. With her courage she solves problems.

With her spirit she changes what doesn't work for her. She says no when she doesn't want to be hugged. She says, "I don't like that person," when she doesn't, and "I like that person," when she does. She takes care of herself. The courage of the universe pulsates through her. She is full of herself.

There are those who are threatened by the girl-child's unique courage. Whether well-meaning or abusive, they will attempt to preach it out of her. They will call her names if she refuses to submit. If she says, "Enough is enough," she is told, "Stubborn and Angry One, say yes when you mean no. Give your anger to God. Forgive. Stay. Stick it out. Fulfill the higher purpose to love, honor, and obey. Pain and suffering are necessary to a woman's life. Bear your husband's bad ways in a spirit of penance. Eve's daughters are passive."

Eventually the Courageous One falls asleep. Occasionally she awakens to remind the woman of what she once knew. These periodic reminders are painful. The woman fills her life with distractions so that she will not hear the quiet inner voice calling her to return home . . . to her own courage.

> The Church taught me pain and suffering. Christ died
> for us. Must we suffer so much to gain salvation? Salvation
> from what? Why can't we just be good as ourselves?
> It seems I'm never good enough. The bad part is
> always there holding me down. If I suffer, then I'm okay,
> then I deserve love because of my pain. Why do I have
> to have pain and be a victim to deserve love?
>
> —Sandi

> My mom has never said, "Enough is enough." My earliest
> memories are of my dad brutally beating her. She continues
> to be a self-imposed victim. She will not take the
> responsibility for changing her life. It's very hard for
> me to look at my mother, she represents the victim part
> of me. She is weak, and her body shows signs of a lifetime
> of battering and the neglect of her health. She
> continues to risk her life and her financial security
> because she cannot imagine a meaningful life without a
> man.
>
> —Erin

Imagine sitting with Erin and Sandi. Add your story to theirs.

• Did you ever hear your mother say, "Enough is enough"? Did she ever refuse to be mistreated? How has your mom's choice to be victim affected your life?

• What lessons have you passed on to your daughters regarding pain and suffering? Do they hear you say no or do they see you tolerate unacceptable behavior?

OUR ORIGINAL INDEPENDENCE

In the very beginning the girl-child is acquainted with the independent Lilith within her. She is pregnant with her own life. It is her virgin time. She is content to be alone. She touches the depths of her unique-ness. She loves her mind. She expresses her feelings. She likes herself when she looks in the mirror. The solitude of the universe pulsates through her. She is full of herself.

There are those who are threatened by the girl-child's unique inde-pendence. Whether well-meaning or abusive, they attempt to scare it out of her. They call her names if she chooses a life of her own apart from the other. She is told, "Selfish One, your time, energy, and atten-tion are to be used in service of others. Forget about yourself. You exist for others. You are to wait for the one who will come. Prepare your body and face for his coming. It is most important that you be desir-able. Your real life will begin when the other arrives. This deliverer will change your life. He will make all the waiting worthwhile. Eve's daugh-ters are always waiting."

Eventually the Independent One falls asleep. Occasionally she awakens to remind the woman of what she once knew. These periodic reminders are painful. The woman fills her life with distractions so that she will not hear the quiet inner voice calling her to return home . . . to her own independence.

> Mother's first child was a boy. He died in infancy. My father died when I was nine. Consequently there were no men or boys in my family. In the memory of my father, the preference for the male survived. Mother idolized him. She didn't develop her own gifts. She kept him alive through her descriptions of him. After his death we moved in with her bachelor brother. She lived

through the males who surrounded her life. By
watching her I learned to do the same thing.

—Laura

Imagine sitting with Laura. Add your story to hers.

• What was your family's attitude toward independent women who
expressed their ideas?

• Were there women in your extended family who preferred life alone? How
were these women talked about? Were you ever encouraged to consider the
possibility of a life without a man?

• As an adult does your fear of being alone drive you from one relationship
to another? Does it make you settle for less? Does it force you to remain loyal
to abusive partners?

• Have you ever called a woman names such as "bitch," "witch," or "ball-
buster" because she refused to apologize for her life, her ideas, and her
power?

• What lessons have you passed on to your daughter regarding her life
choices?

Our Healing

We have given voice to the experiences of childhood that convinced us
that our power, courage, and independence are unfeminine and unnatural. Now we will retrieve the collective story of women from the margins of history and religion. With courage we will retell Eve's and
Lilith's stories, incorporating the healing images of a time when God
looked like us. As the Mother of All Living and the Rebellious First
Woman meet within us, we will recover our original capacity both to
nurture and to take assertive action.

Reclaiming Lilith

> As I descend into my Lilith-self, I am reclaiming my anger
> and strength. I no longer look to men to express my
> assertiveness.
>
> —Annette

We reclaim Lilith by telling the truth of a time when God was a strong woman. We learn of ancient women who did not apologize for their power, courage, and independence. We recall ancient times when women were honored for both their strength and their tenderness, for their capacity both to nurture and to accomplish great things.

We reclaim those ancient ways that taught women to refuse submission and subordination, that applauded women for their assertiveness, and that encouraged women to be independent of men. We reawaken ancient beliefs in a strong and capable Goddess who was trustworthy, who acted on her own behalf and the behalf of all women, and who could say, "Enough is enough" and make it so.

Inspired by a time that once was, we descend into our own lives to reclaim the exiled resources of power, courage, and independence. Lilith, the wild spirit of the dark depths, accompanies us in our descent.

WE RECLAIM OUR POWER

Working with incest survivors, I struggled to find an empowering feminine image that would awaken their own inner power. Many had been encouraged to embrace power in the form of "the masculine within them." This seemed to be an inappropriate image for those who had experienced sexual exploitation at the hands of men. Many found it a disempowering image that triggered memories of their sexual abuse.

The centrality of an admission of powerlessness in self-help philosophies also disturbed me. Men and women bring different experiences to the concept of power. For men to acknowledge their powerlessness means relinquishing the illusion of power with which they have been saturated since childhood. This admission allows them to seek significant connections and mutually supportive relationships within a spiritual, therapeutic, or recovery context.

Women, on the other hand, have been admitting powerlessness most of their lives. Our access to thrones, negotiating tables, boardrooms, pulpits, and presidencies has been limited. Our position has been clear. We are inferior and powerless. Thus the admission of powerlessness, as it has been defined by men, has not been woman-affirming. What women need to do instead is to reclaim their original power.

As women recognize the Lilith within them, they redefine power as the capacity to act on their own behalf, to author their own lives, and to deal with whatever situation confronts them. For men, the admission of powerlessness was essential in order to experience connection with others. For many women, walking into their first therapy appointment, women's support group, or recovery meeting is a powerful act on their own behalf.

Lilith reminds us of what we once knew in the very beginning of our lives. Inspired by her, affirm your original power as you read these words:

I am capable of carrying out any task that confronts me. I have every-thing I need within the grasp of my mind and my imagination. I accom-plish great things—in my home and neighborhood and in the world.

I am a Proud and Uppity One. I am too big for my britches. I do not need the boys' help. I will be a doctor or a mother or whatever I want to be. I am capable. The power of the universe pulsates through me. I am full of myself.

WE RECLAIM OUR COURAGE

Lilith, who is a potentially healing image to support women to take ac-tion on their own behalf and to expect equality in their relationships, was twisted by male-dominated religion into a demon who terrorized men. Likewise her story was twisted into a warning against rebellious wives who leave abusive situations. It is now time for women to reclaim Lilith and her story. She took care of herself. She said, "Enough is enough" and refused to be mistreated by God or man.

Lilith teaches us to embrace our anger and to act with strength on our own behalf. She gives us the courage to leave situations that are abusive. In every aspect of our lives Lilith encourages us: "Be strong. Be powerful. Exert. Initiate. Move." Imagining such a mother, Ferrel wrote, "Every aspect of my life would have been better. I would have a much stronger idea of who I am today, because all of these exertive commands would have pushed me to test myself, to know myself, to experience myself, and to be active in the world."

Lilith reminds us of what we once knew in the very beginning of our lives. Inspired by her, affirm your original courage as you read these words:

I am a warrior. Whatever the difficulty, I know there is a way to face it. It takes no effort for me to summon up my courage, to arouse my spirit. With my courage I solve problems. With my spirit I change what doesn't work for me.

I take care of myself. I say no when I don't want to be hugged. I say, "I don't like that person," when I don't. I say, "I like that person," when I do.

I am a Stubborn and Angry One. I leave when I want to. I refuse pain and suffering. I am active. The courage of the universe pulsates through me. I am full of myself.

WE RECLAIM OUR INDEPENDENCE

Generations of girl-children have been crippled in the expression of their lives because the images of strong, self-contained women have been exiled from religious history. The women's stories that were read in the churches and synagogues of childhood were designed to cultivate and reinforce our helplessness. Convinced of the customary, the girl-child doesn't even consider the option of a solitary life. A life alone is portrayed as a curse, something to be avoided at all costs. It takes tremendous courage for the girl-child to create an original life that is not centered on a relationship.

Rather than twist herself out of shape, Lilith left the customary path and entered the territory of her own experience. We follow her. We travel as she did to the "faraway" place to get to know ourselves. We choose to be alone, whether for an hour a day, a weekend a month, or for a full season of our lives. Whether we are in a significant relationship or not, we take time to nurture and replenish our spirits. In our solitude we relearn the lessons of Lilith, the Independent One. We are reminded of our personal dreams and goals. We develop a relationship with our inner resources.

Lilith preferred life alone to life with a man. With her encouragement some of us reclaim this as an option. Inspired by her courage, we choose abstinence from sexual and romantic relationships for a month or a year, or for a lifetime. In our abstinence we deepen our contentment and satisfaction with our own lives. We reclaim our abundant inner resources. We develop a firm commitment to our own true potential. We have come to believe that a relationship with another will not be deeply satisfying unless our primary commitment is to ourselves.

Lilith reminds us of what we once knew in the very beginning of our lives. Inspired by her, affirm your original independence as you read these words:

I am pregnant with my own life. This is my virgin time. I am content to be alone. I touch the depths of my uniqueness. I love my mind. I express my feelings. I like myself when I look in the mirror. My body and face are my own. I am desirable to myself.

I am a Selfish One. My time, energy, and attention are used in service of my own life. I remember myself. I exist for myself. I change my life if I want it changed. I will not wait for one to come. My life begins anew each moment. The solitude of the universe pulsates through me. I am full of myself.

Reclaiming Our Wholeness

> A feminine God needs to embody the qualities of both Lilith and Eve to be useful for me. I need to draw on my assertiveness and strength, and on my compassion and nurturing every day. I can't live life fully without both.
>
> —Karen S.

Lilith represents our capacity for independent, assertive action. Eve, the Mother of All Living, represents our intimate involvement in the origins of life. In a world that prefers men, the fullness of our power as both nurturers *and* achievers is feared. We've been allowed access to only a portion of our power. If we choose to be involved with the origins of life through our role as childbearer and nurturer, we are denied full economic and social equality. If we choose to exert our intellect, initiate our dreams, and move into the world with ambition, we have had to deny the nurturing mother within us. The connection to our

Original Wholeness has been severed. It is time for women to integrate both aspects of themselves once again: their Eve-like nurturing qualities and their Lilith-like assertive qualities.

Inspired by a time that once was, when women were honored in both their capacity to nurture and their capacity to exert, we imagine Lilith wandering at the edge of the Garden. She meets Eve, the woman who replaced her. We imagine Eve and Lilith eating fruit together and exchanging stories. They play in the earth and imagine their beginnings. They imagine the earth as a womb. In the fullness of time they are born of Mother Earth. They name themselves.

> *Eve shouts,*
> *"I am the Mother of all Living, culmination of creation.*
>   *I hold and nurture life within me.*
> *Welcoming is my womb, nurturing my love.*
>   *In me, you are enclosed and sustained."*
>
> *Lilith speaks,*
> *"I am the Rebellious First Woman.*
>   *Strong is my womb, powerful its thrust.*
> *In the fullness of time I push life from me.*
>   *In me you exert, initiate, and move."*
>
> *In one voice they speak across the centuries,*
>   *"We were woman divided. Now we are one."*

✑ A WOMB PRAYER

At the conclusion of our Mythic Mother retreats, we call upon Eve and Lilith to support us in our daily lives. From Eve we relearn the lessons of the nurturing womb. We acknowledge our limits. We sit and rest awhile. She offers us the serenity to accept the things we cannot change. From Lilith we relearn the lessons of the pushy womb. We acknowledge our power. We thrust forth and push into life. She offers us the courage to change the things we can.

Imagine yourself standing in a womb-shaped circle of women. We are birthing each other into life. We enfold her gently or thrust her forth powerfully, depending on the expressed need of each woman. The womb prayer has three parts: "A Prayer to Eve, the Mother of All Living," "A Prayer to Lilith, the Rebellious First Woman," and "A Collage of Gratitude to Our Mythic Mothers." As you read through it, reflect on this question: "Which Mother do you need today?" They are both present within you. They will hear your prayer.

A Prayer to Eve, the Mother of All Living

Standing in our womb-shaped circle, we ask, "Is there anyone among us who desires the gifts of the nurturing womb? To sit and rest awhile? To have your wounds caressed or dreams held tenderly? To cry on a shoulder? To be granted the serenity to accept the things you cannot change?"

> *Susan answers:* "I need Eve because my parents were so critical. In their desperation to have a perfect daughter, they pushed me to perform. I worked hard to do all the things expected of a good daughter. And I'm still being perfect about it all. I would like permission to mess up a bit. I need Eve's nurturing and acceptance."

> *Jen answers:* "I need Eve. I have a lot of driving energy within me. I am always pushing myself. I never rest. I imagine Eve as an abundantly warm and round woman. I want to crawl into her roundness and be held. I want to feel that I am loved for just being. I would like to rest awhile."

Together we call on Eve. She is within us. We say aloud, "Source of Life, to you we come. Welcoming is your womb. Nurturing is your love. In you we are enclosed and sustained."

One at a time Susan and Jen stand in the center of our womb-circle. We welcome them in our womb. We nurture Susan with our love and acceptance. We rock, support, and enfold Jen. We caress their wounds. We hold their dreams tenderly. We receive their tears. We offer them the gifts of Eve.

A Prayer to Lilith, the Rebellious First Woman

Standing in our womb-shaped circle, we ask, "Is there anyone among us who desires the gifts of the pushy womb? An acknowledgment of your power? The courage to change the things you can? The courage to move out of an abusive situation or to initiate a new adventure?"

> *Ferrel answers:* "I need Lilith to push me to be the creative and outward person I once was. My first major in school was drama. Yet as an adult

I have been anorexic as far as accomplishment is concerned. I've stayed in frustrating clerical jobs, although I have wanted to leave. I need Lilith to push me out there—doing what I want to do, stepping to the front of the stage and showing who I am."

Erin answers: "I have allowed men to dominate me. In my current relationship I still have a hard time speaking up. I give up more power than I want to. I'm loyal. I stay too long. I need Lilith's words 'Enough is enough' to fill me with the courage to get out of the troubling relationship I'm in."

Together we call on Lilith. She is within us. We say aloud, "Source of Life, from you we are pushed. Strong is your womb, powerful its thrust. In you we exert and initiate and move."

One at a time Ferrel and Erin stand in the center of our womb-circle. Our breath quickens. Our womb contracts. We are readying to push Erin forth, out of an abusive relationship that is depleting her energy and life. We are readying to push Ferrel forth into a new career adventure. We encourage each sister to exert, initiate, and move on her own behalf as we thrust her forward into her life. We offer her the gifts of Lilith.

A Collage of Gratitude to Our Mythic Mothers

Now we create a collage of gratitude to Eve and Lilith. They have become images of healing and transformation for us. They have offered us gifts as we have embraced the exiled pieces of ourselves. Imagine sitting in a circle with Karen, Liz, and Laura. Add your expression of gratitude to theirs. Acknowledge the gifts you have received from your Mythic Mothers.

Karen S.: "I am grateful for a mythic female role model who symbolizes the qualities of assertion and initiative often associated with men. Her image has made going about the business of getting what I want professionally less difficult and painful. It is invaluable to realize that these aggressive characteristics are also feminine."

Liz: "I am grateful for Eve and Lilith, who are not idealized objects of pleasure or Hollywood goddesses. They are assertive and powerful women who encourage me to embrace my identity apart from the relationship I am in at the moment. They encourage me to embrace both the passive and the pushy energies within me. They balance me. I am both nurturing and self-confident. These qualities are not mutually exclusive."

Laura: "In praise of Lilith and Eve. In praise of the hard and the soft within myself, within women. In praise of the rigor, honesty, and hardness that cracked the armor. In praise of the powerful thrust from within, saying: Birth yourself, Laura; that is your imperative. Be soft again only when you are open and willing to be whole. In praise of the strength and austerity of your intelligence and its refusal to compromise with lies. In praise of gender-bending role reversals and all the shades in between."

Before moving on, linger awhile with Chapter 8:

THE GIFTS OF THE NURTURING WOMB, THE GIFTS OF THE PUSHY WOMB

Each day this week imagine standing in a womb-circle with a group of trusted women: mythic figures who inspire you, teachers and relatives who loved you in your early years, and friends who support you today. Create a collage or draw a picture of this powerful circle of women. Display it as a reminder of the support that is available to you daily.

The Gifts of the Nurturing Womb

• Do you desire the gifts of the nurturing womb: to sit and rest awhile; to have your wounds caressed, or your dreams held tenderly; to cry on a shoulder; to be granted the serenity to accept the things you cannot change? Acknowledge your need. Write, draw, dance, or sculpt the gifts of Eve that you desire.

• Imagine being nurtured by the inspiration, love, and support of your womb-circle. Imagine being rocked, supported, and enfolded by them. They caress your wounds. They hold your dreams tenderly. They receive your tears. Receive the gifts of Eve.

• Reach out to the women in your life this week. Share with them your need for a tender, nurturing presence. Allow them to be the feminine face of God to you.

The Gifts of the Pushy Womb

• Do you desire the gifts of the pushy womb: an acknowledgment of your power, the courage to change the things you can? Out of what situations do you need the courage to move? Into what new adventures do you need the courage to initiate movement? What situations are calling you to exert yourself? Write, draw, dance, or sculpt the gifts of Lilith you desire.

• Imagine the womb-circle quickening in its breath, contracting, readying to push you forth out of an abusive relationship or a situation that is depleting your energy and life. Into a new adventure of study or positive risk. Imagine the inspiration, love, and support of your circle encouraging you to exert, initiate, and move on your own behalf as they thrust you forward into your life. Receive the gifts of Lilith.

• Reach out to the women in your life this week. Share with them your need for courage, challenge, and support. Allow them to be the feminine face of God to you.

ᵛᶄ LOST AND FOUND

Set aside time each day this week to converse with The Girl-Child You Once Were. Imagine sitting with her in your meeting place. Draw and write responses to the following questions with your nondominant hand:

DAY 1. *Power Lost*

• Describe your Lilith-power. Were you a tomboy?
• For how long were your powerful ways tolerated?
• How did others attempt to squash you? What names were you called? Draw or dance the powerless one you became.

DAY 2. *Power Found*

• Imagine being told by your mother as a child, "You can do whatever you set out to do. Accomplish great things in the neighborhood, in your room, and in your mind. The power of the universe pulsates through you. Be full of yourself."
• Draw or dance the Powerful One you desire to reclaim.

• How might the Powerful One support you in your life today? Write her a letter describing a particular situation in which you need her power. Ask, "Where are you within me?"

DAY 3. *Courage Lost*

• Describe your Lilith-courage, the warrior you once were. Did you speak your mind? Did you say no to things you didn't like? Draw the warrior.

• For how long were your courageous ways tolerated?

• How did others attempt to shame you? What names were you called? Draw or dance the victim you became.

DAY 4. *Courage Found*

• Imagine being told by your mother as a child, "Be strong. Exert. Initiate. Move. The courage of the universe pulsates through you. Be full of yourself."

• Draw or dance the Courageous One you desire to reclaim.

• How might the Courageous One support you in your life today? Write her a letter describing a particular situation in which you need her courage. Ask, "Where are you within me?"

DAY 5. *Independence Lost*

• Describe your Lilith-independence, the self-possessed one you once were. Draw her.

• For how long were your independent ways tolerated?

• How did others attempt to scare you? What names were you called? Draw or dance the dependent one you became.

DAY 6. *Independence Found*

• Imagine being told by your mother as a child, "Touch the depths of your uniqueness. Love your mind. Express your feelings. The solitude of the universe pulsates through you. Be full of yourself."

• Draw or dance the Independent One you desire to reclaim.

• How might the Independent One you once were support you in your life today? Write her a letter describing a particular situation in which you need her independence. Ask, "Where are you within me?"

DAY 7. *Healing Images and Movements*

• Gather images of strong, nurturing women. Display them in your home.

• Gather the images you drew this week of the Powerful, Courageous, Independent One you are reclaiming. Find a special place to display your artwork.

• Choreograph a dance using the movement vocabulary you have developed this week. Dance the Powerful, Courageous, and Independent One you are reclaiming as she emerges out of the powerless, victimized, and dependent one you became.

Mary
The Virgin Mother

The Story

As the face of God changed in my experience, I wondered about Mary. My own memories of her were confusing. She had been both elevated and demeaned. In the Catholic orphanage of my elementary school years, she was presented as the Queen of Heaven. In the Catholic missal I was given there was a "Litany to the Blessed Virgin Mary" that listed forty-eight names for her, including twelve concerning her queenship. The pictures I kept of her in my missal were queenly indeed. She was high and lofty, and surrounded by stars and halos and crowns.

In the Protestant church of my adolescence, there were no statues of Mary, no missals with pictures of the Queen of Heaven, no feasts in honor of the Blessed Virgin, no rosaries or Hail Marys; only church-school plays in which Mary was portrayed as a meek woman with pregnant belly, covered head, and downcast eyes. The Protestants had dethroned Mary, and I had to go into hiding with my love and devotion to her.

Mary's journey from heaven, where she reigned as honored queen, to earth, where she was reduced to obedient handmaiden, was orchestrated by men. Would it be possible, I asked myself, to disentangle her story from the all-encompassing salvation drama of the Father, who sent his son to earth through Mary's womb? Was there a middle space where earth and heaven meet; where the Queen of Heaven, virginal and perfect, meets the Mary of earth, embodied and human?

Contrasting Visions: The Historical Mary and the Second Eve

> Hail Mary, full of grace! The Lord is with thee. Blessed
> art thou among women, and blessed is the fruit of thy
> womb, Jesus. Holy Mary, Mother of God, pray for us
> sinners now and at the hour of our death. Amen.
>
> —The Catholic Daily Missal

Although the God of Judaism and Christianity allows no woman to share his power or throne, Mary is the one sacred female who has come the closest to storming his heavens. She has maintained a powerful and stubborn presence within religious discussion, devotional literature, classical art, and within the hearts of her faithful followers and the anger of her detractors throughout the centuries.

Mary is the religious woman who appears most often in the writings of women. She is remembered with a mixture of awe, anger, and confusion. Many women have spent their lives either emulating or rejecting the image of her presented in the churches of their childhoods. As we acknowledged in chapter 6, most women cannot imagine God as a woman because of the negative and often confusing portrayal of women through word, image, and story in the churches of our childhoods. Like Eve and Lilith, Mary was presented to us through the eyes of men. Catholics and Protestants were offered contrasting visions of her.

The Protestant Mary was confined to earth. She was only valued for the role she played in Jesus' birth. We are not given many details of her life in the scriptural record, only those facts most pertinent to her role as mother of Jesus. Her story revolves around the men in her life— Joseph, her husband; Jesus, her son; and the Lord God, her Master in heaven. She lived in a culture in which women were legally the possessions of men. Before Mary's marriage she was under her father's authority. At her marriage she became the property of Joseph. And when Joseph died, a disciple of Jesus was appointed to care for her. Mary was a good and faithful Jewish adolescent girl, who obeyed the dictates of God and man.

The Catholics raised Mary above life with lofty words about her virginity (Holy Virgin of Virgins) and her immaculate conception (Queen Conceived Without Sin). In catechism classes and sermons there were few references to the human dimensions of her life as the wife of Joseph and the mother of Jesus. Rather it was her participation in the elaborate drama of human salvation reaching back to Eve that was of utmost importance. The unfolding of this salvation drama in the complex imagination, thinking, and writing of the church fathers and theologians inextricably linked the stories of Mary and Eve.[1] In a tragic sense they have been rivals throughout religious history. The image of each was fashioned in reaction and response to the other—by men:

Eve is the Mother of Evil, who was disobedient and sexually sinful. Humanity's fall from grace was instigated by the loss of her innocence and virginity.

Mary is the Mother of God, who was obedient and virginal. Humanity's salvation through grace was transacted through her virgin body.

Eve elevated disobedience. Through the disobedience of this one woman sin entered the world. Eve disobeyed God's command and released death. She refused to obey and ate the fruit.

Mary elevated obedience. Through the obedience of this one woman the savior entered the world. Mary obeyed God's command and released life eternal. She said, "Do unto me according to your will."

Eve elevated sexuality. She committed the sexual act. Her body seduced the good man Adam to join her in sin. She was exiled from the heavens as Whore and Temptress.

Mary elevated virginity. She abstains forever from the sexual act. Her body is eternally covered and beyond desire. She is allowed in the heavens as Madonna and Virgin of all Virgins.

Eve is the Fallen Mother. She experienced suffering in childbirth. She bore children in pain.

Mary is the Sacred Mother. She experienced no pain in childbirth. She bore Jesus joyfully.

Eve is the Human Mother. God gave birth to her.

Mary is the Heavenly Mother. She gave birth to God.

As children we weren't aware of the elaborate theological discussions concerning Mary except as they filtered down to us by way of the songs, prayers, and religious scenes of childhood. It is these that reside within us. Women share their early remembrances of her:

> Mary was a nonperson with no anger and no spine. She was the only female I saw in church, and she was only half human, reduced as she was to only good qualities. This irked my mother and she rejected the Church in part because of it.
>
> —Colleen

> In the front of the church there was a crucifix with Jesus on it, and over to the right, not quite as prominently positioned, was a statue of Mary. That was confusing. Was this ideal woman who I was expected to live up to equal to God or not? I remember very distinctly saying the rosary to her while doing the stations of the cross. I can feel this memory in my fingers.
>
> —Karen H.

> To us Protestants Mary was an object, an empty vessel, just a space holder for the divine Christ. She was insignificant. I remember my mom explaining that "those Catholics" worshiped Mary and how ridiculous that was. After all, she argued, everyone knew that men had all the power and only through Christ could we be saved. I got the impression that "those Catholics" were frivolous and wasting their time praying to "just" a woman.
>
> —Irene

Imagine sitting in a circle with Colleen, Karen, and Irene. Add your story to theirs as you reflect on your earliest remembrances of Mary.

- What were your feelings about Mary? Does she bring up awe? Anger? Confusion?
- Did you want to be like Mary, or did you reject her?

Our Wounds

In the company of courageous women we will give voice to the experiences of our personal and religious past that robbed us of our sexuality and stripped us of our willfulness. As we tell our stories, we will move out of the isolation of a lifetime. This is our first step toward healing.

Chastity at All Costs: Our Twisted Bodies

> It is obvious that the man has had society's blessing to
> build his sexual value system in an appropriate, naturally
> occurring context and the woman has not. During
> her formative years the female dissembles much of her
> developing sexuality in response to societal requirements
> for a "good girl" facade.
> —Masters and Johnson, *Human Sexual Inadequacy*

In the beginning, as defined by men, Eve elevated sexuality. She committed the sexual act. Her body seduced Adam to join her in sin. As a result she was exiled from heaven as Whore and Temptress. Eve's predecessor, Lilith, embodied assertive sexuality. She refused to submit to the man, to lie beneath him. Her unfettered sexuality was her fatal flaw. She is exiled from the Bible as Demon Mother and Tormentor of Men.

In the beginning of Christian history the Queen of Heaven was shaped by men to eliminate the woman's body and its troublesome sexuality. The Sacred Woman elevates virginity; she abstains forever from the sexual act. Her body is eternally covered and beyond desire. The Virgin Mary was robbed of her body and stripped of her sexuality. She is allowed in the heavens only as Madonna and Virgin of All Virgins.

ASSAULTED BODIES

At every point in religious history women's bodies have been assaulted by male priests, ministers, rabbis, theologians, and religious writers. Men have always feared women's bodies. Religious males in particular have had a powerful obsession with them. They have written volumes on the subject. Instead of dealing with their own attitudes, their own sexuality, and their own responses to our bodies, they have twisted us out of shape through their teachings and theologies. Our bodies bear the brunt of their deeply embedded fear of the feminine.

The God created in their image is male. And although theoretically "he" is considered to be asexual and elevated above *all* sexuality, it is clear that he and his male representatives are raised above female sexuality only. Embarrassed by their own sexuality and bodies, and confused by ours, they attribute to the divine the less-embarrassing qualities of power, might, and intelligence.[2]

The maleness of God and the inferiority of women were woven into the religious literature, instruction, and ritual that surrounded us in childhood. According to Aristotle's biology the male form is normative and, when distorted by female matter, it produces an inferior species— woman. Thomas Aquinas, the thirteenth-century Catholic theologian who adopted Aristotle's theories on biology, considered the male as the normative sex of the human species. He believed that the male represents the fullness of human nature, whereas woman is defective physically, morally, and mentally.[3]

When the salvation of humankind required that God "become flesh and dwell among us," it was necessary for God to become flesh in a male body.[4] God would not have chosen to become flesh in a woman's inferior and defective body. And yet it was clear that Jesus had passed through a woman's body on his way to earth. The female body had one value—as a vessel of reproduction for the male seed.

Male theologians reconstructed Mary's womb, however, to eliminate as much of the reality of her womanness as possible. The Queen of Heaven had no womb; the place of Christ's gestation is referred to as a "casket." In the words of one theologian, "Christ is the gleaming jewel contained in the casket which is Mary."[5] The term *casket* conjures up images of a minicoffin or container with satin-covered walls. Its purpose was to protect the Son of God from the defilement of entering life through a woman's messy, bloody, and inferior body. In other words Mary's body had no inherent value except to be used by God the father. Through the casket image men once again denied woman's intimate involvement in the origins of life.

AN UNREACHABLE IDEAL

After her task was completed, Mary was transformed into the Queen of Heaven. She was allowed into the kingdom of God, as the eternal virgin with an unbroken hymen and as sacred mother of the savior son. As virgin and mother Mary served as an unreachable ideal for good girls who desired to emulate her. How could we be mother, requiring the sexual act, and at the same time virgin with an unbroken hymen?

Given the impossibility of Mary's example, we were left with a set of either-or propositions that denied us any sense of wholeness. Either we emulated Madonna Mary, denying our sexuality, or we became Whore Eve, denying our sanctity and worthiness. Either we aspired to be Heavenly Celibate Queen, out of the reach of men's needs, desires, and touch; or we became a mere earthly woman, subject to men's needs and desires, and trespassed by their touch. Either we surrendered as the docile wife of one man, or we became the sexual tormentor of many.

Although many of us left the Church years ago, our bodies have remained shadowed by religion's assault on our self-image and our bodies. As a result of the elevation of Mary's chastity and sacred motherhood, we developed a confused relationship to ourselves. Our bodies—along with their natural desires and sexual inclinations—were twisted out of shape and labeled evil by a religion that preferred men and worshiped a male God. We couldn't begin to imagine a God who had a body and confusing sexual desires and inclinations like ours.

Sitting in a circle, the women share the truth of their lives. One by one they speak out of the silence of a lifetime:

> It is difficult for me to acknowledge my own sexual
> feelings. The attitude of the Catholic church was that sex
> was dirty and only to be tolerated within marriage for
> the propagation of the race. I was taught that Mary
> was rewarded for her chastity and that sexual feelings were
> of the devil. I still hear the warnings of the priests and
> nuns in my mind as I attempt to reconnect with my
> sexuality.
>
> —Robin

I'm embarrassed about anything that has to do with being
a woman. I've gotten the sense that it is not all right
to be a woman and that we are only wanted for certain
things. And we are to do those things quietly and without
being seen. The shame and embarrassment of being
a woman is in everything I do.

I have always felt uncomfortable with my own sexuality.
I feel ashamed of my adult sexual experiences. Mary didn't
have sex. She didn't have the ways of earthly women,
so I really wanted to connect to her, but she felt out
of my reach. I pray that I can let go of men's
imagery of my body.

—Erin

Imagine sitting in a circle with Robin and Erin. Add your story to theirs.

• Reflect on the example of the Virgin Mary and her impact on your body,
natural desires, and sexual inclinations. How was virginity defined by the
Church? By your family? By the culture you grew up in? Did the exhortations
concerning virginity apply to your brothers?

• What feelings, memories, and reactions are triggered by the words *pure
and chaste, virtuous, spotless, clean of heart, death of innocence,* and *impure
thoughts*?

• Did you hear the phrases and words *Boys like virgins better, She's
damaged goods, slut, whore*? Were there equivalent terms for boys and men?

• Was there a double standard in your parents' marriage in terms of marital
fidelity? Who was sexually autonomous and free in your family?

Obedient Woman: Our Twisted Lives

Mary was humble and gentle, and definitely not God. She
obeyed the men in her life.

—Jane

In the beginning, as defined by men, Eve asserted her will against God.
She refused to obey, and ate the fruit. This was the ultimate evil that
plunged all of humankind into sin. She was cursed and exiled from the

Garden of Life. Eve's predecessor, Lilith, embodied rebelliousness. She refused to submit to God or man. Her willfulness was labeled evil and unfeminine. She was exiled from the Bible as the Rebellious First Woman.

In the beginning of Christian history, the earthly Mary was shaped and molded by men to eliminate a woman's capacity for choice and independent action. Without any resistance she allowed her body and reputation to be disrupted. She allowed others to shape her life, destiny, and choices. She was the willing vessel and container for the birth of Christ. She surrendered to God's will.

SURRENDER TO GOD AND EXPERTS

At every point in religious history our willfulness has been assaulted. The image of Mary was shaped according to men's specifications in order to convince us that we are incapable of independent thought and action, of self-determining choice, of the successful implementation of our desires in the world, of controlling our own lives and destinies. As children we are taught to emulate Mary. She was kind and loving; we were to be kind and loving. She surrendered to God's will; we were to surrender to God's will. She was blessed because she obeyed; we would be blessed if we obeyed.

Just as Mary surrendered control of her life and allowed others to shape her destiny, so do we. Convinced that our lives are not our own, we become alienated from our inner sense of what is right and appropriate for us. We become experts at watching the way others live and we shape our lives accordingly. From talk-show hosts, to Ann Landers, to our therapists and trainers, to the countless experts we consult to design our experience, everyone knows better than we do. We spend our lifetimes trying to fit into someone else's idea of what is right for us.

We assemble our bodies according to society's formula of the perfect woman. We form our thoughts and opinions to suit the audience. We limit our feelings to what's acceptable. We formulate our behaviors and actions according to the expectations of others.

Some of us are emotionally crippled as a result of habitually abandoning ourselves into the shapes of others. We become a shapeless blur, our true form in danger of dissolving. Each surrender becomes a mini-abdication of who we are. To author our own lives is not even a consideration.

SURRENDER TO MEN

According to traditional religion, God cursed Eve for her disobedience with the following words: "Your husband shall rule over you." Mary became the penitent Second Eve. Her obedience set the example that required us to be submissive to men, no matter how abusive their presence, or absence, in our lives. It was clear that we were to emulate Mary. After all, only good things were said about her, because she stayed in her place. Lilith was called names for her refusal to stay in her place. And Eve was punished for her disobedience. Clearly we didn't want these terrible things to happen to us.

As a result of the dominance of a creation myth that sees women as subservient to men and as the instigators of evil, we have accepted that it is our fate to be ruled by men. We spend our lives subject to one man after another, beginning with father and brothers, and later, boyfriends and husbands. We cannot imagine life without a man. For some of us a relationship with a man becomes more important than our children, our friends—even more important than our own health and sanity.

We twist our lives out of shape to please men. We learn to like football, to go fly-fishing, to read *Sports Illustrated*, and to cook their favorite meals. We take courses, buy clothes and cars, and reconstruct our bodies and faces based on what we think the men in our lives want. The man's view of the world is central. He acts, we react. He speaks, we listen. He initiates, we follow. A life of our own with definitive boundaries is out of the question. We become the minister's wife, the author's typist, the boss's secretary, the savior's mother.

As a result of the childhood images of the feminine, most of us cannot imagine God as a woman. We believe somewhere in our heart of hearts that women are incapable of independent thought and action, of self-determining choice, of the successful implementation of their desires in the world, and of controlling their own lives and destinies. We believe that women have no will of their own, that they are inferior and need to be taken care of by a man. A woman cannot possibly be God.

Sitting in a circle, the women share the truth of their lives. One by one they speak out of the silence of a lifetime:

I feel like I'm buried deep beneath all the twisted layers.
Twisted by society to get married and to have kids, to stay
in shape and to always look young. Twisted by
education to think the right thoughts. Twisted by the
world of art and design, to create the right image, to
be in style and up-to-date. I found my way into a
support group aching over another abusive relationship
in which I had twisted myself right out of a job, a support
system, and my self-esteem.

—Emily

Before my most recent involvement with a man, I worked
hard to set up a healthy life for myself. When the
relationship began, I vowed that I would not begin
my usual caretaking tasks. However, slowly my
dependence on the relationship grew. I began doing more
than I could manage to keep it going, and this meant I
had to give up the very activities that were so dear to
me. Eventually this constant erosion of who I was
resulted both in tremendous resentment toward this man
and in terror that I might lose him. By this time there
was so little left of me that I truly felt my survival
was at stake.

—Joyce

I have a tremendous need to be accepted and liked. This
makes me want to appear like everyone I happen to be
with so I won't rock the boat, stand out, or challenge
the majority view. This majority might be a
conventional group, such as co-workers or relatives, or a
group of feminist women. The guilt I feel is so great that
I often go along, saying yes instead of no, to avoid
feeling guilty. This guilt is triggered because I
interpret my difference of thought or opinion as not being
nice, so I have to keep trying harder to be nice.

—Sandi

Imagine sitting in a circle with Emily, Joyce, and Sandi. Add your story to theirs.

• In what ways have you twisted your thoughts, feelings, body, actions, and life into the shapes of others? Describe the ways that you have surrendered to others in your imitation of them; in your dependence on their opinions, specifications, and demands; and in your need for their acceptance and approval.

• Describe the ways you have surrendered to the men in your life. In your current relationship whose view of the world is central? Who acts, who reacts? Who speaks, who listens? Who initiates, who follows?

• How have the interests of the men in your life expanded your view of the world intellectually, athletically, and politically? How have your interests, projects, and concerns been received by your lovers? Have they allowed themselves to expand intellectually, emotionally, and spiritually as a result of your interests?

Our Healing

We have given voice to the childhood experiences that have robbed us of our sexuality and stripped us of our willfulness. Now, with courage, we will reclaim the stories of a time when God looked like us. We will incorporate the woman-affirming images of the very beginning into our myths, meditations, and rituals. As we immerse ourselves in these transformational resources, Mary becomes a healing image of the divine within us. In her presence we come home to our Original Willfulness and Sexuality.

Reclaiming Her Story

> The Goddess of the Paleolithic and Neolithic is parthenogenic, creating life out of herself. She is a primeval, self-fertilizing virgin Goddess. The Christian virgin is a demoted version of this virginal deity.
> —Marija Gimbutas, *The Civilization of the Goddess*

Mary was expelled from the Bible after she performed her duty as the passive channel through which Father God sent his only begotten Son to earth. Her experience was not valued, nor did it become part of the orthodox record of the early Church. Nevertheless Mary did reemerge and become a powerful force throughout history. Several factors led to her reemergence.

As Christianity spread through Europe, it had to reckon with the Mother Goddess. She was so deeply rooted in the people's lives and consciousness that the church fathers eventually realized they were powerless to exorcise her. Christianity was unappealing because its God was male and there were no feminine images comparable to the Goddess.[6]

Although Mary had been expelled from the biblical text, she was not forgotten by women. They would not let her memory die. Stories about her circulated among the people and mingled with stories of the Goddess. To women Mary became the manifestation of the Goddess. She became the accessible God who looked like them, who felt, cried, and understood them because she was a woman. Women have always needed to relate to a God who looks like them.[7]

In order to gain converts, the church fathers capitalized on the melding of these two images. Just as the rabbis had swallowed the Goddess into their unfolding myths of creation as Eve and Lilith, so the church fathers swallowed the Goddess, Queen of Heaven and Earth, into their unfolding theology as the Virgin Mary.[8] Layered atop the meager details we have of Mary's life are centuries of imaginative renderings in which she was reconstructed as the Queen of Heaven.

To appease followers of the Goddess, the church fathers wove into the image of Mary some of her qualities. At the same time they eliminated those qualities they found disturbing to their worldview. Mary was stripped of the Goddess's assertiveness and sexual independence.[9] To domesticate the Goddess made perfect sense from the male perspective. However, from a woman's perspective it was a tragic choice, one that presented generations of girl-children with a distorted image of womanhood, in which passivity, chastity, and domestication became the sole ideals of the feminine.

Still, over time, the Queen of Heaven developed a life of her own among the people. She was the Goddess reborn. She refused to stay in her place, as defined by the church fathers. She refused to allow them to dictate the terms of her existence. The people worshiped her as God. Upset, the church fathers attempted to contain her. Eventually, though, they recognized that the worship of the Goddess, reincarnated as the Queen of Heaven, could not be stopped. So they swallowed her festivals, beliefs, and images into their developing theologies. And they transformed the ancient Goddess shrines into the chapels of the Queen of Heaven.

Today we reclaim the Virgin Mother Goddess by telling the truth of a time when God looked like us. We reclaim our woman-history from the *very* beginning! We learn of ancient women who did not apologize for their sexuality and who refused to surrender except to the natural rhythms of life. We recall ancient times when virginity meant a woman who was "one in herself," owned by no man, author of her own life, creatress of her own destiny.[10] We reclaim the ancient ways that celebrated the Goddess and her savior son, her representative on earth who ruled from her lap.[11]

AN ENCOUNTER WITH MARY: RECLAIMING YOUR ORIGINAL AUTONOMY

> Virgin means One in Herself; not maiden inviolate, but maiden alone, in herself. To be virginal does not mean to be chaste, but rather to be true to nature and instinct.
>
> —Nor Hall, *The Moon and the Virgin*

Through ritual, meditation, and guided exploration the God of our understanding moves within us. We imagine a Woman God who is complete in herself and who symbolizes autonomy, willfulness, and creativity. As we glimpse her face, we turn around. Instead of looking outside of ourselves for salvation, we turn toward our own rich inner resources. We come home to our own willfulness, to the creative energy that pulsates through us. We shape our own lives. We name our own gods. She Who Is Complete in Herself challenges us with these words:

I am Mary, the Virgin Goddess.
I stride the earth in willfulness.
I am She Who Is Complete in Herself.

My life is my own. I belong to no man.
I am the author of my own life. I am the creatress of my own
      destiny.

Wrest your life out of the hands of men. Connect with your virgin-self,
      the whole and complete center within you.
Value your will. Be self-determined. Do not allow others to
      dictate the terms of your existence or of your belief.
Design your own life. Name your own gods. Honor all that has
      been demeaned. Receive all that has been cast aside.
Your willfulness is good. It is very good.

I am Mary, the Source of Life.
I stride the earth in fruitfulness.
My watery womb is the fertile birthplace of all that is:
  the dark abyss that swallows the Sun God each evening;
  the chalice from which you drink your wine in sacred ceremonies;
  the sacred belly that receives you each Sabbath.
Out of the moist darkness of my womb new images are born.

In your creativity you are one with me. You are free to choose
      your own form of birthing. Each child is a new image of
      the divine brought into the world by the Mother. Each poem
      and painting, ritual and ceremony, is a new image of the
      divine offered to the world by its Creator.

Blessed are the creative fruits of your womb, springing forth in new
      images and new life. Honor all that has been demeaned. Receive
      all that has been cast aside. The womb is good. It is very
      good.

WE RECLAIM AN ORIGINAL LIFE

Inspired by She Who Is Complete in Herself, we have come to believe
in an inner wisdom aligned with the uniqueness, interests, talents, and
life purpose of our truest self. Reaching back into childhood, we see
that this wisdom faithfully orchestrated our movements from crawling
to walking to running, our speech from sounds to words to sentences,
and our knowing of the world through our amazing senses. The flow of
wisdom has been faithful, calling us home to our truest self even in
those times when we detour from what is healthy and good for us.

In a woman-affirming spirituality we redefine what is meant by *God's will.* She Who Is Complete in Herself values the will. She encourages us to know our own will and to believe that it is valid and achievable in the world. Rather than surrendering to male gods and higher powers, she challenges us to descend into our own inner wisdom and to assert our will in harmony with this wisdom.

Imagine She Who Is Complete in Herself challenging you each morning before you enter the busyness of your life. Incorporate her challenge into your prayer and meditation practice. Speak her words to your daughters, granddaughters, and nieces this day: *Your body is your own. Do not allow society to twist it out of shape. Allow no one access to it without your permission. Your thoughts are your own. Do not allow others to mold them. Your feelings are your own. Do not allow others to express them. Your life is your own. Do not allow it to be shaped by the expectations of others. Author your life without guilt or shame. You were not created to please others. Refuse to surrender except to your truest self and your wisest voice.*

Sitting in a circle, each woman celebrates her truest self and wisest voice. Supported by each other, they have broken out of the conformity of a lifetime:

> O womb of my mothers, empower me to surrender to
> the deepest part of myself. Open my heart that my song
> may come into harmony with your song, that my will
> may come into harmony with your will. Restore me
> to myself that I may experience my greatest joy and highest
> good. I am one with the wisdom of Mother God.
> Blessed be.
>
> —Ferrel

> I am in a subtle process of discerning my own shape. I
> am releasing all the thoughts, feelings, and artistic images
> that had been held captive within me. I thirst for the
> experience of myself. I am in the process of rebirth.
> I am making my own acquaintance through a thousand
> small and large recognitions. Yeah!
> I refuse to surrender my developing autonomy. I
> am becoming responsible, capable of making choices
> and of acting on my own behalf. I do surrender my

exaggerated, charged sense of separateness, based on shame and lingering demons from the past. I begin to trust and love, legitimizing my own life in its bright direction.

—Laura

•

Imagine sitting in a circle with Ferrel and Laura. Add your story to theirs.

• Design an original life. Describe it. Draw it. Sculpt it. Dance it.
• Describe the interests, talents, and life purpose of your truest self.
• Describe the ways in which you are moving from dependency to self-directedness.

WE RECLAIM OUR ORIGINAL SPIRITUALITY

Inspired by She Who Is Complete in Herself, we wrest our spirituality out of the hands of men. We value our willfulness. We are self-determined. We will not allow those who claim to be experts on spirituality to dictate the terms of our belief. We will design an original spirituality. We will name our own gods.

As women reclaim the right to name and imagine the God of their understanding, a wealth of images bubbles up from the experience, strength, and hope of their lives. Hallie describes her newfound freedom with an image: "I imagine an empty table upon which I can try out different images and concepts of a God of my understanding. I discard those that don't feel absolutely right. I keep only those images that are true to my inner depths. I am encouraged that this table is infinitely large and has plenty of room for me to carry out my spiritual explorations."

Some women begin with images from the natural world. They remember their childhood experiences in nature. It is often a woman's intuitive connection with nature's rhythms and cycles that midwives her movement toward the feminine face of God. As you read Emily's writing, reflect on your own childhood experiences in nature; the lessons you learned from its mystery, beauty, and strength; and your ongoing connection to its rhythms and cycles:

So much energy is available to me in the natural world.
I call on her roaring waters when I need strength; on the

brightness of the sun when I'm afraid; and on her
gentle breeze to calm me. Through becoming one
with nature, I embrace my pain and feel it as part of the
world's pain. I embrace my power and experience it
as the life force that flows through me. I accept myself
just as I am, as a part of it all—the cycles, the harmony,
and the rhythm.

—Emily

Others begin with images of the Mother. The first face of God we encounter is of our mother's face. So it is appropriate that we acknowledge
the Source of Life—the source of our life—in designing our own spirituality. For some women, prayers to Mother God are their first attempt
to move beyond the God of their early understanding—their first encounter with the feminine face of God. Listen to Ferrel's poignant
words: "I am praying every morning to Mother God. She is beautiful
and strong. She is transforming my idea of being a woman. Several
times I have spontaneously thanked her for making me a woman."

For some women the image of Mother God is not helpful. Although
they desire a feminine face to their spirituality, painful childhood experiences with their own mothers make it impossible for them to envision
the divine as a loving mother. I invite these women to experiment with
the image of "deeper wisdom." Wisdom, or *Sophia*, the Greek word
for Wisdom, is a feminine face of God in the Hebrew Scriptures. Although she has been obscured over time, she has not been completely
eradicated.

The use of *Deeper* acknowledges that a woman's journey is one of descent. Ascent has been the journey of men. They erect ladders and
monuments, reaching toward the heavens. They name their gods
Higher Power and God of the High Places. Their sins have been pride
and grandiosity. Our "sin" has been self-hatred. Our feminine self was
offered no place in the heavens. Her home is within us. Instead of looking to a God or Higher Power outside of our lives, we look deep within
to reclaim lost or forgotten aspects of ourselves.

The use of *Wisdom* acknowledges that in our descent we rediscover
the original Wisdom that orchestrated our days and our development in
the very beginning of life. We have come to believe that this deeper
wisdom reaches beneath our early injuries. It will restore us to whole-

ness and to a loving relationship with ourselves. In meditation we reflect on Wisdom's presence in our daily lives. In prayer we converse with her about the joys and challenges we face each day.

Sitting in a circle, the women celebrate the naming of their own gods and the designing of their own spirituality. Supported by each other, they have broken out of the conformity of a lifetime:

> I have begun to use the term *Goddess* for the first time.
> This name has amplified as it has reverberated from within,
> growing from a soft, ashamed whisper to a vigorous
> and not-to-be denied expression. I have begun to
> soften my self-criticism and self-rejection in her name.
> When I feel the tendency to brutalize myself, I imagine
> the loving presence of a gentle and inclining figure.
> Not the half-conscious vertical, austere, and phallic
> one of our culture, but one who is tender and full of
> sympathy. Her movement is one of recognition and
> connection.
>
> —Laura

> Through this experience I have affirmed that my spirituality
> will arise from within me. As it takes shape, I will look
> for a spiritual community that closely reflects *my*
> beliefs and experience. I can struggle no longer, thinking
> there's something wrong with me because I don't fit
> into another's belief system and conceptualization of
> God. I have a right to name the God of my
> understanding, not as the ultimate Truth, but as the truth
> that is spoken within my life.
>
> —Annette

Imagine sitting with Laura and Annette. Add your story to theirs.

• Reclaim your creative imagination. Give birth to an abundance of healing images of the divine. Include them in your prayer and meditation practice.

• Compose a prayer, a poem, a song using one or more of your own images.

• Gather together a circle of women and create a "Litany of Many Names" pooling the rich resources of your creative imagination.

✿ AN ENCOUNTER WITH MARY:
RECLAIMING YOUR ORIGINAL SEXUALITY

> When we begin to live from within outward, in touch
> with the power of the erotic within ourselves, then we
> begin to be responsible to ourselves in the deepest
> sense. For as we recognize our deepest feelings, we
> begin to give up, of necessity, being satisfied with suffering
> and self-negation, and the numbness which so often seems
> like the only alternative in our society.
>
> —Audre Lorde, *Sister Outsider*

In the very beginning of her life the girl-child moves through each day
with an exuberant strength, a remarkable energy, and a contagious live-
liness. Her days are meaningful and unfold according to a deep wisdom
that resides within her. It faithfully orchestrates her movements, her
sounds, and her knowing of the world through her remarkable senses.
Her purpose is clear: to live fully in the abundance of her life. Her ordinary life is interesting enough. Every experience is filled with wonder
and awe. It is enough to gaze at the redness of an apple, to listen to the
rain dance, to count the peas on her plate, to touch the parts of her
body that bring her joy. With courage she explores her world. With excitement she explores her body.

In the very beginning of her life the girl-child is acquainted with the
erotic energy within her. Childhood is not a time of sexual dormancy
for the girl-child. From birth she is capable of sexual arousal and orgasm. These are her birthrights as a Child of Life. She loves her body
and her life. She says a big YES to Life as it pulsates through her. She
feels the YES in her genitals. It gives her pleasure to touch her clitoris
and she does it often. She is unafraid of channeling strong feelings
through her. She feels the YES in her heart, her joy, and even in her
tears. It touches every area of her life. The erotic potential of the universe pulsates through her. She is full of herself.

In a world that prefers men, sexuality is defined according to the
needs and desires of men. Eventually the girl-child will be required to
accept a form of sexuality that does not serve her interests. Sex will be
defined as intercourse. Thus her erotic potential will be confined to an

activity that requires a partner. An activity that guarantees physical satisfaction for the man. An activity that, by itself, can be an ineffective way of achieving satisfaction for her. Groomed to sexually service men, she will forget about the wonders of her own body, its rich erotic potential and its capacity for sensual delight and satisfaction.

She Who Is Complete in Herself reminds us of what we once knew in the very beginning of our lives. She calls you home to your body, to your natural instincts, and to your sexual desires. She will inspire your erotic energy and imagination. Enter into her words.

❧ AN ENCOUNTER WITH THE VIRGIN GODDESS: RECLAIMING YOUR ORIGINAL SEXUALITY

I am Mary, the Virgin Goddess.
I stride the earth in nakedness.
No robes hide the beauty of my fertile vulva, my rounded belly,
    and my full breasts.
I am She Who Is Complete in Herself. I am sexual. I live in
    my body. I embrace its desires as my own.
Allow your acquaintance with me to transform your relationship
    to your body.

Your body is your own. It is no one else's. Wrest it out of the hands of men. Live in your body. Trust its natural instincts. Connect with your virgin self, the whole and complete center within you.

Choose to be alone, to reunite with yourself, to touch a long-lost part of you, to hold your body with tenderness and with passion. Embark on an intimate journey with yourself. Experience fullness, self-possession, and satisfaction. Delight in your freedom to be alone, to meet your own needs, and to give yourself pleasure.

Your body is your own. It is no one else's. Experience the pleasure of your body's sensuality. Feel its smoothness and its curves. Touch its lips. Enter its openings. Taste its juiciness. Delight in its natural fragrances. Allow no fantasy of another to accompany you. Self-possessed, give yourself pleasure. Own yourself completely. Explore the edges of your sensuality. Venture to the far reaches of its vibrancy and color.

Feel the fire rise within you. Learn of its ways, its awakening, its path to union. Celebrate the sensations in your genitals. They are calling you to your edges. Imagine a marriage within you. Lover uncoiling to meet lover. Height calling to depth. Earth moving toward heaven. A middle space within you. The two Marys meeting in your body. Breathing in, receive them.

What will you learn from this journey into the depths of you? Will you no longer need a lover? The Goddesses loved themselves to their edges. Self-possessed, they strode the earth. This is my prayer for you, blessed woman:

Rise, Fire, rise. Uncoil within her.
Rise from her depths. Awaken each center.
Unite with her spirit. May joy be the fruit of her union.

Honor all that has been demeaned.
Receive all that has been cast aside.
Your sexuality is good. It is very good.

Sitting in a circle, Wendy, Erin, and Colleen share their sexual healing. They speak out of the silence of a lifetime:

> During a time of abstinence from sexual relationships, I imagined a very caring inner male lover underneath the abusive fantasies of rape and violent partners I had needed to be sexual. The fantasy of a caring male lover was healing for me and worked for a while. I have reached the limits of that image and am opening to a feminine image. In a sense the safe male I created was a step toward the feminine. My next step is to move away from the male completely and begin to imagine an erotic goddess who lives in me, who expresses herself through me, who accepts me as I am.
>
> —Wendy

> I feel the Sexual One within me. She is here, right at my surface. My body is alive with her. My body is tingling, moving, expanding, and evolving. Vulva swells. Fluids fill. Blood moves. Juice circulates. I am thirsty. I gulp her sweetness. I am hungry. I swallow her vastness. My

skin is sensitive to the caresses of the air around me. It
is tingled and teased by the beautiful breath of Mother
Nature's breeze.

It has been so long since I have let go into the Sexual
One. In the beautiful fullness of time, I am open to her,
spread as wide as is physically possible. There is no
fear. I am drinking, tasting, smelling, longing, touching,
absorbing, and jubilantly celebrating this goodness
that is mine, only mine.

—Erin

One evening, after reading about the Goddesses and ancient
religion's celebration of the whole of a woman, her genitals
and sexuality, her anger and wrath, and her power, I
had a remarkable experience with my husband. As we
were making love, the images of the stone Goddesses kept
rising up in front of me. I felt as much in my body as
I've ever been in my life. I felt that every inch of me
was beautiful and that there was nothing to be
loathed or shamed. Something in me was healed that day.
The God of my childhood didn't have sexuality, sensuality,
passion, music, or colors—so I concluded that all
these things in me were superfluous and should be
dried up. Now I realize these are my essence as a
woman.

—Colleen

*Imagine sitting in a circle with Wendy, Erin, and Colleen. Add your story
to theirs.*

• As a child or adolescent, did you ever touch your own body? What did it
feel like to explore its smoothness and curves, to open its lips, and to enter its
openings? Did you ever feel fiery warmth rise in your body? Did you ever feel
tingling sensations in your genitals? Did these feelings scare you or excite you?
Draw the fiery warmth and the tingling sensations in your body.

• Imagine a woman who embraces her sexuality as her own. A woman who
delights in pleasuring herself. Who experiences all of her erotic feelings and
sensations without shame or guilt. Imagine a woman who expects mutuality in
her sexual relationships. A woman who expresses her own needs and desires.

Who is an active participant in each sexual encounter. Close your eyes and imagine yourself as this woman.

• Locate a copy of Audre Lorde's book of essays entitled *Sister Outsider*.[12] Read the essay "Uses of the Erotic: The Erotic as Power" on pages 53–59. Write your own essay, create a dance, or compose a poem in response to her words.

Before moving on, linger awhile with Chapter 9:

✎§ THE MARY OF CHILDHOOD

Set aside time each day this week to converse with The Girl-Child You Once Were. Imagine sitting with her in your meeting place. Draw and write your responses to the following questions with your nondominant hand:

DAY 1. *The Catholic Mary*

• Did you pray to Mary? Pretend you are holding rosary beads. Do your fingers remember moving from one bead to the next saying the Hail Mary and the Our Father?

• Did you ever light a candle at her statue? What were your requests of her?

• If you weren't Catholic, what did you learn about Mary from your friends? Did you ever go to Mass with a Catholic family? Do you remember the statues of Mary?

• Draw a picture of the Catholic Mary.

DAY 2. *The Protestant Mary*

• What were the rumors circulating about "those Catholics"?

• How was she presented to you in church? Were you chosen to be Mary in a Sunday school play?

• Did you want to be like Mary?

• Draw a picture of the Protestant Mary?

DAY 3. *Mary's Body*

• Draw the pictures and statues of the Mary you remember.

• Do you think she had a body under the robes she wore? What did it look like?

DAY 4. *My Body*

• What did God, the Church, the priests, the ministers, or the rabbis think of your body?

• Draw your own body.

DAY 5. *To Be Like Mary*

• Were you a "good girl"? Did you obey your parents and other adults?

• What happened to you or to girls you knew when you disobeyed or did something your own way?

DAY 6. *To Be Like Others*

• As a child whom did you want to be like, to look like, to move like, to talk like?

• Write a story and draw pictures for each: I want to be like ... I want to look like ... I want to move like ... I want to talk like ...

DAY 7. *Free to Be Me*

• Display the challenging words of She Who Is Complete in Herself in your home and workplace today. Personalize the affirmations below to suit your own experience. Repeat them often to yourself. May they heal your wounds. Repeat them often to your daughters. May they prevent the wounding from passing on to another generation of girl-children.

My body is my own. I will not allow society to twist it out of shape. I allow no one access to my body without my permission.

My thoughts are my own. I will not allow others to mold them.

My feelings are my own. I will not allow others to express them.

My life is my own. I will not allow it to be shaped by the expectations of others. I author my own life without guilt or shame.

ஒ THE SEXUAL ONE WITHIN YOU

Inspired by Wendy, Erin, and Colleen, spend this week acquainting yourself with your own sexuality. Gather sensual images of a God who looks like you. Fill your sacred space with them.

DAY 1.

Are you a stranger, an acquaintance, a friend, or a lover of the Sexual One, she who resides in the erotic center within you? Personify the Sexual One—your own sexuality. Write to her every day this week. Ask her, "Where are you within me? What are your needs and desires? How may I embrace you and welcome you to a fuller, more joyous life?"

DAY 2.

Describe the Sexual One through a series of writings. What words express your sexuality?

DAY 3.

Describe your sexuality through a series of drawings. What does it look like? What color is it?

DAY 4.

Describe your sexuality through a series of movements. How does it express itself through movement?

DAY 5.

Describe your sexuality through a series of sculptures. What shape is it? What does it feel like?

DAY 6.

Describe your sexuality through music and sound. What does it sound like?

DAY 7.

Write three reflection pieces today. Ask yourself how your acquaintance with She Who Is Complete in Herself will transform your relationship:

- To your body
- To your sexuality
- To your lover or your desire for a lover

✒ SURRENDER FROM A WOMAN'S PERSPECTIVE

If you have chosen the Twelve Steps as your spiritual guide, set aside time each day this week to reflect on the Steps from a woman's perspective.

DAY 1. *Surrender to a Higher Power*

The central virtue in a shame-based expression of recovery is obedience to a power greater than ourselves. *Turning it over* is the shorthand used at Twelve Step meetings for the surrender called for in the Third Step: "We made a decision to turn our will and life over to the care of God as we understand him."

- How have you understood the surrender called for in the Steps?
- Does your sense of surrender differ according to whether you consider the God of your understanding to be a power outside of you or a wisdom resident within you? In what ways?

DAY 2. *Alienation from Inner Resources*

Being asked by the Third Step to turn our will and lives over to a Higher Power continues the disempowering process that alienates us from our own resources, from our own powers of self-assertion and determination.

- Reflect on Karen S.'s words from your own experience: "As a chronic people-pleaser, I have had no wants, needs, or desires other than to make my parents, lovers, bosses, and friends happy. What's left to surrender?"
- Imagine your sponsor saying the following words in response to your problem or concern: "I support you to recover the rich resources of power, courage, goodness, and wisdom that reside within you as a Child of Life. Let's explore together which of these inner resources you will call upon to assist you with this particular life challenge."

DAY 3. *An Original Recovery*

In a woman-affirming recovery the will is valued. We are encouraged to know our own will and to believe that it is valid and achievable in the world. Rather than surrendering to a Higher Power outside of us, we reclaim the natural resources within us.

• Include the following affirmation in your prayer and meditation practice today: "I value my will. I am self-determined. I will not allow others to dictate the terms of my recovery journey. I will design my own recovery. I will not look outside of myself for salvation. I will name my own gods. I will turn toward the rich sources of creative living that are within me. I will move from dependency on recovery experts to self-directedness."

DAY 4. *Redefining "Turning It Over"*

In a woman-affirming recovery we redefine *turning it over* to include a whole new set of possibilities. Most of them involve getting out of our heads and the inclination to figure things out, and finding the path to our hearts and our deeper wisdom. Add your own alternatives to the list below and practice them this week:

• We turn the problem over to the silence of prayer and meditation. We no longer attack our problems. Rather we listen for the voice of our deeper wisdom.
• Imagining her concern as a pizza, Jen flips it over to see it from a different perspective and to consider a whole new set of options for dealing with it.
• We turn the problem over to the wisdom of our support group or women's spirituality circle by going to a meeting and talking about it.
• We turn the difficulty over by talking to a wise friend. We invite her to support us in discovering the inner resources that are available to us for confronting the situation.

DAY 5. *Personalizing Step 1*

When the God of our childhood understanding dominates our adult understanding, we accept the Twelve Steps as written. In a woman-affirming recovery we personalize the first three Steps to reflect our own understandings of recovery and spirituality. Today we will begin with Step 1.

Practice personalizing the First Step based on a past situation or a current issue. Use this formula: "I cannot change the fact: *(Describe the situation, wound, person). My life has become unmanageable: (Describe the unmanageability)."* Or creatively work the Step inspired by the examples below:

• "I offered my friend healing resources and healthy food options during her recovery from surgery. She refused my suggestions. I am powerless over her lack of readiness for, openness to, and receptivity to my suggestions. My life becomes unmanageable when I try to force my solutions onto my friend's life."

• "I cannot change the fact that I have been wounded by a society that idolized a male God and prefers men. Its intense socialization process has had a crippling effect upon my life and has resulted in a variety of ineffective behaviors that do not support my recovery: I defer to men. I denigrate my feminine qualities. I compete with women."

DAY 6. *Personalizing Step 2*

Personalize Step 2. Reread the recovery exercises in chapter 6. There you were offered a formula for reworking Step 2 based on the God of your understanding.

• "I have come to believe that there is a deeper wisdom at work in each person's life. As I affirm that truth, I am restored to an acceptance of the sacredness of each person's choice to take or leave the resources and suggestions I offer."

• "I have come to believe that there is a deeper wisdom within me that reaches beneath my wounds and my ineffective behaviors. This deeper wisdom will restore me to my original power—I will no longer defer to men. It will restore me to my original connection—I will celebrate women. It will restore me to my Original Goodness—I will embrace the rich resources within me."

DAY 7. *Personalizing Step 3*

Whatever you have come to believe in Step 2 will affect the decisions you make in Step 3. If you have come to believe in a community of support, you will choose to spend time in that community to experience its healing resources. If you have come to believe in intuition as your guiding light, you will develop ways of listening to it and acting on its guidance.

Personalize Step 3 based on what you have come to believe. Redefine *turning it over* to conform with your beliefs and experience.

• "After offering supportive resources to my friend, I will let go of the outcome. I turn my friend over to the wisdom of her own process. Across the distance I choose to honor and respect her sacred journey."

• "I turn toward the deeply wise resources available to me in the women's community in order to be restored to wholeness. One day at a time I choose woman-affirming behaviors. I spend time with women weekly to hear their healing words and to practice new behaviors."

CHAPTER TEN ❧

The Divine Girl-Child

The Story

Just as I had ignored my childhood for many years, consigning its memories to the far recesses of my mind, so, too, had I been convinced through my religious training that the girl-child was not important in the overall scheme of things. As I began to listen to my childhood memories, I became curious about the girl-children of my religious past. Until that time I hadn't even noticed their absence.

Did Jesus Have a Baby Sister?

> Behold you will conceive in your womb, and bear a son, and you shall name him Jesus. He will be great and will be called the son of the Most High.
> —Luke 1:31–32, *New American Standard Bible*

I searched my religious memory and was not able to remember one girl-child's birth that was celebrated in the Bible or Sunday schools of my childhood. The births of John the Baptist, of Moses, of Cain and Abel, and of Jesus readily came to mind. Many religious traditions celebrate the births and childhoods of their savior gods. Krishna is the Divine Child of the Hindus; Jesus, the Divine Child of Christianity. Sadly, though, there was no girl-child whose birth was announced and celebrated by angels, whose coming merited regal visitors and precious gifts, and in whose honor the people of the world gather for a yearly exchange of generosity. On the contrary, daughters were seldom mentioned. In the endless family histories recorded in the Scriptures, daughters and mothers are not included. The fathers "begat" their sons.

I was encouraged to read through the entire Bible yearly in the fundamentalist church of my adolescence. When I would get to Leviticus, the book that outlines the duties of Hebrew priests and the holiness codes of the Hebrew nation, I would cringe. There was so much that I didn't understand about that book. And those things that I did understand frightened me. Listen to Leviticus 12:2–5 (italics added):

> When a woman has conceived and gives birth to a boy she shall be unclean for 7 days, *with the same uncleanness as at her menstrual blood. On the 8th, the boy is circumcised and then she shall spend* 33 days *more in becoming purified.* . . . *If she gives birth to a daughter for* 14 days *she shall be unclean, after which she shall spend* 66 days *in becoming purified of her blood.*

The shame of a girl-child's birth required twice as long a period of purification. And circumcision, the sign of God's covenant with the Hebrew people, excluded the girl-child and emphasized her otherness and inferiority. Without a foreskin she could not participate in this pivotal ceremony of belonging to the Jewish community. Even my young mind could figure out that sons were very valuable and that when God had a choice, he decided to have a son, not a daughter!

While I was in high school, I bought *Strong's Exhaustive Concordance.* This remarkable volume made it possible for me to look up any word and find a listing of all the Bible verses that contained it, along with the number of times it was used in the Bible. Years later I looked up *daughter* and *son, mother* and *father,* and the masculine and feminine pronouns. After carefully counting all the entries listed, this was the disturbing fruit of my labor: *Daughter*—560 times, *Son*—3,420 times; *Mother*—345 times, *Father*—1,685; *she*—760 times, *he*—7,500 times; *her*—1,260 times, *his* and *him*—9,900 times.[1]

Clearly it was the fathers, sons, hes, and hims who showed up more often than the mothers and daughters in the pages of the Bible I read daily throughout my teens and twenties. And the word choices made by the translators of the Bible supported the exclusion of the girl-child from its pages. In passages such as John 16:21, the Greek word often translated *a man* actually means "human being" and would have been more accurately translated *child.*[2]

In the New American Standard Version of the Bible, the word choice is accurate: "Whenever a woman is in travail she has sorrow because her hour is come; but when she gives birth to the child, she remembers the anguish no more, for joy that *a child* has been born into the world." In the New English Bible the word is translated incorrectly: "A woman in labor is in pain because her time has come; but when the child is born she forgets the anguish in her joy that *a man* is born into the world."

The words and images of childhood burrow away in our hearts. They convince the girl-child of her inferiority. They limit her dreams and the expression of her gifts in the world.

Our Wounds

We hold every memory, impression, image, word, event, and formative belief of childhood within us. Nothing has been lost or forgotten. In order to heal into the present, we must retrieve our stories from their hiding places within our personal and religious past. On these pages courageous women give voice to the experiences of childhood that deposited within them a sense of their inferiority as girl-children.

A World That Prefers Men

Before she is born, especially if she will be the firstborn, the girl-child will be imagined as a boy. Books and doctors will speak of her as "he" or "him." The unborn child will be fantasized as a hero, seldom a heroine. She begins her life misnamed in the fantasies of her parents. In contemporary India "May you be the mother of a hundred sons" is a blessing as well as a clearly understood warning to women to produce sons.[3] Is it any wonder, then, that in this technological age, where it is possible to know the sex of the unborn child, that abortion on the basis of male preference is occurring at alarming rates throughout the world?[4]

If the girl-child survives to her birth, she is rarely welcomed with as much pomp, circumstance, and opportunity as the boy-child. While working in a chaplaincy program at Boston City Hospital, I visited a young woman on the maternity floor. She was anxious to tell me of her despair that the newborn was a girl: "I wanted a boy. I remember my childhood. I served my brothers and my father. I poured their coffees and got their beers. I don't want my daughter to spend her life serving men. Boys have a better chance in life. Now all I can pray for is that she finds a good man who doesn't drink too much and who will support her."

This young mother's summation, "Boys have a better chance in life," based on her own experience growing up in the projects of Boston is also true of the education the girl-child will receive. Her summation is supported by the American Association of University Women's report entitled "How Schools Shortchange Girls." It contains disturbing evidence that "girls are not receiving the same quality, or even quantity, of education as their brothers." Two major findings of the report highlight the girl-child's inferior opportunity. She receives significantly less attention from classroom teachers than do boys. And not surprisingly, the contributions and experiences of girls and women continue to be marginalized or ignored in many of the textbooks used in schools.[5]

Since childhood the messages we have received from family, religion, and society have convinced us of our inferiority. We are born into a world that prefers men, and these stories are designed to teach us our secondary place in the scheme of things. We could never be the heroes. We could never be God. Is it any wonder that the rate of depression among women is twice that of men, as reported by the American Psychological Association's Task Force on Women and Depression? This disturbing reality of women's lives, the panel concluded, is a result of women's experience of being female in our contemporary society. Our vulnerability to physical and sexual abuse, bias, and lower wages in the workplace, hormonal changes, and unfulfilling marital relationships were among the causal factors they listed.[6] Depression is an ever-present reality in many women's lives and is one of the most profound evidences of our wounding.

As long as God is male and our experiences, contributions, and concerns continue to be marginalized or ignored in a society that prefers men, we will not have equal access to the pulpits and altars, thrones, boardrooms, and negotiating tables of this world. Our health concerns will continue to be ignored, our bodies found to be "too complicated" to be included in research studies. One out of four of us will experience sexual abuse at the hands of our father, minister, or another trusted male by the time we are eighteen. We will be twice as likely as our brothers to experience bouts of depression and to have our blossoming self-esteem crushed by the time we are twelve. And we will be unprepared economically to live out the length of our days. As long as the image of a God who looks like us remains obscured by the idolatry of God the father, these will remain the realities of a young girl's life.

Sitting in a circle, the women share the truth of their lives. One by one they speak out of the silence of a lifetime:

> As a girl-child, I never understood that I should give
> consideration to "What do I want to be when I grow up?"
> I remember a term paper we were assigned in eighth
> grade in which we were to describe the job or
> profession we wanted. I completed the assignment, but
> I remember thinking that it was make-believe. Being
> somebody was never an option. To this day I struggle
> with the pain of not being able to answer this
> question. Since I was not taken seriously as a daughter
> in the family or as a girl in school, I have a very difficult
> time taking my needs, feelings, abilities, or talents
> seriously. As a result I carry around a lot of contempt
> for myself.
>
> —Ferrel

> I have four birthdays. One is the actual day on which I
> was born. The second one is the date of my birth
> according to the lunar calendar, which is customary
> in Korea, where I was born. The third is the date on
> which my birth was registered. And the fourth is the date
> on which I, as an adult, have decided to celebrate my
> birthday.
>   Why is my birthday so complicated? The answer is
> simple. I was not welcomed into this world as a girl-
> child. I was born sometime in January, but my
> parents did not register my birth until June 30th. I was

placed on my stomach and left alone. I cried all day long because I was dying. To my parents dismay, I became stronger. My voice grew loud and healthy. I did not die. I grew up unwanted. I heard my mother wish that I had been a boy. I tried to please her by acting like a boy and by hating anything that had to do with being a girl. My family home was a threatening environment and I grew up despising myself.

Today in Korea parents know the baby's sex before birth due to modern technology. If the fetus is a girl, an abortion is performed. As a result, there are fewer girls than boys of elementary school age in Seoul, Korea. The society's preference for boys has led it to commit serious crimes against girls. They are not welcomed, and they face life-threatening troubles from their conception. Many grow up to become prostitutes. Others are required to work in the factories of Korea to support their families or to provide money for their brothers' college tuition. Many become domestic servants to support their battering drunken husbands and their children. Throughout their lives these women are betrayed, raped, and harassed by their brothers and husbands.

—Hee Soon

Imagine sitting in a circle with Ferrel and Hee Soon. Add your story to theirs.

• Did your parents expect a son? Was there a preference for a son? Were your brothers welcomed with more pomp, circumstance, and opportunity?

• When I was a teacher, I was astonished at the names chosen for firstborn daughters. Held within their names is a denial of their gender and a reminder of the preference for the male. The daughter of Norman was named Norma. The daughter of Elton was named Eltonette. The daughter of John was named Johnetta. Think about how you were named. What is the story of your name?

• Reflect: In a society that prefers men and worships a male God, the education of the sons is encouraged, the education of the daughters is a stopgap until they marry. Ask yourself: What encouragement did you receive to develop your intellectual capacities? Was education a stopgap until marriage?

• As an adult do you defer to men? Is there a lingering sense of inferiority no matter what your accomplishments?

Our Healing

We have gathered the fragments of our personal stories that convinced us of our inferiority as girl-children. Now we will retrieve more of the collective story of women from the margins of history and religion. Incorporating the healing images of a time when God looked like us, we will retell the girl-child's story. She becomes a healing image of the divine within us. Inspired by her, we embrace our original divinity.

A Time That Once Was

> For God the Mother so loved the world that She sent into its midst The Divine Girl-Child. Whosoever believes in Her goodness, listens to Her wisdom, and celebrates Her power will be awakened to their abundant giftedness as a Child of Life.
>
> —Adapted from John 3:16

We are reminded of a time when God looked like us. We learn of ancient times when the actual birth mother was honored as the giver of life. When it was from her that the line of the generations was traced. When children born of the mother were legitimate and respectable and given her name and social status. When women did not apologize for their girl-children.[7]

Inspired by a time that once was, we reclaim the stories of our personal history. We have not forgotten the past; it remains within us. We can walk through it and heal into the present. This is the promise of the girl-child within us, healing into the present. As the face of God changes in our experience, she becomes our teacher and healer. We listen to her stories, and learn tenderness and compassion. We descend into her wounds, and reconnect to the roots of our uniqueness and our creative ability. We honor her feelings, and embrace our own humanity. As she bubbles forth in the safe life we create for her, our vocations are enhanced by her spontaneity and joy. As we reparent her, we turn from self-hatred toward self-care and self-celebration.

Resources for Healing: An Immersion in Woman-Affirming Images

As I gathered the fragments of the girl-child's story from the far recesses of my ignored past and from the margins of religious history, I searched for stories, songs, and affirmations that celebrated the girl-child's existence. As I found woman-affirming resources, I used them to reparent the child within me and to create healing experiences to offer at retreats, workshops, and religious services.

Each healing experience gives the fragments of our stories a voice—in our spirits through prayer, in our imaginations through images and symbols, in our bodies through movement, in our breath through silence and meditation, and in our communities through healing touch and creative response. Each experience shouts across the centuries, "Girl-Child, we remember you." Each experience whispers into the depths of our woundedness, "Girl-Child, you are good. You are strong. You are sacred. You are wise. You are whole."

I have included the ritual "In Celebration of The Divine Girl-Child" in this chapter. Before presenting the entire ritual as it would be performed at a retreat or Sabbath service, each of the healing resources is described below:

• *A New Birth: Celebration*

In my quest for healing resources for the girl-child, I discovered a medieval infancy narrative celebrating the birth of Christ.[8] I reworked it to be included in a rebirthing ritual. In it the girl-child's birth is announced and celebrated by angels. In her honor we gather to affirm our belief in her goodness, to listen to her wisdom, and to celebrate her power. This narrative has been used in a number of ways: as a celebratory ritual by parents at the birth of their daughters; as a reparenting ritual for women; and as a communal celebration in honor of all the girl-children who have ever lived.

• *A New Song: Welcome*

Long unattended, my creativity revived as I listened to the stories of The Girl-Child I Once Was. The loving gaze of my attention penetrated the silence of years and stirred the gifts of song, dance, and image to life again. Inspired by the birth of my goddaughters, Melanie Jane and Dylan, I wrote my first song, "Hold the Baby." It affirms my love and commitment to the girl-child. Since that time it has been sung as a welcoming chant by parents at the dedication, naming, and christening ceremonies of their daughters and as a reparenting tool for women. It is dedicated to the girl-children of all generations, past, present, and future.

• *New Parenting Skills: Mothers and Daughters*

As we glimpse the feminine face of God, we learn new ways of parenting our daughters and ourselves. We surround ourselves with women's music, images, words, and challenges. We seek out woman-affirming spiritual communities in which the girl-child's birth is welcomed with as much pomp, circumstance, and opportunity as her brother's—communities in which her body and its processes will not exclude her from participation in religious rituals, communities in which she will be surrounded by images of a God who looks like her in the presence of clergywomen and women priests. In this part of the ritual, women share their hopes and dreams for their daughters and themselves.

• *The Mothers Speak*

Words hold tremendous power to hurt or to heal. The sting of childhood words and images contribute to the self-limiting patterns and ineffective behaviors that bring us into therapy, the recovery community, or a woman's support circle. Throughout the book these hurtful words have been pulled out of our histories. We have examined them and spoken them aloud in the company of loving witnesses. In this ritual Eve, Lilith, and Mary speak healing words to the girl-child. Their affirmations welcome her. Their words enlarge her vision. Their challenges acknowledge her truth. Their presence restores her to health.

• *In Praise of the Girl-Child*

We include a collage of gratitude to The Divine Girl-Child in our ritual. She has become a healing image of the divine within us.

✑ IN CELEBRATION OF THE DIVINE GIRL-CHILD: A RITUAL

What follows is the complete script for the ritual "In Celebration of The Divine Girl-Child." Read through the ritual as if it were text. Record the feelings and memories that surface. Later you may want to tape parts of the ritual in your own voice to listen to daily.

Invocation

WOMAN PRIEST: For Mother God so loved the world that she sent into its midst The Divine Girl-Child. Whosoever believes in her goodness, listens to her wisdom, and celebrates her power will be awakened to their abundant giftedness as a Child of Life (John 3:16, adapted).

Call to Worship

WOMAN RABBI: Come let us believe. Come let us listen. Come let us celebrate. The Divine Girl-Child is within us. The Divine Girl-Child is among us.

A New Birth

READER 1: We honor the daughters of history, whose births and accomplishments were not recognized until this age. We honor the unnamed sisters of famous brothers, born into a society that did not acknowledge their birth. Call aloud their names. (Pause while names are said: For example, "Mary's daughters," "Malvena Reynolds," "Virginia Woolf," "Harriet Tubman" . . .)

READER 2: We honor The Girl-Child We Once Were, born into a society that prefers men, a society that at a deep and fundamental level did not honor her coming. She is within us. Call aloud your childhood names. (Pause while names are said.)

READER 3: We honor the girl-children among us, our daughters, grand-daughters, and nieces. We acknowledge and celebrate their births. Call aloud their names. (Pause while names are said.)

DANCE AND VOICE CHOIR:

"The Birthing"

In this hour everything is stillness, there is total silence and awe. We are overwhelmed with a great wonder. We keep vigil. We are expecting the coming of the Divine Child.

In the fullness of time she is born. She shines like the sun, bright and beautiful. She is delightful to see. She appears as peace, soothing the whole world. The voices of many invisible beings in one voice rejoice: She has arrived. The Divine Child is among us. (Pass the word through-out the congregation: She has arrived. The Divine Child is among us.)

Become bold. Lean over and look at her. Touch her face. Lift her in your hands with great awe. Look at her more closely. There is no blem-ish on her. She is splendid to see. (Pause to look at her.) Dance with her. (Pause to dance with her.)

Now come to a still place with her. She is laughing a most joyful laugh. She opens her eyes and looks intently at you. (Pause to look in her eyes.) Suddenly a great light comes forth from her eyes, like a flash of lightning. The light enters you. She enters you. You begin to live.

_____ is born. The Divine Child is among us! She offers us gifts of light and healing. (Pause as each woman's name is read in the above line, after which a cheer goes up to celebrate her birth.)

WOMAN PRIEST (Adapted from "Song of Introduction of the Child to the Cosmos," Plains Indians): Sun, Moon, Stars, all that move in the heav-ens. I bid you hear me. Into your midst has come a new life. Winds, Clouds, Rains, Mist, all that move in the air. Hills, Valleys, Rivers, Lakes, Trees, Grasses, all that are of the earth. Come, one and all. Give your consent, I implore! Make this child's path smooth. Let her travel beyond the four hills, beyond the four directions of the Wheel of the Universe.

A New Song

WOMAN MINISTER: And suddenly there appeared a multitude of heavenly beings singing, Glory to the Mother of All Living and to her Daughter. She will bring peace and inspire goodwill among all people (John 2:13–14, adapted).

READER 1: We sing a welcome song to the daughters of history and to the unnamed sisters of famous brothers. We speak the tender words they did not hear.

READER 2: We sing a welcome song to The Girl-Child We Once Were. We speak the tender words she did not hear.

READER 3: We sing a welcome song to the girl-children among us, our daughters, granddaughters, and nieces. May they hear tender words every day.

VOICE CHOIR:

"Hold the Baby"

(Chorus:) Hold the baby. Tenderly love her.
Hold the baby. Tell her you care.

(Verse 1:) Welcome her joyfully. Shout with a loud voice:
"You belong here among us. We're glad you're alive!"

(Verse 2:) Look down upon her. Bless every movement.
She deserves loving kindness, every day of her life.

(Verse 3:) Surround her with goodness, safety, and laughter.
She is the Divine Child, come among us this day.

(Verse 4:) Look at her closely. There is no blemish.
She is a delight, soothing this world with peace.

(Verse 5:) Cherish the baby, living among us.
Care for her willingly, every day of her life.

(Verse 6:) Celebrate the girl-child, born in all ages.
Come to bring us salvation and grace.

New Parenting Skills

Our Hopes and Dreams for The Child We Once Were

READER 1: As we glimpse the feminine face of God, we learn new ways of reparenting ourselves. As this woman shares her hopes and dreams, imagine The Girl-Child You Once Were as the daughter you have chosen to care for willingly. Reflect on the reparenting you will incorporate into your life.

If I had a little girl . . .
  We would go on adventures every day—to the library and museum, to the mountains and sea. Wherever we go, she will be able to count on three meals a day. Before each meal we will reflect on the good way we are treating ourselves.
  Interesting friends will surround her life. Children and adults of different colors, lifestyles, accents, and beliefs. She will learn that all are held equally by the graciousness of life.
  She will never be left with a baby-sitter unless she or he is a friend of ours and in whose company she feels safe and well cared for. Her room will have lots of windows in it. She will always have a view of the world beyond her room. It will be her own room, and everyone must knock before entering.
  I will surround her with images of women so that she will be proud of her body. I will surround her with art, music, poetry, and books about women. She will hear of men's accomplishments, words, music, and history in the world. Our home will be a space where women's voices are also heard and respected. I will read to her legends of women from around the world, women as powerful and compassionate nonvictims.

Our Hopes and Dreams for Our Daughters

READER 2: As we glimpse the feminine face of God, we learn new ways of parenting our daughters. We surround them with woman-affirming music, images, words, and challenges. We seek out spiritual communities that will welcome our daughter's birth. Communities that will encourage her participation in religious rituals and celebrate images of a God who looks like her. As this woman shares her woman-affirming hopes and dreams for her daughter, Carson, reflect on the conscious parenting you wish to incorporate into your family life:

I hope she likes her name.
I hope she has wonderful female friends.
I hope she loves her body, delights in her sexuality, and creates her own
*   spirituality.*
I hope she feels her power and embraces her anger and creativity.
I hope she owns her intelligence and accepts her beauty.
I hope she feels the unshakable support of her parents.
I hope that she will laugh and laugh, and dance and dance, and sing aloud.
I hope she will put herself first, and love herself as much as I love her, be-
*   cause that would be an unspeakable force!*
I hope that the world will change enough to support her in all these ways.

The Mothers Speak

READER 1: Hear the words of Eve, the Mother of All Living. Speak them daily to the girl-child within you. Speak them daily to your daughters, granddaughters, and nieces:

EVE (WOMAN MINISTER):
Refuse to carry the shame of man within your body.
       Refuse to carry the helplessness of woman atop your life.
Your body is good. Live in it with pride.
Your thoughts are good. Think them with pride.
Your feelings are good. Feel them with pride.
Your life is good. Live it with pride.
Be full of yourself. Brag about your goodness.
       Celebrate your abundant giftedness as a Child of Life.

READER 2: Hear the words of Lilith, the Divine Lady. Speak them daily to the girl-child within you. Speak them daily to your daughters, granddaughters, and nieces:

LILITH (WOMAN RABBI):
Your body is strong. Move in it with courage.
Your thoughts are strong. They create an impact on others. Speak them
       with courage.
Your feelings are strong. They are to be shared.
Express them with courage.

Your life is strong. It will not fall apart. Live it with courage.

Exert, initiate, and move on your own behalf without guilt or shame.

Hold on to your power. Don't let others squash it.

Hold on to your courage. Don't let others preach it out of you.

Hold on to your independence. Don't let others scare it out of you.

Refuse abusive relationships.

Refuse pain and suffering.

Refuse to be submissive and subordinate.

READER 3: Hear the words of Mary, the Virgin Mother. Speak them daily to the girl-child within you. Speak them daily to your daughters, grand-daughters, and nieces:

MARY (WOMAN PRIEST):

Your body is your own. Do not allow society to twist it out of shape. Al-low no one access to your body without your permission.

Your thoughts are your own. Do not allow them to be molded by others.

Your feelings are your own. Do not allow them to be expressed by others.

Your life is your own. Do not allow it to be shaped by the expectations of others.

Author your life without guilt or shame.

Do not live to please others.

Refuse to surrender, except to your truest self and your wisest voice.

In Praise of the Girl-Child

READER 1: Let us create a collage of gratitude to The Divine Girl-Child. We have let go of old images, allowing them to fall to the ground and die. They have nourished the soil, from which has blossomed a God born of our own experience as women. The Divine Girl-Child has be-come a healing image of the divine within us. (Give each woman an opportunity to express her praise of the girl-child.)

> I celebrate The Divine Girl-Child, who has taught me
> self-love and unconditional acceptance and who has brought
> permanent companionship. She has taught me to take
> care of my basic needs: eating, sleeping, and meditation.
> She has made it possible for me to allow pleasurable
> experiences into my life such as massage, pedicures, water,

sun, and touch. Through her I am learning to love
and accept the miraculous functions of my body. And she
has taught me that I have riches to give: my thoughts
and feelings, my present-time awareness, my compassion
and caring for others, and my desire to make our world
a more balanced place for us all to live. I have learned
that I am worthy and beautifully desirable to myself and
others, and I love it.

—Erin

I celebrate The Divine Girl-Child, whose song of welcome
touched and healed me. The thought that I deserve loving
kindness, safety, and laughter every day of my life is
a liberating concept. In the few seconds it took me to
read those words, I have been freed from the layers of
shame that have kept me from believing that I am worthy
to receive good things in my life. You mean I actually
deserve my two wonderfully beautiful children? Yes!
Yes! And as I reflected on their lovely faces when I read,
"Look at her closely. There is no blemish. She is a delight,"
I realized that spiritually I am beautiful and without
blemish too. In fact I'm perfect. It was a deeply
healing moment.

—Colleen

I celebrate The Divine Girl-Child I am rediscovering within
me. Her wonderful traits were not appreciated when I was
a child. They were ridiculed and squelched. Now I
can love and value them—her fun, creativity, devilishness,
spiritedness, silliness, and laughter. She wants to come out
of hiding. I take her contra dancing, swimming, to a kind
therapist, and to dinner with nonjudgmental friends.
She cares about people. She highlights my desire to
bring fun and a sparkle into people's lives. Through her
joy I may yet discover my right livelihood. I remind her
each day, "You are good enough just as you are
without doing anything."

—Emily

READER 2: Let us gather in a closing circle. (Pause as women gather.) Let
us call aloud the names of the girl-children in our lives. As we call aloud

their names, it is our prayer that they may glimpse the feminine face of God and travel a less turbulent path toward self-love, self-trust, and the celebration of their power in the world. (Pause as names are spoken. When there is silence, end with the words "Go in peace.")

Before moving on, linger awhile with Chapter 10:

A RESPONSE: BLASPHEMOUS, HERETICAL, OR HEALING?

Set aside time each day this week to respond to the ritual "In Celebration of The Divine Girl-Child." In certain exercises you may want to converse with The Divine Girl-Child within you. Imagine sitting with her in your meeting place. Draw and write your responses to the following questions, exercises, and reflections:

DAY 1. *In Celebration of The Divine Girl-Child*

Reflect this day on your reactions to the ritual "In Celebration of The Divine Girl-Child." Were you pleased and affirmed? At what points were you uncomfortable? Did you consider the reworkings of Scripture blasphemous and heretical, or healing?

DAY 2. *A New Birth*

Tape "The Birthing." Listen to it in your meditation space. Create a sacred drama in which you enter into the birthing scene. Wrap a beloved doll, a stuffed animal, or a picture of yourself in a scarf. Unwrap her as the scene progresses. Imagine that she is the child you once were. You are allowing her to emerge. Dance with her. Allow her to gaze at you. Celebrate her emergence with a party.

DAY 3. *A New Song*

• Reread the song "Hold the Baby." Write an affirmation to yourself in response to each verse with your nondominant hand. Display these affirmations at home and at work. Repeat them to yourself throughout the day.

• Write a contract committing yourself to at least three specific self-caring actions this day. Sign and date it.

DAY 4. *New Words*

Speak new words to your daughters, granddaughters, and nieces to-day. Incorporate the words of Eve, Lilith, and Mary into your parenting vocabulary. Fill your home with empowering, tender, and affirming words this day.

DAY 5. *New Parenting*

If you have no children, imagine The Girl-Child You Once Were as a daughter you have chosen to care for willingly. Reflect on the reparenting you wish to incorporate into your life as an act of self-celebration. Write down your hopes and dreams for your imaginary daughter and offer them to yourself this day.

DAY 6. *A Healing Image*

Join Erin, Colleen, and Emily and write a hymn of gratitude to The Divine Girl-Child. What gifts has she given you?

DAY 7. *Gratitude for the Girl-Child*

Write a hymn of gratitude to your daughters, granddaughters, and nieces. What gifts have you received from them? Share your gratitude with them this day.

CHAPTER ELEVEN

The One Who Shed
Her Blood

The Story

There were no sacraments or rituals in our childhood churches to celebrate the monthly shedding of our blood, our sacred blood that holds
within it both life and death. As a teenager I learned a hymn, "There's
power, power, wonder-working power in the blood of the lamb. There
is power, power, wonder-working power in the precious blood of the
lamb." We sang a lot about the blood of Jesus. The shedding of his
blood was considered of utmost importance. And yet women have been
shedding their blood for centuries, and I, as a girl-child, learned no
songs celebrating my beautiful and powerful blood. On the contrary the
female body has been denigrated, and an elaborate set of taboos have
been set in place surrounding the girl-child's natural processes: menstruation, childbearing, and menopause.

There's Power in the Blood

> Who can wash away my sin? Nothing but the blood of
> Jesus. What can make me whole again? Nothing but the
> blood of Jesus.
>
> —The Baptist Hymnal

"If you have to wear a dress to be an altar boy, why can't I be one? Girls
look better in dresses anyway," I asked the priest who said Mass at my

elementary school. "God is the father. God is a man, my dear, so only boys and men are allowed at the altar," he explained patiently. Years later I discovered that the official reason for my exclusion from the altar had to do with religion's taboos concerning a woman's body.

Webster defines *taboo* as, "set apart as charged with a dangerous supernatural power; banned especially as immoral or dangerous." My body and its processes were considered immoral and dangerous. As a result I was considered unfit to preside at sacred rituals and to touch the body of Christ. In seminary I read the 1976 Vatican declaration outlining the arguments against the ordination of women. Influenced by Aristotle's definition of woman as a misbegotten male, this document made clear that there must be a physical resemblance between the priest and Christ.[1] Clearly I, as a girl-child, was excluded from the divine.

As the face of God changed in my experience, I searched my religious memory for images of women's bodies and natural processes. I remembered one story I was told in Sunday school. It is found in Mark 5:

> Among them was a woman suffering from a flow of blood for twelve years. In spite of long treatment by many doctors on which she had spent all that she had, there had been no improvement; on the contrary, she had grown worse. She had heard what the people were saying about the Healer, so she came up from behind in the crowd and touched the Healer's cloak. And the source of her bleeding dried up. She was cured.

My Sunday school teachers told me that she had not been touched in twelve years. When I asked why, I was referred to these verses in Leviticus:

> When a woman has her menstrual flow, she shall be in a state of impurity for seven days. Anyone who touches her shall be unclean 'til evening. Anything she lies or sits on during her impurity shall be unclean. Anyone who touches her bed shall wash his garments, bathe in water, and be unclean until evening. (Leviticus 15:19–21)

For twelve years this woman, who was considered incurably ill and permanently unclean, had been exiled from the human community. Her "state of impurity" polluted everyone with whom she came in contact and everything she touched. Given the shame and loneliness of her isolation, it is not surprising that she had spent all of her resources to find a cure.

Our Wounds

Our first step toward healing is to give voice to the experiences of our personal and religious past that deposited within the girl-child a sense that something is wrong with her body and its functions. In the company of courageous women, we will tell our stories. We will move out of the isolation of a lifetime. We will take our first steps toward healing.

Messy Bodies

> Whether it's menstruation, PMS, or pregnancy, women get too messy.
>
> —Susan

As a result of religious taboos that set women's processes aside as dangerous and immoral, the girl-child develops a sense that something is wrong with her body and its functions. A cultic uncleanness accompanies her throughout life. We cannot imagine a God who bleeds like us. These attitudes are not the relics of a distant past. They continue to affect women's lives today. Consider and reflect:

• In contemporary Israel a woman who desires to be legally married must appear before the chief rabbi and declare the date of her last period. The wedding date will be set based on this information in order to assure that she does not enter the marriage "unclean."[2]

• Karen writes of her observations while in Bali on her thirtieth-birthday trip: "I was surprised to find signs in English posted in all the temples that menstruating women were not allowed in the temples. In their culture it's not just menstruating women who are excluded but anyone who is openly bleeding. They don't want blood in their spiritual houses. I thought it incredibly unjust that in such a deeply religious society women were not allowed into the religious houses merely because of their biological functions."

• A woman from Eastern Europe contributed a woman-affirming perspective to a discussion about the fall of communism. One of the reasons it fell, she argued, was that it had not marshaled the resources necessary to provide sanitary napkins for women. Its architects were men and its priorities were forged from men's experience. The male gods of the nations do not bleed monthly. Thus this essential reality of women's lives remains peripheral to men's concerns.

Although there were no signs on our childhood churches excluding us from attendance, the subtle messages we were given made it clear that our bleeding was to be hidden from family and friends. Unlike our Eastern European sisters, we were bombarded with advertisements for an array of feminine products that promised to hide our "messy" blood from public view and to disguise our "disgusting" odors.

These messages convinced us that true women's liberation would come from hiding all evidence that we were women except whatever enhanced our desirability to men. The ads seemed to intimate that if we used enough of these products, we would be able to live as if we were not women. Most disturbing of all, the dangers of these products were not brought to our attention. The potentially lethal side effects were not considered as serious as the messiness of menstruation that the products were designed to eliminate.

Liz writes, "I started my period at ten. I was embarrassed and tried to hide everything that had to do with menstruation. I received very little explanation. My mother viewed menstruation as 'an inconvenience with a lot of washing up to do,' 'a mistake' that we had to deal with, and 'a curse.' I had no sense of it as a life-giving process." Is it any wonder that we cannot imagine a God who bleeds and cramps and must go through all the washing up associated with menstruation? Such a God is unfathomable based on our internalized sense of inferiority.

Sitting in a circle, the women share the truth of their lives. One by one they speak out of the silence of a lifetime:

> Periods have always been a curse. I've dreaded them except
> when I've been concerned about the possibility of
> pregnancy. Only at those times have I been grateful
> for them. I look forward to when I don't have to deal
> with periods anymore, but then I'll have to deal with
> menopause. I constantly hate to be where I am and
> I look to be at another place and dread that too.
>
> —Erin

I was prepared for my period because my mother had talked to me about it for a long time in advance. She gave me the kind of practical information I needed to know. Yet at some point menstruation became something that we women had to keep to ourselves, a secret that we couldn't talk about with boys or men, a burden we were to carry alone.

All the secrets that surrounded menstruation hurt me and crushed the childish excitement that I started out with. By the time I was twelve, I had let a lot of this kind of "crushing energy" into me, and in the process I gave up the joy of my body.

—Colleen

In preparation for my coming period, my mother sent off for a box with an assortment of napkins, belts, and pamphlets. Inside was a book that suggested if you were embarrassed about buying sanitary napkins and couldn't find them on the shelf, that you go to the clerk and ask for "Modess, please." Anyone overhearing you would think you were saying "Oh, yes, please." I got the message this was something you do not talk about.

My period brought with it horrendous, debilitating cramps. I suffered alone and was sure I was being punished. I felt such self-hatred that I would hit myself because I was mad at the pain and misery of it all. I learned well that a good woman hides the unpleasantness so that no one else will be affected. The feeling of filthiness about my body has created a great deal of paranoia in me. For most of my life I didn't feel worthy of a relationship.

—Joyce

Imagine sitting in a circle with Liz, Erin, Colleen, and Joyce. Add your story to theirs.

- Describe your first menstrual experience. Were you prepared? Whom did you tell?

• Reflect on the attitudes of your mother and father, sisters and brothers, and your classmates concerning menstruation. Reflect on the images of the culture concerning menstruation presented on TV, in advertisements, movies, and billboards.

• Can you imagine a God who bleeds and cramps as you do?

Our Complicated Bodies

> I have battled self-hatred and self-doubt throughout my
> life. I have denied my female self, body, and qualities.
> There is always a sense of shame attached to being
> female.
>
> —Sandi

As a result of our immersion in the exclusively male words and images used for God and the religious stories and myths that have held sway over our imaginations since childhood, the girl-child develops a sense that something is wrong with her body. She does not look like God. She is other and defective. A woman's wounds are most often acted out on her own body. It is her body that bears the scars of her intense self-hatred. Some are embarrassed by their breasts, thighs, and curves and will starve themselves in order to eradicate all roundness. They will attempt to look like adolescent boys. Others will be groomed as sex objects and will spend inordinate amounts of time and money twisting their bodies, hair color, noses, and breasts into the acceptable sexual shapes of the culture.

In desperation women ask, "Why is it that men wake up in the morning and are enough? Why is it that we wake up and must add to our faces, adorn our bodies, and cover our scents and roundness in order to be enough—and we still fall short?"

A participant in a spirituality group comments on one of the complications of having a female body. Hers is a very practical and personal reflection, one that is echoed in many women's writings: "I wear a bra not because I need one but because I have adapted myself to society's expectations and I don't like people staring at me when I don't have one on. A woman cannot just accept her body for what it is. On the one hand I love it. On the other I feel weird about my body and go through tremendous conflict over what to wear each morning. I can't wear something really tight because then I would have to deal with men responding to me as a sexual object and not as an intelligent woman. Being a woman is a complicated matter in this society." Is it any wonder that women cannot imagine a God who has a troublesome body like theirs?

As a result of our culture's immersion in the exclusively male words and images used for God and the religious stories and myths that have held sway on our *societal* imagination, women's health concerns have consistently been ignored by the medical establishment. Historically our bodies have been considered too complicated to be included in health-research studies. In a world that prefers men, it is the organs of the man's body vulnerable to disease and stress that are researched to develop effective drugs and technologically sophisticated surgical procedures and instrumentation. His body, created in the image of God, is of greater value than the woman's. Her reproductive organs and breasts are dispensable to modern medicine.

Our early training convinces us that we cannot understand our complicated bodies. That it is only men who have the skill and intelligence to become experts on women's bodies, most particularly in gynecology and obstetrics—the two areas in which they will never experience first-hand the reality of being a woman. Eighty percent of all gynecologists are men.[3] A recurring theme in women's writings concerns the discomfort they have felt at the hands of male gynecologists. Jen writes of her experience: "Since adolescence I have felt abused every time I visit the gynecologist. Something inside of me says to get the hell out of there, but I am petrified to try something new—such as a female doctor. I was taught from the time I was a preteen that men are the experts about our female problems. Even as I write these words, I see how ridiculous it sounds."

Sitting in a circle, the women share the truth of their lives. One by one they speak out of the silence of a lifetime:

> I have not developed a relationship with my feminine
> natural processes. My major wound has been alienation
> from my body, including menstruation and childbearing.
> I never seriously considered giving birth to my own child.

I aborted my one pregnancy when I was twenty-nine.
Deprived of nurturing my own biological children, I
turned those needs into codependent behaviors with family
and friends.

To naturally mother was not of value to me until
now, when I am close to menopause. Coming to
grips with the fact that I will not have children has been
painful. In order not to be seen as a weak female underling,
I felt I had to make my mark in the world whatever
the cost. Eventually that quest became so empty that
I had a breakdown. Now that I am healing and accepting
my feminine processes, I want a new relationship with my
body.

—Hallie

My family of origin transmitted a sense of disgust about
my bodily functions. Anything that had to do with my
body I learned to hide at an early age. I didn't want
anyone to know that I had to go to the bathroom,
that I was too hot, too cold, or even that I was thirsty.
I was taught to endure physical discomfort and not to talk
about it.

I picked up the sense that if I inconvenienced
anybody, I was being naughty and that I didn't have the
right to express my needs. Eventually I lost the sense of
what my needs were. I still hide the fact that I have
to go to the bathroom. I don't like to expose my
body. I'm embarrassed if someone sees me in a bathing
suit, so I seldom go swimming.

—Liz

Imagine sitting with Hallie and Liz. Add your story to theirs.

- What were you taught as a child about your body and its processes?
- Have you had difficulties with male doctors? How did this make you feel
about your body and your right to proper health care?
- List the ways your woman body is complicated or troublesome.
- How have your wounds been acted out on your body?

• How have you twisted your body into the acceptable sexual shape of the culture?

• Can you imagine a God with a troublesome body like yours?

Our Untouchable Bodies

> As soon as I grew out of the "cute stage," all touching stopped.
>
> —Liz

Touch is essential to our healthy development. In our mother's womb it soothes and comforts us. Our trip down the birth canal is supported by the laboring action of our mothers as their bodies push, pull, and hug us into life. And it is clear from the experience of "foundling babies" who wasted away from lack of touch that touch is much more essential to our survival as young infants than a sterile environment. A woman's sense of uncleanness is accentuated by the quality of touch that was or was not present in her childhood home.

When some of us were growing up, touching only occurred through discipline—the slap across the face and the spanking. We grew up deprived of affectionate touch. Nancy writes, "I cannot remember having been touched as a child by either parent except to be disciplined. I remember my mother taking my hand when I was a teenager, but it was so unnatural, I almost died of acute embarrassment and stiffened, so she dropped it."

Even for those who were touched affectionately by their parents, touch was seldom extended beyond early childhood. As the girl-child matures and grows out of the "cute stage," her parents become uncomfortable with her developing body, and most touching abruptly stops. She creates stories to make sense of this withdrawal of affection. She becomes convinced that it is because she is now dirty, smelly, and ugly and that her growing breasts and pubic hair and the new sensations she is experiencing in her genitals have made her untouchable to her parents. [In the next chapter we will see how the incestuous touch of a parent compounds the shame already taking root within the young girl's body and life.]

We internalize the culture's denigration of our feminine processes and become untouchable to ourselves. Susan's words are echoed in many women's stories: "It's not okay for me to touch my own body. I didn't look at it or touch it until the birth of my first child."

Sitting in a circle, the women share the truth of their lives. One by one they speak out of the silence of a lifetime:

> My mother never spontaneously hugged or kissed me. I
> felt happiest when I was sick because then she would touch
> my head to feel my temperature. Today my hunger to
> be touched is stronger than my need for sex. I can't
> get enough of it. Yet touch is unfamiliar to me. I forgive
> myself for accepting sex when what I really wanted was
> to be touched and held.
>
> —Karen H.

> My father never touched me after age five. He was
> extremely uncomfortable with my development through
> puberty. And yet he was attentive in a strange way.
> According to him, the only thing I had going for me
> as a girl-child were my looks, so he would periodically
> insist that I stand in front of him for a weight inspection.
> He checked to see if there were any parts of my body
> touching. If anything was touching—calves or
> thighs—these were the "fat places," and he encouraged
> me to bicycle more and eat less.
>
> I loved being sick as a child because I would lose
> weight and the fat places would disappear. When I
> weigh myself now, the image of "parts touching" comes
> back to me. I inspect myself as my father once did. To
> this day my dad's first comments when we visit have
> to do with my appearance. He is still inspecting me
> and says, "You're looking slim" or "You've gained some
> weight."
>
> —Irene

Imagine sitting in a circle with Karen and Irene. Add your story to theirs.

- Recall the times you were touched as a child. What was the quality of each touch? Affectionate? Disciplinary? Functional?
- When did your family stop touching you with affection?
- How have you become untouchable to yourself?
- Keep track of the touches you receive this week. Do you continue to be touch-deprived?

Our Healing

Our first step toward healing has been to give voice to the childhood experiences that have deposited within the girl-child a sense that something is wrong with her body and its functions. And now, with courage, we will immerse ourselves in transformational resources inspired by a time when God bled like us. The One Who Shed Her Blood becomes a healing image of the divine within us. In her presence we will enter into loving partnership with our bodies and into supportive community with other courageous women.

A Time That Once Was

> we need a god who bleeds now
> whose wounds are not the end of anything
> —Ntozake Shange, *A Daughter's Geography*

As an adult I wondered about The One Who Shed Her Blood in the New Testament story from Mark 5. I gathered the fragments of her story from my childhood memory. She has no voice in the story. Her name is not mentioned. Her story was told only as it related to the more important story of the Healer. I tried to imagine her feelings and the details of her life. For twelve years she was never touched or hugged. She had no visitors. Her furniture and bed were considered unclean. She took no trips to public places. She was not allowed to pray in the synagogue. Her presence was considered a contamination.

I allowed her pain to touch mine. For most of my life I felt untouchable to myself and others. A veil of shame separated me from the human community. At times I longed for reconnection. I searched for a magical insight or treatment that would exorcise the flawed part of me. And yet there were other times when my shame felt like a warm protective covering. I hid behind it so that no one would awaken my childhood memories of severed connection and incestuous touch.

It was in circles of women that my childhood memories were coaxed out of hiding. It was in circles of women that my shame was washed away. I wondered if the male writers of The One Who Shed Her Blood's story had overlooked the women in her life. Did she visit with them in secret? Did they tell each other stories late at night under the stars?

I gathered woman-affirming images from the very beginning when God was woman, when she bled like us. I learned of ancient women who did not apologize for their bleeding. I read of ancient ways that held the woman's blood to be magic, flowing in harmony with the moon. I was told of ancient beliefs that celebrated the Great Mother, whose "moon-blood" thickened within her and then spilled from her to create all that is.[4] I wove the healing images of the very beginning and the fragments of The One Who Shed Her Blood's forgotten story and my own into a performance piece.

In the name of Eve, Lilith, and Mary, our Mythic Mothers, we ask The One Who Shed Her Blood to break out of the confines of traditional religious interpretation. We ask her to tell her own story. Enter into this fragment of the forgotten. Swallow her story into your own.

᪥ AN ENCOUNTER WITH THE ONE WHO SHED HER BLOOD: MOONBATHING

Longing . . .
I see them in the distance. I watch them.
  They visit each other's homes. They converse in public places.
  They touch and speak, eat, love, and live together.
I see them in the distance. I watch them live out their days.
  They are in a clearing of light, listening to healing words.

It has been twelve years. I long to draw near.
My eyes are weary from watching them at a distance . . . longing.

Hiding . . .
Hiding from a painful touch of long ago.
  My blood keeps me safe.
Filled with its warmth, it has become my friend.
  I cover my body. I watch it grow.
  No touch will penetrate the uncleanness of my blood.
My hands are tired of concealing my shame . . . hiding.

I rise up and go into the night.
In its darkness my eyes and hands rest.
The moon calls to me.

She tells me of a time when a woman's blood was sacred. There were no shameful separations. She tells me of a time when a woman's body was honored. There were no painful touches.

The Moon tells me of ancient women who did not apologize for their bleeding, of ancient times when the color of royalty was the dark red wine color of our beautiful blood, of ancient ways that held the blood to be awesome, for it was shed without pain. I learn of ancient beliefs that celebrated the Great Mother, whose "moon-blood" spilled from her to create All That Is.

My eyes closed, I find myself in a clearing of light with women from every age. Their song calls to me: "You who stand apart, come close. You who are out of touch, come near." They throw no stones, instead they offer me flowers and they touch me with healing and light. They sing to me: "It is right and good that you are beautiful and full."

Together we moonbathe.
Together we dance.
In the dance I shed my shame.
  I am washed clean of my shame in the light of the moon.

Imagine sitting in the clearing of moonlight with The One Who Shed Her Blood, sitting in a circle of women from every age.

Swallow Her Pain into Your Own Story

- What do you long for?
- What do you hide from?
- Describe your own "veil of shame." How has it separated you from the human community?
- To what lengths have you gone to find a cure? List all the "cures" you have tried.

Swallow Her Healing into Your Own Story

- How does the truth of another time when a woman's body was honored and her blood held sacred heal you?
- List the healing resources that you have used to wash away your shame.
- Reflect on the women who have been a healing presence in your life. How did they regard their bodies and processes? What new perspectives have they given you?

A Healing Community

> There's a river of birds in migration. A nation of women
> with wings.
>
> —Libana

In our retelling, The One Who Shed Her Blood found healing in the community of women. She was offered a safe space in which to shed the tears of a lifetime and to tell her story. She was empowered to move into life unashamed and to enlist all of the woman-affirming resources available to her. Inspired by the circle of women, she bravely walked through the crowd and touched the Healer's cloak. This was a forbidden act—an unclean woman touched the Rabbi.

There is a tremendous acceleration of our personal healing and growth when we open ourselves to the support, understanding, and empowerment that are available within a community of women. Initially women tend to be suspicious of one another. We carry within us a lifetime of attitudes and fears designed to keep us separate.

Colleen describes the fear she brought into a women's spirituality group: "I was groomed to compete with all women. I have felt tremendous jealousy in the past. I don't know how to release myself from it. At the very core of it I am afraid that our closeness will violate the tenet that I must compete with women. There's a fear that if I get too close to women, I will be attracted to them, and then my lesbian phobia comes up. I have to do a lot of healing around my relationships with women."

Competition among women is woven into the fabric of a society that prefers men. We compete for the attention of the gods. At some point during our work together I encourage women to inventory their competitive attitudes and behaviors toward other women. They acknowledge the women they have been jealous of; the ones they have gossiped about; those they have called names or slandered; those with whom they have competed for the attention of a man. They describe the behaviors and then look beneath them for the underlying motivation. Was it their own insecurity about their body or appearance? Was it unexpressed anger, fear, or self-loathing?

Over time these ineffective behaviors begin to dissolve as women share with one another from their common experience, strength, and hope. For the first time in their lives women begin to trust other women, to know and be known by them, and to relax in their presence. Most had only identified with their femininity through the touch, awakening, and arousal of men. They had not known that they could experience being a woman in the company of other women. In a woman's circle we redefine the meaning of the old stereotyped ideas of what is feminine. We embrace qualities that have been considered male. We develop a vocabulary for our feelings as we turn inward rather than outward to unravel life's complexities.

As the face of God changes, women begin to spend more time in the company of women and less time swirling around men. They become the feminine face of God to each other. In one another's presence the tears of a lifetime can be shed, the forgotten stories can be remembered and spoken aloud, and our former dignity and power as women can be reclaimed. We are empowered to move into life unashamed. Inspired by a circle of women, we boldly enlist the healing resources that are available to us. We commit the forbidden acts of embracing each other as sisters and of offering each other healing touch and empowering words.

In each other's presence we are reminded of the community of women that reaches far back in time. We acknowledge this wider community of which we are a part. We awaken to women of every age— their ideas, music, and stories. We delve into women's history, art, and spirituality. We discover that we are surrounded by a courageous cloud of witnesses; their ancient stories and images become healing resources for us now.

Sitting in a circle, the women share the healing of their lives. One by one they speak out of the isolation of a lifetime:

> I am beginning to understand that it is the community
> of women that can abide with me, that can comfort me,
> and that can provide me with a kind of security that
> a male lover could never do (though I still struggle
> with this). The point is that I am a woman. Practically
> speaking this means that the struggles and triumphs that
> other women experience as they go through their lives
> can inform my life in a way only women can.
>
> —Ferrel

> My deepest and most comfortable relationships have been
> with women. Yet I painfully acknowledge that for most
> of my life it was necessary for me to feel more
> attractive than another woman in order to include her
> in my life. She must pose no threat. There must be no
> possibility of competition between us. I instantly sized up
> women, and when I felt myself to be out of their
> league, I became intimidated, jealous, and filled with
> hate. I expressed these feelings indirectly through gossip
> and a critical attitude.
>
> I am making amends daily. I am developing
> intimate and honest relationships with beautiful,
> powerful, intelligent, and spiritual women. I no longer see
> them as a threat. They are a part of me, and together we
> all become beautiful and strong. I am learning to love
> women as I learn to love myself.
>
> —Erin

I have long been a seeker of truth. Before being in this women's community I was not aware of how strongly this search had been influenced by the male images of my religious past. Nor was I aware of how these male images prevented me from validating myself as a woman. It had never occurred to me before to look toward something nurturing, strong, and feminine—to a God who looks like me. I avoided learning about Goddess religions. But I have realized *at last* that what they offer is far more in alignment with what I'm seeking. Now I am drawn to articles, books, and films that deal with women's spiritual quests.

—Joyce

Imagine sitting with Ferrel, Erin, and Joyce. Add your story to theirs.

• Reflect on this statement from your own experience: "Competition among women is woven into the fabric of a society that prefers men. We compete for the attention of the gods." What attitudes have kept you from reaching out to women for inspiration, support, and challenge?

• Are you a member of a women's circle? If you are in a circle, list the gifts you have received from the women in your group. Acknowledge the attitudes and behaviors toward women that you have confronted in order to remain in solidarity with your sisters. If you are not in a circle, have you considered joining one? List your concerns. Consider starting your own group with a few trusted friends. Use the readings, exercises, rituals, and prayers in this book as a starting place.

A Healed Connection to Our Bodies

Who cannot love herself cannot love anybody.
Who is ashamed of her body is ashamed of life.
Who finds dirt or filth in her body is lost.
Who cannot respect the gifts of life
given even before birth can never respect anything fully.
—Anne Cameron, *Daughters of Copper Woman*

Inspired by a time when a woman's body was honored and her blood was sacred, we continue the journey home to our bodies. Through ritual, meditation, and guided exploration we imagine a Woman God with breasts, curves, and thighs. We reclaim the images of a time when God looked and bled like us. We ask, "How might our sense of ourselves and our attitudes toward our bodies be transformed in her presence?" The women answer:

• We imagine our body as the sacred temple of the Spirit of Life. As a community of support within us. As a harmonious partnership of cells, tissues, organs, and systems. As an exquisite resource, a faithful ally, a trustworthy companion.

• We enter into a partnership with our body, consulting it through each season of our lives. Through prayer and meditation we improve our conscious contact with our body. We become fully aware of the feelings, sensations, and signals our body has been sending us for years as faithful reminders of the way home. We embrace our body as a loyal and long-term companion from whom we have been estranged.

• We no longer find it necessary to twist ourselves into the shapes of the male God. We embrace our bodies as sacred. We like ourselves when we look into the mirror. When we awaken each morning, we look into a full-length mirror and affirm, "I am enough this day. Just as I am, I am enough. There is no blemish." And then we read a litany of transformation in which we celebrate those parts of us that the culture has judged and that we have despised.

• A God who bleeds like us transforms our relationship to all of the sensations that accompany menstruation. We no longer denigrate our natural processes. We call upon our natural cycles to support the energy of our lives. We celebrate the coming of our period and cherish each day the blood flows from us. We honor our beautiful blood.

• When our periods are delayed, we ask our body, "What are you trying to say?" And during our periods we honor our body's Deep Wisdom. We dialogue with it through imagery, writing, and movement. We ask our body, "What pillows of support do you need during this time? How might I support you?" We no longer fight our body's needs. We tenderly acknowledge them and then meet them.

Sitting in a circle, the women share the healing truth of their lives. One by one they speak out of the isolation of a lifetime:

On a daily basis I affirm the goodness of my body as it
looks right now. This ongoing affirmation is essential
because daily I'm bombarded by images of the perfect
body and by messages that my life will be perfect if
I just lose ten pounds. The daily assault on my body is
very painful. More often than not, though, I am completely
happy with my body, its feelings and its sexuality, and
how it looks as well. In this healed frame of mind I
don't want to change a thing. I don't want to begin a new
exercise or diet regimen. I want to go on living.

At the same time, I have learned to love and
admire other women's bodies. Today I honor that
there is an essential rightness and beauty about each person's
body. I had never been exposed to that perspective before.
I had been taught that a woman needs to look a
certain way to be good and acceptable.

—Colleen

Through talking about my natural bodily processes with
women, a healing light has shone into the darkness and
the shame that have surrounded my body since
puberty. In the company of women I expressed my
fear of aging, of uselessness, and of having been unfulfilled
as a woman. I have been given gifts of insight that have
helped me to accept the facts of my life, the choices
I have made, and that I will never have my own
children. I have been given the courage to explore my long-
term alienation from my body. I have bought a copy
of *The New Our Body, Our Selves.* The community of
women has helped to repair the broken connection to my
own femaleness. I now believe that I am part of the
divine.

—Hallie

As a result of this experience I have come to a deeper sense
of self-worth, not just as a human being but as a woman.
With the support of my community of women I am
learning to give myself a higher quality of self-care. I
am learning to say no to situations that exhaust my energies

and to slow down when the pace of my everyday life becomes so frenetic that I'm unable to hear the voice of my deeper wisdom.

I'm learning to accept my female body and its natural processes. I am shedding my sense of shame about menstruation. I am beginning to feel the mystery of the cycles of life and death that move through me. As I heal, I find that I am able to look at myself in the mirror. I spend more time in the bath. I am taking dance lessons and receiving massage. And I am embracing my body's inevitable aging with compassion and gratitude. There are still negative feelings that come up with each of these self-caring actions. It will take a while to heal my long-standing body shame.

—Liz

Imagine sitting in a circle with Colleen, Hallie, and Liz. Add your story to theirs.

- In the presence of The One Who Shed Her Blood, how might your sense of yourself and your attitude toward your body be transformed by her healing gifts?
- What self-caring actions will you include in your week to honor your body?
- What healing rituals will you include in your life to celebrate the shedding of your beautiful blood?
- The Goddess supports us to discover the unique gifts in each cycle of our lives. What are the unique gifts menopause has brought to you?

Before moving on, linger awhile with The One Who Shed Her Blood.

✌§ HEALING THE INNER ADOLESCENT

Set aside time each day this week to converse with your Inner Adolescent. Imagine talking to her as if you were having a conversation with an adolescent daughter or niece in a comfortable meeting place. With your nondominant hand, draw and write responses to the following questions:

DAY 1. *Messy Bodies*

• Describe your first menstrual experience. Were you prepared for it? What kind of support did you receive from your family and friends?

• How did it feel to bleed? Did you talk about it with your girlfriends?

• Did you get your period before or after your girlfriends? How did this make you feel?

DAY 2. *Developing Breasts*

• How did it feel to develop breasts? When did you first wear a bra?

• Did you develop breasts before or after your girlfriends? How did this make you feel?

• How did Dad respond to your breasts? How did Mom respond?

• How were your breasts spoken of? Were they too small, too large? How did you feel about them?

• Draw your breasts. Do you like them?

DAY 3. *Changing Body*

• What size was your body? Did you want to be smaller or bigger than you were?

• Did you ever feel pretty enough? Thin enough? When did you begin feeling not enough?

• When did you begin to mask your face, cover your woman scents, and hide your roundness?

• How did boys respond to your body? How did your girlfriends respond to your body?

• Draw your body. Do you like it?

DAY 4. *Touch in the Family*

• Until what age did your father hug, hold, and lovingly touch you?

• Did his touch ever feel uncomfortable? Was it ever sexual?

• Until what age did your mother hug, hold, and lovingly touch you?

• Did her touch ever feel uncomfortable? Was it ever sexual?

• Why do you think your mother and father stopped holding, hugging, and lovingly touching you?

• Did your brothers or sisters touch you? Were their pats, hugs, and hits affectionate or uncomfortable?

DAY 5. *Touching Yourself*

• Did you ever touch your own body? Did you explore its smoothness, its curves, lips, and openings?

• When did you first hear the words *vagina, genitals, clitoris, horny, sex*?

• Did you ever feel fiery warmth rise in your body? Did you ever feel tingling sensations in your genitals? Did these feelings scare you, or excite you? Did you talk to anyone about these feelings?

• Draw the fiery warmth and the tingling sensations in your body.

DAY 6. *Boys*

• Who was the first person to touch your breasts? Your vagina? Your naked body? How old were you?

• How did this touch feel to you? Was it comfortable or frightening?

• Who instigated the touch? Were you forced, or did you participate freely?

• Did you talk to anyone about these experiences?

DAY 7. *Healing into the Present*

• Write a self-celebration of those parts of your body that you despised in adolescence. Look into a full-length mirror five times today and affirm, "I am enough this day. Just as I am, I am enough. There is no blemish." And then read your self-celebration aloud to the image in the mirror.

• Talk to a good friend, your therapist, your spiritual guide, or your sponsor about each of the exercises you completed. Read your writings to that person. Show him or her your drawings. Together create a ritual of healing for your Inner Adolescent. Incorporate the transformational resources included in this chapter.

✑ RECLAIMING THE WISDOM OF YOUR BODY

If this is the week of your period, incorporate the following woman-affirming actions and reflections into your week:

DAY 1. *Body Wisdom*

Honor your body's Deep Wisdom today. Dialogue with it through imagery, writing, and movement. Ask your body, "What pillows of support do you need during this time? How might I support you?" Do not fight your body's needs; tenderly acknowledge them and then meet them. If you need to rest, then rest. If you need to be by yourself, cancel your appointments.

DAY 2. *Blood Red*

• In solidarity with our sisters around the world who have no access to pads, make your own. The irony must always be acknowledged that we have a choice—they do not.

• Wear bright red clothing today.

DAY 3. *Heart Center*

According to Eastern teachings, the body has seven energy centers, called chakras. The fourth chakra is the Heart Center. It is connected to our capacity to love, to open, and to give. There is an acupressure point located at the Heart Center on the sternum between your breasts. Place the fingertips of each hand there. This powerful acupressure point strengthens the blood and calms anxiety. The Chinese call it the Sea of Tranquility, or the Sea of Blood.

Begin and end today with the following "Heart Center Movement Meditation." Because the breath is involved, it will be easier for you to read the words silently rather than speaking them aloud. As you become familiar with the opening and closing movements, improvise and create your own movement meditation.

(*Breathe in with fingertips on sternum.*)	Heart of Life,
(*Breathe out as arms open outward.*)	To you I am opening.
(*Breathe in as you place fingertips on sternum.*)	Healing is your touch,
(*Breathe out as arms open outward.*)	Flowing is your love.
(*Breathe in as you place fingertips on sternum.*)	In you,
(*Breathe out as arms open outward.*)	I bleed, and touch, and live.

DAY 4. *Time of Power*

Take time off today to acquaint yourself with the special powers that are available during your period. Write to The One Who Shed Her Blood. Speak to her of your feelings. Ask her to share her wisdom with you. Draw your Heart Center. Open to the heart of your life through poetic imagery. Move the cramps through your body as you stretch and breathe deeply.

DAY 5. *There Is No Blemish*

Create a writing, drawing, dance, or sculpture in which you celebrate those parts of your body that the culture has judged negatively and that you have come to despise. Look into a full-length mirror today and affirm, "I am enough this day. Just as I am, I am enough. There is no blemish." And then read your self-celebration aloud to the image in the mirror.

DAY 6. *A God Who Bleeds Unto Life*

Imagine a God who bleeds as you do. Draw a picture of her. Display it in a special place with the other drawings that have emerged through our work together.

DAY 7. *In Celebration of Woman*

Create a celebratory ritual with your adolescent daughters, granddaughters, and nieces in which a woman's body is honored and her blood held sacred. Invite postmenopausal women to preside at the ritual as they did in ancient times. They were considered the wisest of the wise because they permanently withheld their "wise blood" within them. Invite them to share with the younger ones the wisdom of a woman's body. Read the woman-affirming stories of Eve, Lilith, and Mary. Wear red, eat red foods, light red candles, and decorate your sacred meeting place with bright red paint and glitter.

✒ AN INVENTORY: TRANSFORMING COMPETITIVE ATTITUDES AND BEHAVIORS

If you want to explore more deeply your relationships to women, set aside time to do the following exercises:

DAY 1. *An Inventory I*

Inventory your competitive attitudes and behaviors toward women. Below is a sample inventory. It was written by a women's spirituality-group participant who took the challenge to confront her competitive behaviors and to move beyond them.

List the women you have been jealous of; the ones you have gossiped about; those you have called names or slandered; those with whom you have competed for the attention of a man. Describe the behaviors and then look beneath them for the underlying motivation. Was it your own insecurity about your body or your appearance? Was it unexpressed anger or fear? Was it your own self-loathing?

> I was jealous of my friend's wife while visiting their home recently. She is a very organized and competent cook and hostess. I felt intimidated by her. And I was unwilling to admit that I wanted to spend time with my friend, who is her husband, rather than with her. I expressed my dissatisfaction and jealousy indirectly through criticism and smoldering anger.
>
> —Sandi

DAY 2. *An Inventory II*

Continue your inventory.

Determine if an acknowledgment to the person is called for. If it is, write a statement of your intention to mend the broken relationship.

> When we are together again, I want to make amends to myself by acknowledging my need to spend more time with my friend. She has been in my life for many years, and time with her is very important to me. I want to make amends to her by acknowledging that part of the discomfort she and I experienced was due to my

jealousy, my feelings of inadequacy, and my resentment
of her competence. I will make amends by expressing
appreciation for her gifts.

—Sandi

DAY 3. *An Inventory III*

Complete your inventory today.

If a direct acknowledgment is not appropriate, determine how you
might make amends through your changed behaviors in the present.

> I will make indirect amends by strengthening my
> relationships with women and giving them support rather
> than focusing on receiving the approval of men. At
> work my colleagues and I are struggling to keep from
> feeling inferior to men, so we compete with each other
> for their attention. I can make amends by learning to
> express appreciation and support and by affirming our
> solidarity as women.
>
> —Sandi

DAY 4. *Communities of Support*

• What are the communities of support that surround your life? Describe each of them.

• Reflect on the ways you will strengthen your relationships with women this week by giving them support rather than competing with them for the attention and approval of fathers, bosses, professors, or boyfriends.

• Describe the specific ways you will express your appreciation, support, and solidarity to the women at work, in school, in your family, in your church, and in your aerobics class.

DAY 5. *Healthy Connections*

Incorporate the following woman-affirming behaviors into your relationships this day:

• I will remind my sisters of their goodness. I will encourage them to include self-celebration in their daily meditation practice.

• I will remind my sisters of their inner resources. Rather than giving advice, I will ask, "How might I support you to act on your own behalf? How might I support you to deal with each situation that confronts you? How might I support you to author your own life, relationships, and spirituality?"

• I will honor women's bodies and natural processes. With my sisters I will develop rituals in which menstruation, childbirth, and menopause are celebrated.

• In mixed groups that are focused on men's concerns and accomplishments, I will look into the eyes of women to acknowledge their presence. I will listen to women's stories and concerns. I will ask women questions rather than defer to the men in the group.

• I will refuse to become involved in triangular relationships in which I will be pitted against another woman while we both swirl around one man.

• I will support women. I will use my time and talents in service of women. I will compliment the successes of the women in my life.

• I will remind my sisters of the resources available in the community of women. Rather than giving advice, I will ask, "How might I support you to reconnect with the communities of support that surround your life?"

DAY 6. *Our Heritage Is Our Power*

Judy Chicago's art project *The Dinner Party* celebrates the contributions and achievements of 1,038 women. The project is described and illustrated in a powerful book you will find in your local library or women's center. Read one entry a day to reconnect to your woman history.

DAY 7. *An Immersion in Women's Reality*

Begin a month-long immersion today. Surround yourself with women's ideas, history, stories, books, films, art, music, and spirituality. Allow yourself to become immersed in a woman's reality. Reflect on how these woman-affirming resources make you feel about your life, body, relationships, dreams, and goals.

WEEK 1. *Women's History*

Gather more of the fragments of women's stories from the margins of history and religion. The following books will inspire your quest for a heritage, a history, a noble lineage that reaches back to the very beginning: *When God Was a Woman* by Merlin Stone; *The Once and Future Goddess* by Elinor Gadin; *The Dinner Party* by Judy Chicago.

WEEK 2. *Women's Ideas*

Women experience and know the world differently than men do. Reclaim your unique woman-intelligence and bring its gifts into the world. Allow the works of these creative thinkers to inspire you: *Kiss Sleeping Beauty Good-Bye* by Madonna Kohbenschlag; *Women's Reality* by Anne Wilson Schaef; *Of Woman Born* by Adrienne Rich; *Sister Outsider* by Audre Lorde; *Blood, Bread, and Roses: How Menstruation Created the World* by Judy Grahn.

WEEK 3. *Women Writers and Poets*

Allow the brilliance of women's words to inspire your own writing. Be full of yourself! Write a novel. Compose a poem. See *A Daughter's Geography* by Ntsoke Shange; *Getting Home Alive* by Aurora Levins Morales and Rosario Morales; *Cries of the Spirit* by Marilyn Sewell; *The Temple of My Familiar* by Alice Walker.

WEEK 4. *Women Artists, Dancers, and Musicians*

Surround yourself with women's music, images, and movements this week. In response allow the creative fruits of your womb to thrust forth. Consider these images: *The Dinner Party* and *The Birth Project* by Judy Chicago. Consider this music: "Shadows on the Dime" by Ferron; "A Circle Is Cast" by Libana; "City Down" by Castleberry and Dupree; Consider these movements: *The Spirit Moves* by Carla De Sola.

CHAPTER TWELVE

The Wounded Healers

The Stories

While gathering the fragments of my forgotten childhood, I encountered stories from my religious past that startled me. They were terrible
stories of nameless and voiceless women, of women whose stories I was
not told in the churches of my childhood and adolescence. These stories were passed over in Sunday school and seldom mentioned from the
pulpit.

The stories of King David's conquests were well known, yet no men-
tion was made of his daughter, Tamar, who was raped by Amnon her
brother. I was taught in exacting detail about the adventures of kings
and priests. Yet the abusive treatment of their unnamed wives and con-
cubines was seldom given any attention except in passing as supporting
detail. And no one, either in the Bible text or in the pulpit, expressed
outrage at the treatment of the women in these tragic stories.

Yet the churches of my childhood included a regular ritual in which
they honored the broken body and the shed blood of Jesus Christ. A
wounded male was honored, his broken body ritualized. Wounded
women went unnamed, their broken bodies brutalized in the silence.

Texts of Terror

> As a child I knew there was a woman in God's life because
> when it rained, the kids in the neighborhood told me that
> God was beating his wife, and the raindrops were her
> tears.
>
> —Erin

The stories of Tamar and The One Who Was Cut into Pieces tell the truth of a woman's life, a truth unspoken in the churches of our childhoods. Through them we see clearly the sad realities of the girl-child's life throughout the centuries and catch glimpses of our own forgotten stories. Phyllis Trible, whose book *Texts of Terror* inspired my work, describes the life of the girl-child in ancient Israel: Less desirable in the eyes of her parents than a male child, a girl remained close to her mother, but her father controlled her life until he relinquished her to another man in marriage. If either of these male authorities permitted her to be violated, she had to submit without recourse.[1]

I have invited hundreds of women and men to enter into the courage, pain, and healing of the stories of Tamar and The One Who Was Cut into Pieces. Most have accepted the invitation. With courage they had drawn, danced, written, and wept through these stories. Among those who have participated have been many who were not survivors of rape and incest themselves: daughters who entered the stories in remembrance of their mothers and grandmothers, who lived in a time when the sin of incest was not named; partners and friends of survivors of rape and incest, as an expression of their support and solidarity; fathers, as a commitment to deal with their ingrained attitudes toward women and to respect their daughters' bodies.

Groups of women have also participated as a ritual of remembrance in honor of Tamar, The One Who Was Cut into Pieces, and the myriad unnamed daughters of history who experienced incest and rape. Therapists have joined us to explore their own histories and attitudes toward abuse. And ministers have participated as an act of repentance for ignoring the stories of women in their sermons and ministries.

I invite those of you who are not survivors of incest and rape to enter into these stories on behalf of your daughter's future, a friend or lover's healing, your grandmother's silence, the courage of your clients, or the untold stories of your parishioners. Imagine the experience as an expression of solidarity and support, a ritual of remembrance, a healing prayer, an act of repentance. In order to enter, you must be willing to witness great pain; to examine your own attitudes; and to explore your own story.[2]

Among the survivors who have entered into these stories have been women who had only a quiet suspicion of childhood abuse, their memories buried beneath years of denial. We remain asleep to our history and its impact on us until we are ready to awaken. In the fullness of time we descend into our history. In the fullness of time we remember. In the fullness of time our wounds heal. Listen to a story that I have shared with many survivors:

> A camper noticed a moth pushing, straining, and struggling to get out of its cocoon. It was a disturbing sight to the camper, and when she could take it no longer, she extended the tiny slit-opening of the cocoon. The moth was freed; it fell to the ground and died. The camper was devastated; her intention had been to help. She consulted encyclopedias upon arriving home and found out that the struggle she had observed was essential to the moth's metamorphosis. Its struggle against the walls of the cocoon strengthens its wings and releases fluids that enhance the beauty of its colors.

Inspired by this story, I investigated the moth's life. The life cycle of the moth from egg to adult is orchestrated by a remarkable inner sense of right timing that leads it to each new transformation. This inner timing allows for the emergence of the larva to coincide with the adequate growth of the plants that will be its food. It orchestrates the outgrowing of each of its skins, and the securing of a refuge where it will remain until the conditions are ready for its survival as a fully formed adult moth.

The camper was not aware of the sacredness of struggle and the trustworthiness of the timing of the moth's cycle. She cut open the cocoon. This premature release led to the moth's death. Awash in her own discomfort, she had arrogantly intruded in the moth's life cycle. Yet the moth had been content in the midst of its own trustworthy process, a process essential to its development.

Like the moth each of us is an emerging healthy adult whose process is orchestrated by a finely tuned inner timing. In the fullness of time, when a behavior begins to hamper, press, and squeeze us, we twist and turn until we burst out of the old skin and are freed at a deeper level of our existence. Each time a memory is ready to be acknowledged out of decades of denial, it gnaws its way to the surface through a dream or a sensory memory, through a movie, or by reading the stories of others. In the fullness of time it is remembered. The trustworthy timing of our inner wisdom leads us to each new transformation when we are ready.

Tamar's Story

As you read the story that follows, imagine sitting in your women's support circle, Bible study, or therapy group. Tamar has been invited to tell her story. She is a part of the circle of women that extends back in time.

As you read, take note of phrases of particular significance to you, the ones that touch your body, that cause your heart to tremble or to rage, the ones that trigger a memory. Some women have found it helpful to highlight these phrases as they go along. Others jot them down in their journals. Later you will be asked to find a movement, image, and sound to express each of these phrases. However, feel free to stop at any point in the story to give voice to whatever needs expressing. Draw your outrage. Write your memory. Dance your body's response.

Of the many people who have experienced Tamar's story through my work, only one woman had heard this story during childhood: "My great-aunt was a preacher. She sat me on her lap with her great big King James Bible and said, 'There are some things in this book that men won't tell you; some stories that won't be told in the church. This is one from II Samuel chapter 13.' And then she read Tamar's story to me." (italics added)

Now, David's son, Absalom, had a beautiful sister named Tamar, and Amnon, another of David's sons, fell in love with her. Amnon lay down and pretended to be ill. When the King came to visit him, he said, "Sir, let my sister, Tamar, come and make a few cakes before my eyes, and let her serve them to me from her hands." So David sent a message to Tamar in the palace: "Go to your brother Amnon's quarters and prepare a meal for him."

Tamar came to the house of her brother. He was lying down; she took some dough and kneaded it, and she made the cakes before his eyes. She baked them and she took the pan and she served them before him. But Amnon refused to eat and ordered everyone out of the room.

When they had all left, he said to Tamar, "Bring the food to the bedroom so that I may eat from your hands." Tamar took the cakes she had made and brought them to Amnon in the bedroom. But when she offered them to him, he grabbed hold of her and said, "Come to bed with me, my sister."

But she answered, *"No brother, do not violate me, we do not do such things in Israel; do not do this foolish thing. Where could I go and hide my shame? And you would sink as low as any fool in Israel. Why not speak to the King for me? He will not keep me from you."*

He did not want to hear her voice. He was stronger than she. He raped her and laid her.

Then Amnon was filled with utter hatred for her; truly greater was the hatred with which he hated her than the desire with which he desired her. He said to her, "Get up and go."

She answered, *"No, it is wicked to send me away. This is a greater evil than all you have done to me."*

He did not want to hear her voice, but summoned the boy who attended him and said, "Get rid of this woman. Put her out and bolt the door after her." [She had on a long-sleeved robe, the usual dress of virgin daughters of the King;] And the boy put her outside and bolted the door after her.

Tamar threw ashes over her head, tore the long-sleeved robe that she was wearing. She put her hands on her head and she went away, sobbing as she went. Her brother Absalom asked her, "Has your brother Amnon been with you? Keep this to yourself. He is your brother; do not take this deed to heart." So Tamar remained in her brother Absalom's house, desolate.

PAUSE AND REFLECT

• Find a movement, image, and sound to express each of the phrases you have marked. Draw your outrage. Write your memory. Dance your body's response. Shout out your feelings. Take your time and allow each phrase to be fully expressed.

• What fragments of your own story are touched by Tamar's? Terror in the ordinariness of life? Coercion and capture? Shame and desolation? Humiliation, secrecy? Family lies? The preference for the brother?

• Write your story in the form of a passage from the Scripture, describing your experience in the third person. Narrate the details of the story, including any dialogue. Use Tamar's story from II Samuel as a guide.

• After writing your story, read through it as you did Tamar's. Read it as if it were the story of another. Take note of the phrases that touch your body, that cause your heart to tremble or to rage. Underline them with a felt-tip pen.

Stop at any point in the story to draw your feelings or to dance your body's response.

• Tape your third-person narrative or have a friend read it to you. As you listen, imagine that it is being read aloud in church or synagogue as the scriptural text for the day. Write a sermon, essay, or poem expressing your feelings and outrage as you hear the story—your story.

The Story of The One Who Was Cut into Pieces

As you read the following story (from Judges, chapter 19), imagine sitting in your women's support circle, Bible study, or therapy group. Now it is The One Who Was Cut into Pieces who has been invited to tell her story. Listen carefully, because she is given no voice of her own in the scriptural record. She whispers in this fragment of her forgotten story.

As you read, mark the phrases of particular significance to you, the ones that touch your body, that cause your heart to tremble or to rage, the ones that trigger a memory. Stop at any point in the story to draw your outrage, write your memory, or dance your body's response.

A Levite[3] had taken himself a concubine[4] from Bethlehem in Judah. In a fit of anger she had left him and had gone to her father's house. Her husband set out after her with his servant and two asses to appeal to her and bring her back. The girl's father welcomed the Levite, and he stayed with him for several days, and he was well entertained during their visit. On the fifth day the Levite rose and left with his concubine and servant.

They traveled until sunset overtook them. They turned in to spend the night in Gibeah, and sat down in the town square; but nobody took them into his house for the night. Meanwhile an old man was coming home in the evening from his work in the fields. He looked up, saw the traveler, and said, "You are welcome in my home. I will supply all your wants. You must not spend the night in the street." So he took them inside. They washed their feet, and ate and drank.

While they were enjoying themselves, some of the worst drunken scoundrels in the town surrounded the house, hurling themselves against the door and shouting to the old man, "Bring out your guest so that we might have intercourse with him."

The owner of the house went outside to them and said, "No, my friends, do nothing so wicked. This man is my guest; do not commit this outrage. Here is my daughter, a virgin; let me bring her out to you. Rape her and do to her what you please; but you shall not commit such an outrage against this man."

But the men refused to listen to the old man, so the Levite took hold of his concubine and thrust her outside for them. They raped her savagely again and again, abusing her until the morning. At daybreak they let her go and she fell at the threshold of the old man's house and lay there till morning.

The Levite, her master, rose in the morning and opened the door of the house to set out on his journey, and there was his concubine lying at the door with her hands on the threshold. He said to her, "Get up and let us be off"; but there was no answer. So he lifted her onto his ass and set off for home.

When he arrived there, he picked up a knife, and he took hold of his concubine and cut her up limb by limb into twelve pieces; and he sent her mutilated body through the length and breadth of Israel.

PAUSE AND REFLECT

• Find a movement, image, and sound to express each of the phrases you have marked. Draw your outrage. Write your memory. Dance your body's response. Shout out your feelings. Take your time and allow each phrase to be fully expressed.

• What fragments of your own story are touched by The One Who Was Cut into Pieces? The preference for the husband? Betrayal? Rape? Mutilation? No voice? No advocate?

• Write your story in the form of a scriptural passage, describing your experience in the third person. Narrate the details of the story, including any dialogue. Use the passage from Judges as a guide.

• After writing your story, read through it as you did her story. Take note of the phrases that touch your body, that cause your heart to tremble or to rage; highlight them. Stop at any point in the story to draw your feelings or to dance your body's response.

• Tape your third-person narrative or have a friend read it to you. As you listen, imagine that it is being read aloud in church as the scriptural text for the day. Write a sermon or essay or poem expressing the outrage you experience as you hear the story—as you hear your story.

Our Wounds

It is essential that we give voice to the experiences of our personal and religious past that wounded our bodies and silenced our voices. In the company of Tamar and The One Who Was Cut into Pieces, we will tell our stories and acknowledge the societal and religious realities that have shaped them. This is our first step toward healing.

Broken Bodies

> The body has been made so problematic for women that it has often seemed easier to shrug it off and travel as a disembodied spirit.
>
> —Adrienne Rich, *Of Woman Born*

A girl-child's birth into a society that prefers men and worships a male God assures that she will be sexually harassed in some way during her lifetime. No woman is exempt. Her sexual harassment will begin in early childhood at home and continue on the playgrounds and in the classrooms of school.

By the time the girl-child leaves childhood and adolescence, she will be convinced that women are inferior to men and vulnerable to their powerful sexual urges. She will become a woman by negotiating the dangerous geography of sexualized male violence. She will be afraid to walk alone at night. She will be subjected to catcalls and whistles. Her body will be the focus of dirty jokes. All that she has experienced from conception will intensify her vulnerability to rape and incest. One out of four girls is sexually abused before she reaches eighteen. In the United States a rape is committed every six minutes.

RAPE

The story of The One Who Was Cut into Pieces involved a senseless act of brutality, the dimensions of which are never dealt with in the text. Throughout the story and throughout religious history, the unnamed woman's concerns are ignored:

• Her anger at the Levite did not sensitize her father to the problems she was having in the relationship. He ignored his daughter and catered to the Levite.

• The Levite did not appear to have any qualms about his own behavior in volunteering his concubine for the drunken mob's amusement. Such behavior in a society that prefers men was considered normal.

• The ultimate mutilation of The One Who Was Cut into Pieces at the hands of the Levite was not in protest of the brutal treatment she received by the townsmen. It was in outrage at the townspeople's inhospitable and disrespectful treatment of his personal property. She was his property!

• The Scripture itself expresses no moral outrage at the treatment of The One Who Was Cut into Pieces. And the reading of this story in our childhood churches was never accompanied by sermons of outrage. It was passed over quickly as the more important stories of kings and conquests were read.

The fear of rape is ever present in a girl-child's life. From the time she is quite young, stories enter her consciousness from the media and from the whispers of relatives and kids on the block that she could be raped. As a result a fear of men and their sexual power is deposited within her. As she grows older, she will order and reorder her life based on this fear. It will deeply affect the choices she makes. She will adapt her lifestyle to guarantee the illusion of safety and her sense of security that rape will not happen to her. Yet deep inside she knows that no matter what precautions she takes, rape could happen at any time to any one of us.

• Jean carefully chooses the shoes she will wear each day to ensure that she can outrun an assailant. She also chooses clothes that will not stand out—"quiet clothes," she calls them, so as not to attract the attention of men. She ties her long hair up under a hat.

• Susan writes, "High heels intensify our vulnerability, so I carry them in my bag and wear running shoes. I have been told since I was a child that what I wear could arouse a normally peaceful guy. 'Boys will be boys,' my mother always said."

• Jen writes, "I know rape happens everywhere. I always put at least three locks on each of my doors and special rods on each window. Then and only then will I spend even one night in a new apartment, no matter how safe anyone tells me the neighborhood is."

INCEST

Tamar's story is tragic. It offers no happy ending. In the ordinariness of everyday life her brother pretends and her father commands. She obeys her father and she serves her brother. In the ordinariness of life Tamar is betrayed, captured, violated, and then rejected. She is raped and told to keep it a secret.

Tamar carries the shame alone in the desolation of her heart. She carries the sin of her brother within her violated body. Robbed of her sight, once clear and focused, her eyes are downcast, unable to sustain contact. Robbed of her voice, once proud and noble, her mouth is tightly closed, words imprisoned within her throat. Robbed of the dignity once worn proudly atop her strong shoulders, her hands hide her assaulted body, fearful of exposure.

Meanwhile her father and brothers go on with business as usual—wars, rivalries, and conquests.

Tamar's story is the story of at least 80 percent of the women who find their way into treatment centers to deal with their chemical dependency.[5] Alcoholism in the family of origin intensifies the probability of incest occurring, and once our bodies have been exploited by the trusted "higher powers" of our childhood, we ourselves often turn to alcohol, drugs, or food to forget.[6]

The act of incest deposits a profound shame within us. We come to believe that our bodies are flawed, that even our souls have been tainted. When shame screams loudly enough from the depths of our woundedness, some of us mutilate ourselves in an attempt to quiet its voice. We hit our bodies. We starve them. We cut them. We do battle with them. We act out the rage and anger of the early abuse, not toward the perpetrator but toward ourselves. In some wounded way we feel that these acts are our penance for being so very bad to deserve the awful things that were done to us.

RELIGION: AN ACCOMPLICE IN OUR ABUSE

Our personal stories of incest and rape, taken together, become much larger than ourselves. Each is a thread in the much broader societal and religious patterns that underlie the violence against women in a society that prefers men. Traditional religion's elevation of a male God condones men's sexual access to their wives and children. A 1989 United Nations report concluded that violence against women is a function of the belief, fostered in all cultures, that men are superior and that the women they live with are their possessions or chattel they can treat as they wish.[7]

This pervasive attitude has its roots in the stories and myths we have explored together. In all of them the male body has been exempt from responsibility: "Boys will be boys. They can't help themselves," girls are taught. One wonders if the sexual harassment and abuse of women is a man's reward for having been created in the image of his God?

Sitting in a circle, the women share the truth of their lives. One by one they speak out of the silence of a lifetime:

> My father touched my breasts in front of the whole family,
> beginning when I developed them at age twelve. I was
> too insecure and guarded to speak of my discomfort.
> I was innocent and used. I didn't know the truth of
> what was happening to me. When I was forty years old,
> a therapist asked me if I had been abused and I said no.
> I was silent and in denial. I didn't forget; I just didn't
> know it was abuse. And yet my body knew, so I
> began eating in order to disappear. This is the paradox:
> I disappeared by eating and becoming fat. My body size
> was always an issue with my parents. I was angry at
> my father most of my life. And of course anger was
> not acceptable, so the eating intensified.
>
> My vision of myself was wounded. I felt ashamed and
> embarrassed by my huge breasts. Breasts that my
> father touched jokingly and derived pleasure from.
> Breasts that all men looked at before they looked me in
> my eyes. Breasts that two men I did not know squeezed.
> I hit my breasts and hated the largeness of them. I
> wanted them to go away. I was never encouraged to
> appreciate my fullness. I did not explore the sexual
> pleasure that my breasts could give me until much
> later in life, through experiencing the love and touch of
> another woman. My breasts were numb and dead for thirty
> years.
>
> —Robin

One day the police came and took my mother away. They
pulled and pushed her into the police car as my
father and I stood in the doorway and watched. I was
thirteen years old. At one point my mother looked at me
and swore she would never come back to our house
because it was all my fault that she was going away.
It was my fault that my father was sexually abusing me.

Around that time my father, no longer satisfied with
fondling me, began forcing me into physical
intercourse. It *was* all my fault. Didn't my father tell
me nine thousand times that he couldn't help himself?
Something about me was so powerful and bad that this
man could not stop doing evil things to me. The evil
I caused was so great that it drove my mother insane,
so that on that day she was dragged away to be forcibly
locked up in a state mental hospital.

I was shamed to the innermost core of my being.
All evidence of who I was had to be suppressed. To
assert myself, to be visible in any way, to express my
individuality, sexuality, or creativity meant the risk of
driving the people around me insane. Consequently
I have been very careful to hide from life, choosing
dead-end jobs and dead-end relationships and putting
light-years between myself and the expression of who I
am. Now I am forty-eight years old and I have
struggled for years to discover something that could
give me even a small sense of myself as someone whose
life has purpose and meaning. This society and my father
stripped me of knowing even the shadow of my
strength and creativity as a woman.

—Ferrel

Imagine sitting in a circle with Ferrel and Robin. Add your story to theirs.

No Woman Is Exempt

• Reflect on the following statement from your own experience: "All
girl-children grow up to become women by negotiating the dangerous
geography of sexualized male violence."

• Describe the ways you have been sexually harassed, beginning with childhood experiences at home and at school. Include situations that we tend to take for granted: fear of walking home alone at night, being subject to catcalls and whistles, having your body be the focus of dirty jokes.

• How was the fear of men and their sexual power deposited within you in childhood? Have you ordered and reordered your life based on this fear? How has it affected the choices you make every day? How does it affect where you live and where you go or do not go during the course of a day? How does it affect your safety and security measures, your wardrobe? Do you have a curfew—an hour you must be home to be safe?

Our Broken Bodies

• Was your vision of your own body wounded by early experiences of molestation, incest, and rape?

• Where in your body do you carry the shame of these deeply wounding experiences?

• How has your body borne the brunt of the abuse?

Seeking Support

Talk to a good friend, to your minister or rabbi, to your therapist or sponsor, about each of your responses. Read your writings to them. Show them your drawings. Ask your supportive listener to write a sermon, essay, or letter that expresses his or her outrage at the ways your life has been limited and your body assaulted in a world that prefers men.

Silenced Voices

> Amnon did not want to hear her voice.
> —II Samuel 13:14, 17

> The woman should keep silent in the church. For
> they are not permitted to speak.
> —I Corinthians 14:34

The statistics are alarming and yet we have wished to erase the reality of rape and incest from our memory. Until the 1980s the denial of sexual abuse was rampant in the psychiatric community, in religious institutions, and in the family—even among women survivors themselves. Perhaps if we ignore it long enough, we thought, it will go away.

How many of our voices have gone unheard throughout the centuries? Tamar was told by the brother who raped her, "I don't want to hear your voice." Even her good brother, Absalom, told her after the rape, "Keep this to yourself. Don't take it to heart. He is your brother." Tamar was left alone with the truth, her text of terror locked away within her. It was a muted crime, ignored in the family except as it intensified the sibling rivalry between her brothers. She was left alone with the shameful secret and carried the consequences in her desolate body.

In II Samuel 13:21 we read of David's response to Tamar's rape, "When King David heard all these things he was angry. And he did not rebuke Amnon his son because he loved him since he was his firstborn." David's silence has been religion's silence. Its priests, ministers, and rabbis have minimized the reality of sexual abuse and domestic violence in their congregations. Thus silence and denial continue the myth that "such things do not happen in good Christian-Catholic-Jewish families."

In addition, religion has failed to tell the women's stories that were allowed to remain within its own sacred texts. The stories of Tamar and countless unnamed women had disappeared from our memory until recently. Because religion has closed its eyes and ears to women's stories, many survivors of childhood incest have had to search for healing resources outside of the religious community.

When abused women find their way into a therapist's office, they are often confronted with disbelief. Until recently the psychiatric community was trained to be skeptical of stories of sexual trauma. According to Freud, the memories of women concerning sexual contact with their fathers were just wishful fantasies—all little girls fantasize about sleeping with their daddies. Consequently women continue to be reabused when they seek help from professionals who do not believe their stories and deny their realities. How much easier to think of sexual abuse as a fantasy, to consign it to the imagination . . . of the woman.

Silenced by our families, our churches, and the therapeutic community, we then silence ourselves. Those of us who have experienced incest and sexual violence can make it disappear from our memories for years.

We become very skillful at pushing the event down and pretending it didn't happen. We, too, find it much easier to erase it from our memories, to consign it to the imagination, to deny our own painful reality. We lose our voices.

This isn't surprising when we consider the ways in which our voices have been assaulted throughout religious history. The girl-child is taught to mistrust anything that flows from her life. She is told that what she knows is not true, that what she feels is not real, and that what she sees is not there. She is encouraged to turn her life over to others and to trust their truth, their reality, and their ways. Daughters are taught to be quiet and good and that they are to blame for anything that happens to them.

Sitting in a circle, the women share the truth of their lives. One by one they speak out of the silence of a lifetime:

> My grandfather was regarded as saintlike. He loved his grandchildren. We were all Grandpa's babies. Grandpa had a special relationship with the babies; he never spanked or yelled at them. He was a small man with a kind face. He was very patient. He made his own bread and cheese. He bathed my grandma.
>
> But he had a quirk or two. He liked to burn things in the fields (which is a common trait of pedophiles) and he molested babies. He was my family's great white hope, unlike the crude men on my father's side. My mother believed he was a saint.
>
> I was able to keep the early memories a secret to myself until my forties. Then the memories of my grandfather's abuse of me surfaced. When I told my mother that I had been molested by my grandfather, she didn't believe me. It was the last straw for our relationship. She was once again put in the position of choosing between her daughter and the men, living and dead, in her life. And she chose the men. I need to keep speaking the truth to myself whether she believes me or not.
>
> —Christine

> I was sexually molested by two men, a teenager and a middle-aged man. They took advantage of my innocence

and vulnerability. I was left to handle it in silence
and with strength. I was proud that I could keep it
a secret from my father. He would have killed me. He
was certain that I was deceiving him by doing all the things
that bad girls do. No matter what I said, he would
turn my truth into lies. He made me feel very dirty
and uncomfortable with my body and its functions. He
was intrusive, and yet he expected me to acknowledge and
respect his boundaries.

I was afraid that I was responsible for the
molestations. I felt very powerful at age seven. I denied
my sexual abuse. I minimized it. I felt dirty and I chose
masturbation as the way to re-create the abuse; it
brought both pleasure and shame. I was left with no
voice and no power. I carry shame in my gut, solar plexus,
and ovaries. I'm tired of carrying this weight and holding
my stomach tight. I pray to let go and release myself.
I deserve pleasure and to reclaim my sexuality and my
power.

—Erin

Imagine sitting with Christine and Erin. Add your story to theirs.

In the Family

- Describe the ways in which your voice was assaulted in your home.
- Were you abused as a child? Did your abuser threaten to hurt you if you told?
- Did you try to tell anyone what was happening to you? Did they believe you?

Religious Community

- Describe the ways your voice was assaulted through your religious training.
- Was your father's aggressive behavior taken for granted and your mother's helplessness encouraged?
- Did the Church or synagogue offer healing resources to you or to your family?

Therapeutic Community
- Trace your interactions with therapists over the years.
- Was your story met with skepticism? Disbelief? Embarrassment? Validation? Belief?

Keeping Secrets at Our Own Expense
- How long were you able to keep the early memories a secret from yourself? What strategies did you employ in order to forget?
- Are there still secrets you carry alone in your heart?

Seeking Support
Talk to a good friend, to your minister or rabbi, to your therapist or sponsor, about each of your responses. Read your writings to them. Together write a sermon, essay, or letter that expresses your outrage at the lack of support you received to tell your story. Then write words of gratitude for those in your life today who support your truth, who listen to your stories, and who applaud your courageous strides toward healing.

Our Healing

We have given voice to the experiences of our personal and religious past that wounded our bodies and silenced our voices. Now, with courage, we will reclaim the stories and images from the very beginning, when a woman's body was honored and her voice celebrated. We will incorporate these woman-affirming resources into our myths, meditations, and rituals. Tamar and The One Who Was Cut into Pieces will become healing images of the divine within us. In their presence our bodies will be restored to wholeness and our voices will be set free to shout out the truth of a lifetime.

A God Who Looks Like Me

> If I had been surrounded by the feminine face of God,
> I would not have had such enormous self-hatred.
>
> —Sandi

We are reminded of a time when God looked like us. We reclaim the story that reaches back before the Hebrew and Christian Scriptures were written. We discover that we are surrounded by a courageous company of women. Their ancient stories and images become our healing resources.

We learn of ancient women who did not apologize for their bodies or their voices. We recall the ancient times when reverence for the Goddess gave women status, a voice, and fair treatment. We read of ancient ways and laws stating that if a man raped a woman, he was to be put to death.[8] We reclaim those ancient beliefs in a strong Goddess who did not stand by patiently as those created in *her* image were raped, battered, molested through incest, and robbed of their self-love and self-trust.

Those of us who experienced incest or rape were broken into pieces. We want our bodies back, free of shame. We want our stories back, out of the silence. We want our feelings back, out of denial. We want to be restored to wholeness and to a loving relationship to ourselves. We want to have the full use of the amazing resources that dwell within us as Children of Life.

The One Who Was Cut into Pieces becomes our Wounded Healer. She rises in us each time we choose our wholeness. Her broken body is resurrected as we speak out of the silence and reclaim each dismembered piece of our history, our bodies, and our lives. She offers us gifts of healing as we enter into her presence through meditation, reclaiming the images of a time when God looked like us.

What follows is a meditation entitled "An Encounter with The One Who Was Cut into Pieces: Gathering the Fragments." To prepare, create an altar in the center of your sacred space with a red candle, a chalice (or wineglass) filled with grape juice, and a plate with twelve pieces of bread representing the broken body of The One Who Was Cut into

Pieces. Place a red scarf on the altar as a symbol of the river of women's blood that has flowed for centuries.

Gather six items to represent the lost years and experiences of your life (photos from a childhood album, a collage of magazine pictures . . .). Gather another six to represent your broken body (scarves, pieces of clay shaped as parts of your body). Scatter the twelve items around your sacred space.

❧ AN ENCOUNTER WITH THE ONE WHO WAS CUT INTO PIECES: GATHERING THE FRAGMENTS

I am The One Who Was Cut into Pieces.
My body broken. My blood shed for your wholeness.
Take back your life . . . every year of it.
Take back your body . . . every precious piece of it.
Take back your story . . . every experience of it.
Be restored to wholeness.

Gather all the fragments of your broken life.
Claim the despised years. Remember the severed experiences.
Gather them from the far reaches of your years.
   Move through your sacred space and gather the lost experiences
         and years.
   Bring each fragment of your brokenness to the altar, your
         healing center.

Gather all the fragments of your broken body.
Claim the despised part. Remember the severed part.
Gather them from the far reaches of your years.
   Move through your sacred space and gather the broken pieces
         of your body.
   Bring each fragment of your brokenness to the altar, your
         healing center.

I am The One Who Was Cut into Pieces.
My body broken. My blood shed for your wholeness.
May your broken life and your shed blood be unto you
         wholeness.
   Take and eat of the bread, a symbol of your broken life and body.
   Take and drink of the juice, a symbol of your shed life-blood.

Sit quietly at your altar, the healing center within you.
From it radiates a light that soothes, heals, and empowers.
Breathe into your wholeness.
> Breathing in . . . My body is whole.
>> Breathing out . . . There is no blemish.
> Breathing in . . . My life is whole.
>> Breathing out . . . There is no blemish.
> Breathing in . . . I am restored to wholeness.
>> Breathing out . . . I am restored to a loving relationship to myself.

A God Who Looks Like Us

As survivors of sexual violence glimpse the feminine face of God through ritual and meditation, and through woman-affirming stories, myths, and images, their healing deepens. In her presence they move from brokenness to wholeness. The women who share their healing stories have done the work described in chapters 1 through 12. They have worked through each story that has brought us to this point. Their healing has taken time and tender patience.

Sitting in a circle, the women share the healing of their lives. One by one they speak out of the silence of a lifetime:

> A Woman God who looks like me would have been my advocate. I would not have wasted forty-seven years on diets to fit in, on anger because I couldn't fit in, and on depression trying to figure it all out. In this community of women I have finally realized that the standard held up for me to emulate was male-defined.
>
> In this community of women I have been allowed to be, to feel comfortable in my own skin, to feel my feelings, and to risk intimacy with other women. I have felt nurtured as part of a community. Through this experience the pieces of the puzzle of my whole life have come together. My life "clicks" now. I have a perspective on it. I am the center of it. I am no longer confused. I make decisions on my own behalf. I like myself. I feel holy and whole as a woman.

> —Robin

The source of my healing was demonstrated to me as I was working on drawings inspired by my search for the feminine face of God. Twice after drawing sessions I experienced a feeling of completeness. I have heard people talk about an empty hole in the soul. God knows, I have felt that painful emptiness all my life. But for a few moments while working on my drawings I felt complete. Although the feeling was brief, I now know it is possible to heal the ache in my heart.

It does not surprise me that my healing would come from creating art. As I was growing up, art came *from me*—it was the only thing that had nothing to do with my father. I drew until my father began having intercourse with me. After that everything was shameful, including my drawings. So my healing has to do with reclaiming art and the feminine face of God. Art connects me to my original identity and worth as a person apart from my father. And through searching for the feminine face of God, I have for the first time in my life considered the possibility of woman, of me, as sacred. I now believe it is a blessing to be born a woman.

—Ferrel

Imagine sitting in a circle with Robin and Ferrel. Add your story to theirs.

• Tape Gathering the Fragments and set aside a time to enter into it today. Reflect afterward in your journal: How are you reclaiming each dismembered piece of your history, your body, and your life? What action might you take this day on behalf of your wholeness?

• Take a piece of clay and sculpt a God Who Looks Like You. Honor in the sculpting those parts of your body that were abused and violated as well as those severely judged by the culture and despised by you.

• Personify the God Who Looks Like You. Write to her every day this week. Ask her, "Where are you within me? How may I experience more of your healing presence in my life, body, and creativity?"

A God Who Says, "No More!"

> Women's most feared power over men is the power to say
> no. To refuse to take care of men. To refuse to service
> them sexually. To refuse to buy their products. To
> refuse to worship their God. To refuse to love them.
> Every rapist knows that sex can be forced, but no power
> in the world can force love from any woman who wishes
> to withhold it.
>
> —Barbara Walker, *The Crone: Woman of Age,*
> *Wisdom, and Power*[9]

Amnon did not want to hear Tamar's voice, but our religious leaders must hear her voice now and tell her story. They must move out of denial for the sake of the young girls attending their services this week. The startling reality is that some of them are not safe even in their fathers' arms.

Perhaps if the religious institutions of our childhoods had listened to Tamar's story and allowed her firm *no* to challenge its ways, our stories would have been encouraged out of the silence of denial and shame much sooner. Her *no* was a courageous act on her own behalf. With great clarity of vision in a dangerous moment she challenged her brother's behavior and named it as a violation, as a foolish thing, and as low, wicked, and evil. She is the only one in the whole of the Hebrew Scriptures to name his sin! Let us remember her words:

"No, brother, do not violate me, we do not do such things in Israel; do not do this foolish thing. Where could I go and hide my shame? And you would sink as low as any fool in Israel. Why not speak to the King for me? He will not keep me from you."

He did not want to hear her voice. He was stronger than she. He raped her and laid her.

Then Amnon was filled with utter hatred for her; truly greater was the hatred with which he hated her than the desire with which he desired her. He said to her, "Get up and go." She answered, "No, it is wicked to send me away. This is a greater evil than all you have done to me."

As Tamar's truth is told, our truth is told. As we swallow her story into ours, hers becomes a healing story. We receive the courage to say no and the resources to tell our own stories out of generations of silence. Tamar's *no* shouts across the centuries each time we speak out of the silence to tell our own stories; each time we express outrage at the jokes that denigrate our bodies and at the pornography that defiles and mutilates them; each time we support a friend to leave a sexually abusive relationship; each time we demand that the fathers of our daughters deal with their powerfully destructive attitudes toward women's bodies; each time we challenge our religious leaders to tell the whole story in their teaching and preaching.

We are joined by Eve, Lilith, and Mary. Their voices rise from the depths of us. With Eve we say no to shame, to scapegoating, and to mother-bashing. With Lilith we say no to abusive relationships, to pain and suffering, and to anything that denies the self. With Mary we say no to twisted lives and bodies, and to surrender except to our truest self and to our wisest voice. Together our voices accumulate the power to topple the systems that condone violence, incest, and rape.

Inspired by Tamar, we affirm the Lilith-courage of our daughters, granddaughters, and nieces. We applaud the girl-child's voice as she affirms,

> *I am a warrior. Whatever the difficulty, I know there is a way to face into it. It takes no effort for me to summon up my courage, to arouse my spirit. With my courage I solve problems. With my spirit I change what doesn't work for me. I say no when I don't want to be hugged. I say "I don't like that person" when I don't, and "I like that person" when I do. I take care of myself. I am a Stubborn and Angry One. I leave when I want to. I refuse pain and suffering. I am active. I say no. The courage of the universe pulsates through me. I am full of myself.*

The Scripture tells us that Absalom was the father of three sons and one daughter. He named his daughter Tamar, after her beautiful aunt. For the sake of our nieces and our daughters, we must tell our stories. Imagine Tamar walking up the aisle this Sabbath. She looks into each woman's eyes and says, "Take back your sight. See yourself as beautiful and full. Take back your voice. Shout out your truth! Take back your dignity. It was not your sin. It is right and good that you are woman. Refuse to carry the sin of your father and brother within your body."

In response each woman in the congregation affirms with courage, "I take back my sight. I see myself as beautiful and full. I take back my voice. I will shout out my truth. I take back my dignity. It was not my sin. It is right and good that I am woman. Father, Brother, I will no longer carry your sin within my body. No more!"

One after another the women rise from their seats and tell their stories—stories of menstruation, of childbirth, of menopause. Stories of violation, shame, healing, and courage. The women's stories fill the space. And in the telling the space becomes sacred.

Sitting in a circle, the women share the truth of their lives. One by one they speak out of the silence of a lifetime:

> I've had numerous dealings with my family in which I
> have revealed the truth of my incest experiences. I feel
> great resistance from them and from within myself as
> I acknowledge the truth and as we keep it a living
> awareness in our relationships for the sake of my nieces.
> In the face of my fear that they will abandon me, I have
> gone ahead and spoken the truth because the
> covenant I have made to honor my truth is now my
> greatest commitment.
>
> —Ferrel

> As a child it was not all right for me to say no. And this
> made me vulnerable to sexual abuse. I carried this
> fear into adulthood as the sexual abuse continued. I received
> from Tamar the freedom, courage, power, and capacity
> to say no. I have released myself from self-imposed
> limits. I am in a joyous process of experimentation
> and expression. It's like breathing fresh air. I no longer
> feel closed in and trapped. I feel more energetic. I have
> redirected my energy back to myself. I realize that my
> center is life-giving and to move away from it is
> death for me. I realize how very powerful I am. I feel solid
> on the inside. There is an energy bubbling within me.
> It is on the verge of exploding in a loud voice that
> announces with certainty to the universe, I AM.
>
> —Erin

Imagine sitting in a circle with Ferrel and Erin. Add your story to theirs.

- In what ways do you say "No More!" in your life?
- Include one of the following courageous acts in your week:

Tell a trusting friend or relative a story you've kept secret.

Express outrage at the jokes said in the office that denigrate a woman's body or life.

Challenge a friend to say "No more!" and leave an abusive relationship.

Demand that your daughter's father deal with his destructive attitudes toward women's bodies.

Challenge your minister, priest, or rabbi to tell the stories of Tamar and The One Who Was Cut into Pieces. Volunteer to preach a sermon of outrage.

Encourage the Lilith-courage of your daughters, granddaughters, and nieces. Give them your blessing to say no.

Before moving on, linger awhile in the healing presence of Tamar:

⋐§ THE HEALING PRESENCE OF TAMAR

Set aside time each day this week to be with The Wounded One within you. Include her in each of the healing resources offered here. May she heal into the present through tender and compassionate self-care. Incorporate the following experiences into your daily life:

DAY 1. *Reclaimed Body*

- Where in your body do you carry the shame of deeply wounding experiences? Draw your body. Mark the places that hold your shame.
- Now transform the drawing. Reclaim each shame-filled part with a healing color or image. Honor them in a special way through your drawing.

DAY 2. *The Battle's Over*

- List the ways you have done battle with your body. Match each abusive action with a commitment to a specific self-caring action. Incorporate these healing actions into your week.

DAY 3. *Reclaimed Vision*

- Hear Tamar speaking these words to you today: "Take back your sight. See yourself as beautiful and full."
- Incorporate this affirmation into your day: "I take back my sight. I see myself as beautiful and full."
- Be aware of the ways you are reclaiming your clear vision. See yourself without blemish this day!

DAY 4. *Reclaimed Voice*

- Hear Tamar speaking these words to you today: "Take back your voice. Shout out your truth!"
- Incorporate this affirmation into your day: "I take back my voice. I will shout out my truth."
- Be aware of the ways you are reclaiming your strong voice. Speak your truth this day!

DAY 5. *Reclaimed Dignity*

- Hear Tamar speaking these words to you today: "Take back your dignity. It was not your sin."
- Incorporate this affirmation into your day: "I take back my dignity. It was not my sin."
- Be aware of the ways you are reclaiming your dignity. Refuse shame and guilt this day!

DAY 6. *Reclaimed Goodness*

- Hear Tamar speaking these words to you today: "It is right and good that you are woman."
- Incorporate this affirmation into your day: "It is right and good that I am woman."
- Be aware of the ways you are reclaiming the goodness of woman. Refuse to be belittled and set aside this day!

DAY 7. *No More!*

- Hear Tamar speaking these words to you today: "Refuse to carry the sin of your father and brother within your body."
- Incorporate this affirmation into your day: "Father, Brother, I will no longer carry your sin within my body. No more!"

• Be aware of the ways you are reclaiming your body as your own. Refuse all burdens that are not yours to carry this day!

Before moving on, linger awhile in the healing presence of The One Who Was Cut into Pieces:

✌ THE HEALING PRESENCE OF THE ONE WHO WAS CUT INTO PIECES

Set aside time each day this week to be with The Wounded One within you. May she heal into the present through tender and compassionate self-care. Incorporate the following meditation into your daily life.[10]

Imagine that you are in an ancient forest. Take a few deep breaths. Imagine that you have roots like the trees that surround you. You are as grounded, as connected to Mother Earth as a tree. You are held, supported, and nourished by her. Imagine your breath rising from the rich Earth beneath you with each inhalation. Release the breath into the cool and moist air around you with each exhalation.

Weave an affirmation into each breath:

My body is holy. There is no blemish.
My body is whole. There is no blemish.

The weather is refreshing and you are following The One Who Was Cut into Pieces down a path known only to her. She takes you to a clearing, a wide open space deep in the forest. Look around the clearing and find a seat on a rock or in the soft cool grass. Make yourself comfortable. The One Who Was Cut into Pieces will lead you in a gentle walk of acknowledgment over and around your body. Follow her suggestions with tender touch, expressive movement, or in the stillness of your imagination. Imagine her saying:

You are enough. You are blessed. Hold nothing in. Allow your body to take its shape. Love the shape of your body. Inhale and affirm, My body is holy. Exhale and affirm, My body is whole.

Come home to your body. Love it. No more pounding, twisting, sculpting.

Love your flesh, love it with your heart and soul. Love it now with your touch.

Pay special attention to the areas it is difficult to acknowledge—a scar, a place trespassed by another, a layer of protective fat, an untouchable part. Are you ashamed of certain parts? Proud of others? Breathe into any discomfort without judgment. Notice what is true for you without shame.

Begin at the top of your head. Acknowledge your head. Move it. Massage it.

Love your hair. Touch it now. Stroke it. Twirl it. Bless its curls, its straightness, its color, its texture.

Love your eyes. Bless their color. Massage your eyelids and eyebrows. Open and close them. Honor your unique view of the world.

Love your ears. Bless their shape and size. Massage them. Love your unique reception of the world.

Love your nose. Bless its shape and size. Breathe in and out slowly. Honor the Breath of Life as it passes through you.

Love your mouth and lips. Trace the shape of your lips. Love the sounds of your mouth. Make a sound.

Love your neck. Stroke it. Hold it up high. Massage it tenderly.

Love your shoulders. Raise them to your ears. Listen to them. Is there tension? What are your shoulders saying to you about the pace and shape of your days? Release them, and all they carry, with love.

Love your arms. Raise them up in front of you. Pat your hands together. Shake them. Kiss them.

You are enough. You are blessed. Hold nothing in. Allow your body to take its shape. Trace the shape of your body. Inhale, My body is holy. Exhale, My body is whole.

Love your breasts. Firm, sagging, full, flat, beautiful as they are. Trace the shape of your breasts.

Love your abdomen. Fill it with your breath. Honor its roundness. Allow it to take its shape.

Trace your pubic triangle. As you do, celebrate your connection to Woman God. She who has breasts, thighs, and a vagina like yours.

Trace the shape of your bottom. Honor the shape of your bottom. Massage it tenderly in appreciation for its faithful support of you.

At your own pace, create a Meditation of Acknowledgment. Slowly move, touch, or imagine each of the remaining parts of your body, your thighs, knees, calves, feet, and toes. Breathe deeply as you acknowledge your body and listen to it.

To bring closure to your Meditation of Acknowledgment, inhale deeply. Imagine the breath rising up from the rich Earth beneath you, as you say in your heart: **My body is holy.** Release the breath into the cool and moist air around you, as you say in your heart: **My body is whole.**

Sit quietly until you feel ready to write or draw in your journal. Acknowledge all the feelings, sensations, and memories that surfaced for you. Share your experience with a trusted friend.

The Wise Old Woman

The Story

The God of our childhood was changeless. He stood outside the realities of our existence. He was the giver of life and remained untouched by death. Death was an enemy of life, a consequence of humanity's fall from perfection. It was to be overcome.

Her intimate participation in the origins of life forgotten, it is the old woman who reminds us of death. For it was the woman Eve who brought death into the world, and her daughters bear the curse in their aging bodies.

The Face of Death

> For the wages of sin is death.
>
> —Romans 6:23

As the face of God changed in my experience, I searched for the old women in my religious past. In my childhood the old women attended Mass every day. They cared for the orphans. They volunteered to bake cakes for the charity bazaars. They sewed the altar cloth by hand. They prepared the priest's food and cleaned his toilet. But it was the male priests who presided at the daily Mass.

In my adolescence the old women sewed the drapes for the Sunday school. They attended every prayer meeting and Bible study group.

They prepared the food for church banquets and dinners. They serviced the church. But it was the male minister who presided at each service.

In college it was the old women, the maids and nannies, who shouldered the parental and hospitality burdens of the wealthy. They carried the pain of their own children while they dried the tears of the white folks' kids. They catered the special dinners and cleaned the toilets of church and home. These were the bent-over women, who bore the racism of generations atop their shoulders.

I remember Sarah, the wife of Abraham. Consumed with having a son, she sought to be built up through her slave, Hagar. Young and fertile, Hagar bore the outcast son. Sarah, old and barren, laughed when God told her she would have a legitimate one. Old woman and young woman engaged in a dance of bitterness and suffering, encircling the man and his sons.[1]

I remember Naomi and Ruth, wise and brave women, mother and daughter-in-law committed to each other in the absence of their husbands. Their story revolves around the finding of a new husband and the birth of a grandson to carry on the deceased male's name.[2]

I remember old Anna, the prophetess. She was a widow. Unrelated to any man, she was as illegitimate as the fatherless, but God sustained her in the service of the temple. He was the protector of widows.[3]

It was clear that a woman's power, if she had any to begin with, diminished as she grew older. Very few listened to her voice, to her stories, to her wisdom. Every old woman eventually became a shut-in, alone and poor. While men grow old with dignity, women alone grow old with disgrace.

Our Wounds

In the company of courageous women we will give voice to the experiences of our personal and religious past that deposited within us a dread of growing old. As we tell our stories, we will move out of the isolation of a lifetime. This is our first step toward healing.

The Dread of Aging

> In real life, signs of old womanhood are not supposed
> to be seen.
>   Women are socially and professionally handicapped
> by wrinkles and gray hair in a way that men are not.
> Instead of aging normally through their full life cycle,
> women are constrained to create an illusion that their
> growth process stops in the first decade or two of
> adulthood.
>
> —Barbara Walker, *The Crone of Age,*
> *Wisdom, and Power*

As we have journeyed through the truth of a woman's life, beginning
with her birth, traveling through the creation myths and symbols that
have shaped her, venturing into her body's unfolding cycles and
rhythms, and exploring her vulnerability to rape and incest, we have
caught glimpses of the dread of aging that fills women's writings. This
dread has accumulated power and force along the way.

The Old Woman is the culmination of all she has experienced since
childhood. All along, it has been the natural occurrences of our lives
that have been unacceptable: our "girlness," our bleeding, and our
changing bodies during puberty and pregnancy. It makes great sense
that we would be forced to continue the battle with our woman-bodies
on a new frontier, the aging process. As our bodies change, we twist
them out of shape in order to live up to society's expectation that a
woman never grow old.

Sadly our self-hatred has reached such depths by this time that many
women will do anything to get rid of the evidence of their aging, often
employing violent means. Some become obsessed and keep track of
their wrinkles with a magnifying glass. Others submit to regular and
painful injections of collagen. Still others resort to cosmetic surgery—
the knife cutting away unwanted pieces of themselves, a bit of nose
here, a piece of thigh there, a double chin, an unwanted bulge, wrinkle,
or spot. Few celebrate their changing face and body. We can't imagine
a God who ages as we do.

Disguising the signs of aging consumes a great deal of a woman's energy. This means that there is little left to deal with the economic and social factors that threaten her survival in a world that prefers men. Her money has been spent on clothes, diets, and dyes instead of being set aside for the future. Her focus has been riveted on getting and then keeping a man, who will be her salvation, security, and companion into old age. The overwhelming reality is that most women grow old alone, outliving all of their "saviors" and outlasting their saviors' bank accounts.

Consider and reflect:[4]

• Among the elderly who are poor, more than three out of four are women. Most women earn less than most men, so they build up less in savings, pensions, and Social Security. They also live much longer.

> I don't want to grow old alone. One of my most fearsome images is seeing myself as an elderly woman living alone in a cold tenement listening to the heater turn on and off.
>
> —Teresa

• A lifelong homemaker earns no Social Security protection of her own. Even though she has worked for decades in the home and has contributed substantially to her family's economic well-being, she receives only a spousal benefit equal to half of the benefit her husband receives.

> The feeling of "not being enough" has intensified through the years, and as I age, the world reinforces that message. I am afraid of being swallowed up and then spit out as no longer desirable or useful. If I do not have a family to make it all worthwhile as I grow older, I think I will die.
>
> —Ann

• About 75 percent of Americans in old-age homes are women. In three decades the number of elderly Americans living alone will balloon from 8.8 million to 15.2 million, with four out of five still being women.

> I feel like I don't exist when I'm not attached to a man.
> As I age, the likelihood of finding a suitable partner
> diminishes. This scares me because I do not want to
> grow old alone.
>
> —Joyce

• By the year 2020 poverty among older Americans will be almost entirely confined to women living alone. Unless pervasive job segregation and sex and age discrimination are checked, the decades ahead will bring little improvement in wages or in the economic status of succeeding generations of women in midlife and older.

> I support myself and take care of my car, home, office,
> taxes, bills, and health care. At times it gets overwhelming,
> but I've been doing it about twenty years. Getting old
> scares me. I fear that I will lose control of some part
> of my body and I won't be able to care for myself.
>
> —Mary

• According to the Screen Actors Guild, the average male SAG member earned 60 percent more than the average female. Of actors in their fifties, men earned 150 percent more. "It looks to me as though females get hired along procreative lines. After forty, we are kind of cooked," says Carrie Fisher.[5]

> The natural occurrences of life have not been acceptable
> to me. Currently I am fighting my own aging process.
> I have given birth to two wonderful children, and my
> body is changing. Unable to accept these changes, I
> batter my body into shape in order to live up to society's
> expectations of maintaining a youthful body.
>
> —Erin

Sitting in a circle, the women share the truth of their lives. One by one they speak out of the silence of a lifetime:

> When I look in the mirror, I don't see myself as a forty-
> three-year-old woman with lines and roundedness and
> drooping places. I look in the mirror and think,
> "This isn't me. Inside, I'm still twenty-five." Intellectually

I honor the aging woman and yet when I look at her in the mirror, I deny her reality. I'm still influenced by the culture's definition of what is acceptable, and attractive.

—Rebekah

There are many things about my body that I can't put into words because of the intense pain involved. They truly affect my ability to be close to others and they cause me to feel unacceptable as a human being. My age has long been a difficulty. The value placed on youthful women in this society is constantly reinforced at the dances I attend as I see old geezers, namely guys my age and older, in hot pursuit of women in their twenties. In that group, women who are fifty-something are largely invisible as dance partners and as potential life partners as well.

—Joyce

My father told me that the only value I had was a temporary sexual value. He said that when I got old (and I'm now well beyond the age he meant), I wouldn't have any value at all. His words contributed to my ever-present terror of growing old. When I was twenty-five, I felt just as terrified of aging as I am now at forty-six.

Other than being of sexual value, I don't know I exist. This has made relationship addiction a daily plague. I haven't been involved in a relationship for four years, yet men still control my attitude toward myself. It doesn't matter if they're in my life or not, the terror of aging and my obsession with their response to me is present just the same.

This woundedness is so deep that it will be a sign of tremendous healing if I do not pursue cosmetic surgery in the coming years. It's healing to admit the truth in a circle of women.

—Ferrel

Imagine sitting in a circle with Rebekah, Joyce, and Ferrel. Add your story to theirs.

- What was your father's attitude toward your mother's aging? Toward your aging?
- What were your mother's attitudes toward aging? Were there any fears that she passed on to you?
- Did your mother prepare economically for her own future? How have you prepared for your future?
- As an adult what are your fears of aging? Are you more involved in disguising the physical evidences of aging than you are in developing your gifts, sharing the wisdom of your years, and preparing a financially secure future for yourself?

Our Healing

We have given voice to the experiences that deposited within us a dread of growing old. Now we will gather more of the fragments of our collective story from the margins of history and religion. With courage we will retell The Wise Old Woman's story incorporating the powerful images of a time when the accumulation of a woman's years was celebrated. The Wise Old Woman becomes a healing image of the divine within us. As we embrace her, we will recover our Original Wisdom and Beauty.

A God Who Ages Like Me

> There is an enormous gulf between a society like this and earlier pre-patriarchal societies where elder women were founts of wisdom, law, healing skills, and moral leadership. Their wrinkles would have been badges of honor, not of shame.
>
> —Barbara Walker, *The Crone of Age Wisdom, and Power*

We are reminded of a time when God looked like us. We discover that we are surrounded by a courageous company of women. Their ancient stories and images become healing resources for us. We learn of ancient women who did not apologize for their later years. We recall ancient societies that celebrated the accumulation of a woman's years and that respected a woman's wise blood. We read of ancient ways in which only postmenopausal women could preside at rituals and sacred rites.[6] We learn of ancient beliefs in the Triple Goddess—Maiden, Mother, and Crone.

Just as the changing face of the Moon transforms the night sky, so the changing face of God transforms our images of aging and death. The God who looks like us changes as we do. In the fullness of time she becomes the Crone Goddess, who wisely brings an allotted life span to its end. She represents old age, winter, and the waning moon. She holds life and death as one within her. Neither is elevated or despised in the endless cycle of birth, life, death, rebirth.[7]

Inspired by her, ancient women didn't view death as a passage to heaven but as a return to the earth. These women weren't obsessed with aging and death. The old ones among them were considered as awesome as the earth's sacred sites. They were revered because they held the wisdom of the earth within their cracks, crevices, lines, and years. Each woman honored the face of the Goddess in her own changing face.

We invite The Wise Old Woman to be present among us at our community gatherings. Imagine sitting in a circle with women of all ages, affirming, "In wisdom, we acknowledge that everything changes. 'Seed becomes fruit; fruit becomes seed. In birth, we die; on death, we feed.'[8] The Wise Old One honors both life and death. Neither is elevated or despised. They are a part of the cyclical nature of reality. That which is born will die, and that which dies nourishes life in its many forms. Our capacity to embrace death is determined by the depth to which we have welcomed life. We honor all that has been demeaned. We receive all that has been cast aside. Life and death are good. They are very good."

In Celebration of The Wise Old Woman: A Meditation

In meditation we reclaim the images of a time when God looked like us. What follows is a two-part meditation entitled "In Celebration of The Wise Old Woman." The Wise Old Woman offers us gifts of healing as we enter into her presence through meditation. It is from her body that we came. It is to her body that we return. From her body we catch a glimpse of our future. And from ours she is reminded of the past. Together we tell the whole truth of a woman's life.

In part I of the meditation you will be invited to pay attention to the accumulation of your years, to bless the bruised years and to celebrate the bright ones. May you embrace the emerging Wise Old Woman as you acknowledge all of your years without shame. In part II you will be invited to transform each of the dreaded changes of age into a celebration. May you embrace the emerging Wise Old Woman as you bless your body without shame.

Below is the complete script for the meditation. Read through it as if it were text. Draw or write the feelings and memories that surface as you read. Eventually you may want to tape the meditation in your own voice. Many women listen to it daily as a healing resource.

PART I. *Gathering the Years*

The Wise Old Woman calls us to fill up the years of our lives.

Move forward through the years of your life, beginning with your birth. Pay special attention to the years that hurt you. Draw the painful years. Write about the bruised ones. Dance the wounded years. Bless each one of these years by adding. Add a healing color to your drawing, a healing symbol to your writing, or a healing movement to your dance.

Now travel again through the years, counting each year as you move along. This time pay special attention to the years that delighted you. Draw the delightful years. Write about the comfortable ones. Dance the bright years. Celebrate each one of these years by adding a celebratory color to your drawing, a celebratory symbol to your writing, or a celebratory movement to your dance.

Gather all the years of your life into a bundle, the bright and the bruised. Bring that bundle of years to your altar. Display your drawings and writings. Dance your "Dance of Life." Call out your age without shame. Fill the sacred space with the accumulation of your years.

Sit quietly at your altar. Breathe into the fullness of your years.

Breathing in . . . I gather my years.
    Breathing out . . . There is no blemish.
Breathing in . . . The bruised and wounded years.
    Breathing out . . . There is no blemish.

Breathing in . . . The bright and comfortable years.
Breathing out . . . There is no blemish.
Breathing in . . . I gather my years.
Breathing out . . . I release all shame.

PART II. *Loving Our Changing Bodies*

Stand and breathe deeply. Imagine that you are in an ancient forest. Imagine that you have roots like the trees that surround you. You are as grounded, as connected to Mother Earth as a tree. You are held, supported, and nourished by her. Inhale deeply. Imagine your breath rising up from the rich earth beneath you as you say in your heart, "**My changing body is holy.**" Release the breath into the cool, moist air around you as you say in your heart, "**My changing body is whole.**"

Follow The Wise Old Woman to a sacred clearing in the forest. She invites you to sit with her beside the Stream of Life. Hear her words: "Reach into the stream. Bless your body with its healing waters. Take a gentle walk over and around your whole body. Acknowledge the changes. Celebrate the changes. I am emerging within you. There is nothing to fear."

At your own pace create a meditation of acknowledgment. Beginning at your feet and slowly moving to your head, acknowledge each change that is occurring: the lines, wrinkles, cracks, and roundness; the loosening, lowering, and stretching; the changes in color, shape, and texture. Embrace The Wise Old Woman who is emerging. Bless your body without shame.

When you are finished, imagine sitting in a circle with Wendy, Erin, Dana, and Irene. Add your affirmations to theirs as you transform the changes you dread into a celebration of the coming of the beautiful old woman.

Wendy at thirty-two is delighting to discover:

Wise muscles that tell me to go more slowly and thoughtfully through life.

Silver strands that fall from my hair, reminding me that I have just said something wise. I am awed by each strand's silver beauty. I keep them in a red cushioned box, covered with silver beads. They are my strands of wise maturity.

Laughter lines around my eyes that remind me of all the funny stories

I have heard and of all the radiant and sunny days I have squinted to enjoy.

Erin at thirty-five is rejoicing to discover:

My extended belly, which represents the challenges of life that have stretched me beyond the limitations of childhood.

My textured legs and pumping veins that have supported my weight and the weight of two babies.

My defined face, one that has sharpened with experience.

My shoulders, which tense and signal times to meditate and to release.

My bottom, which is much looser now. I have let go, I am not so tight and guarded.

Dana: The older woman is showing herself to me as I look in the mirror each morning. I see character lines around my eyes and mouth, a delicate double chin, serenity spots on my hands, a bountiful soft belly, and small sacks of wisdom under my eyes. I welcome these changes.

Irene: I have finally made a sort of peace with my physical body. I've ceased longing for the air-brushed image of youth portrayed in the media. The delicate spidery lines on my legs tell the stories of each of my pregnancies. I know when each one appeared and their significance in my present life. They remind me of my importance. I once held and nurtured a life within my body.

The Wisdom of the Old Woman

> Wisdom cries aloud in the open air. She raises her voice
> in public places. She calls at the top of the busy streets,
> and proclaims at the open gate of the city.
>
> —Proverbs 1:20

Ours has been a journey of descent into the uncharted territory of our inner life and resources. We have reclaimed our goodness (Eve), our power (Lilith), our willfulness and our sexuality (Mary), our sacredness (The Divine Girl-Child), our natural processes and our sisters (The One Who Shed Her Blood), our bodies (The One Who Was Cut into Pieces), and our voices (Tamar).

Now we rediscover Wisdom in our descent. In chapter 9 you were introduced to her. We learned that Wisdom (or Sophia, which is the Greek word for Wisdom) was actually a feminine face of God in the Hebrew Scriptures. She had been obscured but not completely eradicated over time.

I sought out Wisdom's presence in religious history. I found her in the Gnostic Christian versions of the life and work of Jesus. These writings were considered heretical by the orthodox Christian church and were not included in the Bible. Many feminine images of the divine are included in Gnostic writings, so it is not surprising that women found their way into this early Christian community.

The Gnostics embraced the first creation story in which man and woman were created simultaneously in the image of a male-female God. This belief led to greater equality among women and men and created more opportunities for women to assume leadership positions. In Gnostic writings Sophia was present at creation; all things were conceived in feminine power and wisdom.[9] Sophia taught Adam and Eve self-awareness. She guided them to food and assisted them in the conception of their children.[10]

And Sophia holds the seeming contradictions of a woman's life within her:

> *I am the first and the last. I am the honored one and the scorned one.*
> *I am the whore, and the holy one. I am the wife and the virgin.*
> *I am (the mother) and the daughter. . . .*
> *I am she whose wedding is great, and I have not taken a husband.*
> *I am knowledge, and ignorance. . . . I am shameless; I am shamed.*
> *I am strength, and I am fear. . . . I am foolish, and I am wise. . . .*
> *I am godless, and I am one whose God is great.*[11]

I searched for Wisdom's presence in my life and found her each time I listened with laughter and tears to the stories of a lifetime shared in a writing class at the senior center. She spoke to me each time I listened with respect to the experience, strength, and hope of the wise old women in Al-Anon. She was there each time I was challenged by the courageous deeds of wise old women rabbis and ministers. She whispered in my ear each time I noticed the natural beauty of wise old Quaker women who choose to honor the changes of age with dignity and grace.

I sought Wisdom in the company of the women I work among. Inspired by her presence, we reinvented the act of prayer as a conversation with Wisdom. We reinvented meditation as a reflection on Wisdom's presence in our lives. Through prayer and meditation we seek to improve our conscious contact with the deeper wisdom within us, praying only to come into harmony with her ways.[12]

Meditation: a Reflection on Wisdom's Presence Within Us

Below is a passage from the Hebrew Scriptures describing the attributes of Wisdom. As you read it, reflect on the ways your life might have been different if you had been surrounded by these feminine qualities from your birth. Reflect on how the presence of Sophia might affect your life this day.

> For in Wisdom there is a spirit, intelligent and holy; subtle, free-moving, and lucid; spotless and clear; working no harm and loving what is good; eager and unhindered; beneficent and kindly; steadfast and unerring; all-powerful and all-surveying. For Wisdom moves more easily than motion itself; She pervades and permeates all things. Like a fine mist she rises from Power, permeating all intelligent, pure, and delicate spirits.
>
> She is the brightness that streams from everlasting light, the flawless mirror of Active Power, and the image of Goodness. She is more radiant than the sun and surpasses every constellation. Compared to the light of day, she is found to excel; for day gives way to night, but against her no evil can prevail. She spans the world in power from end to end, and orders all things benignly.
>
> —(Wisdom 7:22–30, adapted from *The New English Bible*)

Colleen reflects on how her life might have been different if she had been surrounded by images of Divine Wisdom from her birth. Add your reflection to hers.

> If we had been immersed in images of a Woman God,
> all of the women who surrounded me in my youth would
> have had their power, dreams, and anger. They would
> have been able to protect themselves. I feel sad at all
> the lost possibilities. My fluidity and feminine intelligence
> were not valued. Being loving, quiet, and practically
> invisible were the traits that seemed to be espoused
> by the Church, my father, and his friends. As a result

my concept of womanness has been so far from whole.
In Woman God the lost possibilities of youth are reclaimed.
I, as woman, am divine. I am self-defined and
complete in myself.

Prayer as Conversation with Our Deeper Wisdom

Wisdom resides in the depths of us, below the turbulence of our mind's activity and the fluctuations of daily living. She reaches beneath our early injuries and our ineffective behaviors. She predates our socialization by religion, society, and family. She is available to us in the stillness. She is trustworthy and the one to whom we open in prayer. Experiment with the following meditation to improve your conscious contact with her.

Imagine that you are sitting in a clearing within the forest of your life. A stream surrounds the clearing, and you hear the music of its flowing waters. You are awaiting a visitor—an image that represents your deeper wisdom. She may come to you as a particular person, someone who is a wise presence in your life. She may appear as a teacher, grandmother, sister, friend. Wisdom may also come as a mythic figure who has served as a healing image through this study, The Wise Old Woman, Lilith, Eve, Mary, or The Divine Girl-Child.

When she arrives, dialogue with her through writing or drawing. Tell her of a confusing situation, a troubling relationship, disturbing memories. Tell her of your need for guidance, perspective, clarity, courage, or serenity. If you know what you need, ask her for it. If you don't, trust her to know and tell you.

In the stillness that follows the writing, allow her to speak to you. If an image forms, draw it. If a message wells up from the depths of you, write it down. Do not edit it as it comes. Simply write down whatever comes to you.

As Annette moved through this meditation, she envisioned a Mother Spirit. She shared with the Mother her fears and insecurities about what lay ahead after seminary graduation. The Mother replied from the depths of Annette's spirit:

You are the greening of my spirit in the world. You are a verdant pasture, a wildflower in bloom. You are my daughter and I love you. I created you to bring beauty and truth to my world. You are embodied in my love. I have given you my spirit to be my eyes and hands in the world. I wanted to run

through open fields in the summertime, to breathe the mountain air, to touch
another in loving concern, to heal the hurts in the world. So I created you.
It saddens me when you don't realize the gift you are to me. I am always
here, lovingly present within you. I will never leave you.

Imagine

> There was a time when you were not a slave, remember
> that. You walked alone, full of laughter, you bathed bare
> bellied. You say you have lost all recollection of it,
> remember! You say there are not words to describe it;
> you say it does not exist. But remember! Make an effort
> to remember! Or failing that, invent.
>
> —Monique Wittig, *Les Guerilleres*

Inspired by Sophia, I created a ritual presentation entitled "Imagine." I
invite women and men to imagine how their lives might have been different if the Mother of All Living, The Divine Girl-Child, The One
Who Sheds Her Blood, Tamar, The One Who Was Cut into Pieces,
and The Wise Old Woman had been present in the churches, synagogues, and homes of their childhoods. It has been performed in
church services, recovery centers, women's retreats, and ritual circles.

Interested participants join me for a two-hour "work in progress" ses-
sion the day before the service, presentation, or retreat. In the large
group we work through each section of the ritual using many of the exercises, reflections, and meditations found in this book. Then we divide
up into small groups according to interest. Each small group creates a
movement piece and practices the readings for a particular portion of
the ritual. The next day we facilitate the larger group's ritual experience.

For many congregations and groups this is their first encounter with
the feminine face of God, their first immersion in a woman-affirming
symbol system. The reaction is always mixed. As we stand at the door
after each service to greet those who were present, some women brush
by, threatened and offended. Their self-loathing makes it impossible for
them to tolerate such an intense gaze at the beauty of their lives, bodies,
and blood. Others have tears in their eyes because they were so moved
by the ritual's profound affirmation of a woman's reality.

Below is the complete script of the ritual. Read through it as if it were text. Imagine being in your childhood church. Draw or write the feelings and memories that surface. As you read, you will be reminded of your journey through the book. Each of the women you have met you will meet again.

✒ AN IMMERSION IN WOMAN-AFFIRMING IMAGES, STORIES, PRAYERS, AND SONGS: THE IMAGINE RITUAL

CLERGYWOMAN: The Wise Old Woman invites us to imagine a childhood in which we were surrounded by woman-affirming stories, images, songs, and rituals. She invites us to imagine how our lives might have been different if we had been introduced to the Mother of All Living, The Divine Girl-Child, The One Who Shed Her Blood, Tamar, The One Who Was Cut into Pieces, and The Wise Old Woman in the churches, synagogues, and homes of our childhoods.

READER 1: Imagine a creation myth in which the Mother was present. Imagine if you as a girl-child had heard the following words in the synagogue, church, or home of your childhood:

DANCE AND VOICE CHOIR:
In the beginning was the Mother.
On the first day she gave birth to light and darkness. They danced together.
On the second day she gave birth to land and water. They touched.
On the third day she gave birth to the plants.
        They rooted and breathed.
On the fourth day she gave birth to land, sea, and air creatures.
        They walked and flew and swam.
On the fifth day her creation learned balance and cooperation.
        She thanked her partner for coaching her labor.
On the sixth day she celebrated the creativity of all living things.
On the seventh day she left space for the unknown.

READER 2: Together let us pray.

ALL:
Our Mother, who art within us, we celebrate your many names.
    Your wisdom come.
    Your will be done, unfolding from the depths within us.
Each day you give us all that we need.

You remind us of our limits and we let go.

You support us in our power and we act with courage.

For thou art the dwelling place within us,

the empowerment around us,

and the celebration among us.

Now and forever more.

READER 1: Imagine a Divine Girl-Child whose birth was announced and celebrated by angels, whose coming merited visitors and precious gifts, and in whose honor the peoples of the world gather for a yearly retelling of the story of her birth. Imagine if you as a girl-child had heard the following words in the synagogue, church, or home of your childhood:

DANCE AND VOICE CHOIR:

In this hour everything is stillness, there is total silence and awe.

We are overwhelmed with a great wonder. We keep vigil.

We are expecting the coming of the Divine Child.

In the fullness of time she is born.

She shines like the sun, bright and beautiful.

She is delightful to see. She appears as peace, soothing the whole world.

The voices of many invisible beings in one voice rejoice:

She has arrived. The Divine Child is among us.

Become bold. Lean over and look at her. Touch her.

Lift her in your hands with great awe.

Look at her more closely. There is no blemish on her.

She is splendid to see.

Dance with her. Now come to a still place with her.

She is laughing a most joyful laugh.

She opens her eyes and looks intently at you.

Suddenly a great light comes forth from her eyes,

like a flash of lightning.

The light enters you. She enters you. You begin to live.

_____ is born. The Divine Child is among us!

READER 2: Together let us affirm,

ALL: For Mother God so loved the world that she sent into its midst The Divine Girl-Child. Whosoever believes in her goodness, listens to her wisdom, and celebrates her power will be awakened to the abundance of gifts within them. [Adapted from John 3:16]

READER 1: Imagine the sacraments and rituals of childhood commemorating the monthly shedding of a woman's blood, her sacred blood that holds within it both life and death. Imagine singing songs and spirituals that celebrate the beautiful, powerful blood of woman. Imagine that you as a girl-child had sung these words in the synagogue, church, or home of your childhood.

VOICE CHOIR:
There is power, power, wonder-working power
     in the blood of the woman.
There is power, power, wonder-working power
     in the precious blood of the woman.

ALL:
Would you be free from the burden of lies?
  There's pow'r in the blood, pow'r in the blood.
Would you receive deep healing within?
  There's wonderful pow'r in the blood.

There is pow'r, pow'r, wonder-working pow'r in the blood of the woman.
There is power, power, wonder-working power in the precious blood of
    the woman.

Would you be wiser much wiser than now?
  There's pow'r in the blood, pow'r in the blood.
Shame's stains are lost in her life-giving flow.
  There's wonderful pow'r in the blood.[13]

READER 1: Imagine the sermons and readings of your childhood churches and synagogues including the stories of violence against women. Imagine Tamar and The One Who Was Cut into Pieces being invited to each service. Imagine healing rituals that acknowledge a woman's wounds and offer resources of hope and transformation.

A DANCE AND VOICE CHOIR:
Hear a tragic story: (The voice choir reads the story of The One Who Was Cut into Pieces from Judges 19. As it is being read, the dancers will scatter twelve scarves throughout the meeting place.)
    The One Who Was Cut into Pieces offers you wholeness. Her body broken, her Blood shed for your healing. May she be unto your life and health. Gather all the fragments of your broken body. Claim the despised part. Remember the severed part. Gather them from the far reaches of

your years. (*Dancers move through the space and gather the scarves. Bring each one to the altar.*)

Take and eat of your broken body. Swallow the broken parts. Take and drink of your shed blood. Swallow the Fluid of Life. (*Dancers distribute the bread and drink.*)

May your broken body and your shed blood be unto you wholeness of body. Affirm aloud, "I am whole. My body is whole."

The One Who Was Cut into Pieces offers you wholeness. Her body broken, her blood shed for your healing. May she be unto you life and health.

READER 1: Imagine the rituals and sacraments of the churches and synagogues of our childhoods presided over by wise old postmenopausal women who, as in ancient times, were considered the wisest of the wise because they permanently held within them their life-creating wise blood. Imagine that you as a girl-child had heard these words from the wise old woman every Sabbath.

A CIRCLE OF CRONE GUIDES: Let us gather our years. The Wise Old Woman, from her Fountain of Wisdom, calls us to celebrate the years of our lives.

Move forward through the years of your life, beginning with your birth. Pay special attention to the years that hurt as you pass through them. Bless the bruised and wounded years. Call out those years. (*Wait for group to call out the years.*)

Now travel again through the years, beginning with your birth. Pay special attention to the years that delight you as you pass through them. Celebrate the bright and comfortable years. Call them out. (*Wait for group to call out the years.*)

Gather all the years of your life in a bundle, the bright and the bruised. Bring that bundle of years into this room. Call out the years you have lived. Fill this sacred space with your years.

May you fill up the years of your life without shame.

READER 2: Together let us remember,

ALL: In the name of the Mother of All Living (*touch your womb center in honor of our intimate connection to the origins of life*),

and of the Divine Daughter (*touch your breasts in honor of The Divine Girl-Child's developing body*), and of The Wise Old Woman (*touch your eyes in honor of the wise vision she offers*).

As it was in the very beginning, may it be now (*open your arms to receive All That Is*).

READER I: How would your life be different if you had been introduced to the Mother of All Living, The Divine Girl-Child, The One Who Shed Her Blood, Tamar, The One Who Was Cut into Pieces, and The Wise Old Woman in the churches, synagogues, and homes of your childhood? Join Sharyn, Erin, Hallie, and Laura. Add your story to theirs.

SHARYN: Surrounded by the images of a strong Woman Goddess, our feminine experiences and our very bodies would have been validated. We would have learned to enhance our attractiveness because we liked ourselves, not because we needed others to like us.

ERIN: My life would definitely have been different if I had been presented with the full picture. I believe there would be balance in our world, and an awareness of connection rather than separation. We would all be empowered to live out of our fullness rather than out of an empty hole.

HALLIE: Perhaps if I had been well grounded in a spirituality that held women's blood as sacred; if I had attended religious ceremonies in which Adonai and the Shekhina were celebrated as the masculine and feminine faces of a divine presence; and if I had been brought up in a culture that valued the totality of the feminine experience to the same degree it valued the logical, external, and athletic aspects of the male experience, I would not have rejected motherhood throughout my life.

LAURA: In the company of women I have begun to accept the coming of a complex and rich old age. Those soft, petallike, and vacuous prepubescent images of the fashion magazines and movies have begun to look hollow and sterile to me. I think of the many years in which my mother dyed her hair with cheap dyes and finally, close to eighty, surrendered to her long white hair, so fragile, lovely, and genuine. I encounter unforgettable old women. Through them I begin to embrace the vitality and wealth of old women. The body deteriorates, and yet I now understand how one's sensuality can acquire the depth and richness of a full life. Shame dissolves as we affirm our essential loveliness as women.

Before moving on, linger awhile with Wisdom:

✌ PRAYER AND MEDITATION: WISDOM'S ONGOING PRESENCE

Set aside time each day this week to spend with the Wise One within you. Incorporate the following experiences into your daily life:

DAY 1. *An Ongoing Presence*

Think back to the presence of Sophia in your childhood and adolescence. Who were the wise old women who taught you wisdom in the secret of your heart—a loving aunt, a kind nun, an unconditionally loving grandma, a wise neighbor? Who are the wise old women who surround your life today?

DAY 2. *An Intelligent and Holy Presence*

"For in Wisdom there is a spirit, intelligent and holy; subtle, free-moving, and lucid; spotless and clear; working no harm and loving what is good; eager and unhindered; beneficent and kindly; steadfast and un-erring; all-powerful and all-surveying." (Wisdom 7:23–24, adapted from The New English Bible)

• Mark the phrases in the foregoing statement that have a particular significance to you. Write a song, draw an image, create a dance in response to them.

• Personalize the verses "For in me there is a spirit, intelligent and holy; subtle, free-moving . . ."

• Carry these personalized affirmations into your day. Consult them. Decide which quality is needed in any given situation and then call upon your inner wisdom to provide it.

DAY 3. *A Graceful and Fluid Presence*

"For Wisdom moves more easily than motion itself; she pervades and permeates all things. Like a fine mist she rises from Power, permeating all intelligent, pure, and delicate spirits." (Wisdom 7:24–25, adapted from The New English Bible)

• Mark the phrases of particular significance to you in this passage. Write a song, draw an image, create a dance in response to them.

• Are there areas of your life that feel awkward, stuck, unmovable? Reflect on how Wisdom's graceful, fluid presence might support you this day.

DAY 4. *A Bright and Radiant Presence*

"Wisdom is the brightness that streams from everlasting light, the flawless mirror of Active Power, and the image of Goodness. Wisdom is more radiant than the sun and surpasses every constellation. Compared to the light of day, she is found to excel; for day gives way to night, but against her no evil can prevail. She spans the world in power from end to end, and orders all things benignly." (Wisdom 7:26–30, adapted from The New English Bible)

• Mark the phrases of particular significance to you. Write a song, draw an image, create a dance in response to them.

• Are there areas of your life that feel shadowed, covered, fearful of exposure? Reflect on how Wisdom's bright and radiant presence might support you this day.

DAYS 5, 6, AND 7. *A Conversation with Wisdom*

Spend time each day improving your conscious contact with Wisdom.

• Imagine sitting in a clearing within the forest of your life. You are awaiting an image that represents your deeper wisdom.

• When she arrives, dialogue with her through writing or drawing. Tell her of a confusing situation, a troubling relationship, disturbing memories; of your need for guidance, perspective, clarity, courage, or serenity. If you know what you need, ask her for it. If you don't, trust her to know and tell you.

• Pause and listen. Allow her to speak to you. If an image forms, draw it. If a message wells up from the depths of you, write it down.

≈§ GATHERING THE GIFTS OF YOUR JOURNEY

Spend a week reviewing your writings and drawings from each chapter. As you journeyed through the truth of a woman's life, what gifts did you receive from each of the women you have met in this book? Write your response in the form of a prayer or letter to each of them. In what ways did each of them become the feminine face of God to you? Through what exercises, writings, meditations, and experiences did each of them touch your life?

DAY 1. *Eve, The Mother of All Living*

In her presence we reclaimed our original Mother and goodness.

DAY 2. *Lilith, The Rebellious First Woman*

In her presence we reclaimed our original power, courage, and independence.

DAY 3. *Mary, The Virgin Mother*

In her presence we reclaimed our original autonomy and sexuality.

DAY 4. *The Divine Girl-Child*

In her presence we reclaimed our original sacredness.

DAY 5. *The One Who Shed Her Blood*

In her presence we reclaimed our original connection to our bodies and to our sisters.

DAY 6. *Tamar and The One Who Was Cut into Pieces*

In Tamar's presence we reclaimed our original voice. In the presence of The One Who Was Cut into Pieces, we reclaim our original wholeness.

DAY 7. *The Wise Old Woman*

In her presence we reclaimed our original beauty and wisdom.

PART IV ❧

Having Had a Spiritual Awakening

CHAPTER FOURTEEN

Awakened to Healthy Connections

Woven into this chapter are conversations with several of the women whose stories you have read throughout this book. Women who have faithfully explored their religious past. Women who have courageously designed their own spirituality. Women whose lives have been transformed.

Initially these women were reluctant to enter our in-depth explorations. They feared that the level of awareness and anger triggered would make it impossible for them to relate to men again. Now, many months and years later, they acknowledge with gratitude that their journey home to themselves has enhanced not only the quality of their own lives but the quality of their relationships as well. Daily they are bringing the gifts of their awakening into their relationships with male friends, lovers, and colleagues. Celebrate with us the fruits of our healing and our hard work.

A Middle Space: Shared Independence

> Human love . . . consists in this:
> that two solitudes protect and border and greet each other.
> —Rainer Maria Rilke, *Letters to a Young Poet*

Inspired by Lilith, several of the women whose stories you will read chose abstinence from sexual and romantic relationships for months or years. In their abstinence they have deepened their contentment and satisfaction with their own lives. They have developed a firm commitment to their own true potential. Certain they will no longer abandon themselves, they are once again venturing into relationships with men.

Now, however, they're looking for potential partners at a slower pace. The old franticness based on an aching emptiness has dissolved. They are no longer blinded by their neediness. Their eyes are open. Their senses are engaged. They are eager and excited about exploring relationships with men. From a place of fullness they look, sense, and determine what works for them and what doesn't. Their choices are wiser today because they trust what they see and what they sense, they trust their own deeper wisdom. They are drawn to very different kinds of men these days: to men who take responsibility for their own emotional, spiritual, and practical needs; to men who have a wide circle of support and maintain it. In these new relationships women are finding it possible both to show up for their own lives while still being significantly involved with a man.

Others who are in long-term relationships are choosing to be alone at specific times—for an hour a day, for a weekend a month, or for a full season of their lives. They are taking the time to nurture and replenish their spirits. In their solitude they are reminded of their personal dreams and goals. When they reenter their relationships after an hour, a day, or a month, they are grounded again in their primary commitment to themselves. They are no longer willing to give men their total attention. They are discovering a middle space in which they are able to both honor their own needs, dreams, interests, and projects and yet remain significantly involved with their partners.

I encourage couples to choose the way of shared independence. To see themselves as two individuals, separate and unique in feeling, thinking, and experience, each bringing a rich and colorful solitude to their partnership. In choosing the way of shared independence, each becomes the protector, the guardian of the other's solitude. Our capacity to protect a lover's solitude means that we are able to accept aloneness. The aloneness of love is far more valuable than the togetherness of dominance and conformity. I spoke the following words at Wendy's wedding:

Wendy and Richard, encourage each other to spend time alone to nour-ish your solitude. "Two solitudes protect each other."

Times of aloneness are essential to the health of a relationship. Insti-tute times of personal retreat early in your partnership lest you become deluded that you cannot survive without the other, even for a weekend. Don't become imprisoned by your affection. Keep your solitude.

Guard the distance between you. Refuse to allow your lover to slip into your shadow. Lovingly support her to stay connected to the distinc-tiveness of who she is. Remind him of the beauty of his solitude. At times the distance may seem unbridgeable. In these moments, too, you must guard the distance. You must leave the distance alone. In the full-ness of time you will make your way back to each other. You will find a place to meet. You will touch again. A distance born of love holds within it exquisite gifts for your relationship.

Guard the differences between you. To love is to allow what is differ-ent to exist and to be itself. To love is to accept the otherness of the be-loved. To love is to refuse to violate the mystery of the beloved. Delight in each other's individuality, in the distinct shape of her thoughts, of his feelings, of each other's unique experience of life. Honor the boundaries that define your unique individuality. Say clear yeses and nos to each other. Yes, you will bump into each other's borders. Yes, you will hurt each other. Learn to say "Ouch." And learn to make amends for trespassing.

"Two solitudes border each other."

You met because your solitudes border each other's. You have shared interests and convictions. The healing paths you have chosen to travel are parallel. Along the fertile borders of your solitude where your lives meet, plant a garden together, a sacred garden. Sow the seeds of kindness and tenderness and truth there. Cultivate the garden of shared interests and concerns, of common challenges and treasured friends.

Wendy and Richard, human love consists in this: that two solitudes protect and border each other.

Sitting in a circle, the women share the gifts of their awakening:

> For a long period of time my wedding vows just wouldn't come. I was in conflict because the romantic, idealistic vows didn't fit for me. And then it became clear that my commitment to Richard needed to be prefaced by a clear commitment to myself. I wrote a vow to myself

even though it didn't seem like the ordinary way vows
were to be written and said.

As it turned out, my vows were absolutely in sync with
the flow of the ceremony. My wedding wasn't just an
event in which I was getting married to a man. It
was my life taking its next right step. So, bringing a
commitment to myself into the ceremony rounded out
the experience for me. The wedding became a part of
the circle of my life, rather than an isolated commitment
to a man. It felt complete.

—Wendy

My solitude is comfortable. I embrace my aloneness. The
life I have now will stay intact no matter what man or
men are in my life at any given time. I will always
keep spaces open for myself. A relationship, or many
relationships, are but a small part of the whole of me. I
choose the ways I want to fit men into my life schedule.
No longer does my life revolve around them. I turn
all my energy toward myself: my spirituality, my
women friends, my job, and my children. I am the center
of my universe from which all else flows. I no longer
service men with my life and energy.

—Erin

In the past I believed that being in a relationship with
a man was the only important function I had in the world.
I expected to receive my total identity from him. I
expected him to take care of me and make me a
visible person. I just didn't exist without a man, period.
Then, when I began my search for myself, I abstained from
being in a relationship for six years. During that time
I found my identity. So here I am at forty-eight, I
know who I am; I have a rich, full life, and along comes
this nice guy, but I don't know what to do with him. I'm
struggling with where and how to fit him into my
life.

In the past I'd meet a man and in thirty seconds we
would be in a full blown relationship. In my current
relationship, I am staying awake. I feel my fear, my

anxiety, my concerns. I have needs, desires, and wants of
my own. I am no longer a blank slate to be filled in
by a man. I have filled in the contours of my own
life. Some things about our interactions work for me and
some things don't work. I'm telling my truth. This
relationship isn't happening in an instant. I'm showing
up for it, and that's probably very good news and it's
awkward as hell.

—Ferrel

In my women's group I was encouraged to create an
original life, one that worked for me without necessarily
including a man. I'd go home and sit in my bathtub
and think long and hard about that concept. It took
a while before I could even imagine implementing it. It
was such a new idea for me. Slowly I'm doing it, though.
I'm creating an original life. I've changed careers. I've
bought a condo. I've developed a spirituality that
satisfies me. I have lots of friends with whom I share
intimate moments. I have personal projects that I set time
aside for every day.

The old neurotic longing for a lover seems to be
gone. Last week a woman friend came over to visit after
a period of estrangement in our friendship. We talked about
what had happened between us. In our honesty we
shared a wonderful intimacy. While I was with her, I
realized that what I'm really longing for is closeness and
emotional intimacy, and that I'm no longer looking to men
exclusively to have those needs met.

I still keep a personal ad in the paper. It's very
interesting to date different men. Just recently I dated a
doctor who has a lot of nice qualities. On our last date,
though, we talked deeply and personally enough so
that I understood why I wasn't attracted to him. I let
him know that I wasn't going to continue to see him. I
don't have any interest in just killing time with somebody
just because he's a man. I have a life to live.

—Jean

The Birth of Tenderness: The Mother Loves Her Sons

> The Mother of All Living saw all that she had given birth to and it was very good.
>
> —"An Encounter with Eve"

The most surprising fruit of our healing has been the birth of tenderness toward men. Having embraced our own strength, we no longer need a knight in shining armor who is all powerful. We can now allow men to be human. They can be vulnerable and needy. As we have become more tender toward our own woundedness and aware of our own ineffective behaviors, our partners feel freer to bring their wounds into the relationship. They can be vulnerable. They can share their struggles, doubts, and fears without worrying about us falling apart or taking it personally.

Just as we have begun to witness our own lives with great compassion, we now offer that compassion to men. We are no longer enemies who use each other's vulnerabilities as a weapon. We become allies and partners in our mutual healing process.

Women are now entering new relationships with more compassion and less anger. Couples locked in the historic "battle between the sexes" become willing to find new ways of relating as partners, not enemies. Today, when a couple becomes aware of a problem in their relationship, they consider it a challenge to be worked out instead of an excuse to blame, shame, emotionally batter or leave each other. There is a new voice within the relationship that says, "This challenge will offer us gifts if we face into it. Together we have everything we need."

Of course the challenges we face now are of a very different quality than before we began our work together. The women in the circles you have joined throughout the book are no longer available for abusive relationships, in which life-threatening crises were the norm. They are no longer willing to use their precious life energy in managing crisis and conflict. Instead they choose graceful relationships that deepen in satisfaction and contentment. They choose men who are willing to develop the relationship skills necessary to dance gracefully through challenging moments.

The women whose stories you have read have experienced tremendous healing as they have awakened to the truth about themselves. However, their personal healing is only the beginning of the journey. The ultimate salvation of the world depends upon the coming together of the masculine and feminine. It depends upon developing a new kind of balance in which women and men are able to offer their combined strength, wisdom, and compassion in the service of humankind.

As each couple finds their way to a sacred meeting place beyond right and wrong, beyond blaming and shaming, beyond one-up and one-down, the world becomes a safer, saner place for all of us. I invite couples to personalize the following prayer-affirmation in ways appropriate for them, and to include it in their family discussions and meditations:

Our Commitment to Each Other

I respect the distance placed between us.
You are a unique reality. I will not confine you within my
      formulas and definitions.
You are an unfathomable mystery. I will not try to figure you out.
You are a free person. I will not seek to possess you.

Your journey is sacred. I will not judge or tamper with it.
I will guard and protect your solitude.
I will honor your boundaries.
I will greet you often in the sacred garden we plant together along
      the fertile borders of our solitude.

An Affirmation of Our Partnership

We are partners.
Together, we call upon the Deeper Wisdom,
   to help us find our way through each issue
     that will cause us frustration,
   to help us find a middle space
     between our inevitable differences,

to help us find a sacred meeting place beyond right or wrong.
Together, we trust the Deeper Wisdom to show us
a way in which we will both win,
a way that is comfortable for both of us,
a way that will bring us both greater healing and joy.
May our partnership flourish, one day at a time.

Sitting in a circle, the women share the gifts of their awakening:

As my own spirituality has deepened, I've become more
accepting of who I am. I've befriended the ebb and flow
of my own receptivity to a partner. I've acknowledged
my relationship foibles and ineffective behaviors. As
a result, I have a deeper acceptance of my partner, his ebb
and flow, and his ineffective behaviors. I know now that
there's a Deeper Wisdom at work in his life as well as
my own. I can't script his life so that it fits with my
script. I let go of his life.

I recite an affirmation at least once a week: "My partner
has the right to live his own life and to walk his own
path. He has the right to make his own mistakes. His
choices are good, as are my own." I don't want him to
interfere with the steps I take, and I have no right to
undermine the steps he takes. This shift in my
attitude has been a tremendous boon for our
relationship. It has changed our footing in a basic way.

—Colleen

I have found a sacred respectful place to meet men in
which we share, notice, breathe, and embrace each other.
They have been wounded as we have been. They are
on the path to healing as we are. I no longer feel
compelled to be their healer. I can support them to heal
themselves in the presence of other men. I also want to
be able to regard with compassion those men who are
severely wounded and act out in abusive behavior. I
will no longer choose them as lovers, but I do want to
find a place to hold them in prayer and in hope.

The men who are coming into my life reflect the
deepening of my self-awareness and self-love. As I

become more grounded in my own life, I find myself more comfortable with men. I want to be in their presence. I want to be challenged in my interactions with them. I want to be healed through our healthy exchanges. I find that men are very wise. I used to think that women were the only bearers of wisdom, but I'm discovering the unique wisdom and healing men offer me and the wider world.

—Erin

I used to need each lover to be everything to me. If he was totally together, then I'd be okay. He was the competent one who made up for my incompetency. This dynamic was played out with a man I almost married. He was a knight in shining armor, a charismatic leader, everything I thought a man should be. I latched on to him. He was the answer for me. But when his armor cracked, I ceased to love him in the same way because he didn't fit my perfect picture anymore. The end of that relationship was the most blessed event of my life. It forced me to finally acknowledge that everything I longed for and admired in that man was present in me.

The man I eventually married doesn't fit my pictures in any way. He falls apart regularly. He is human and vulnerable. Currently he is wrestling with tough family-of-origin issues. All of the old ways of being that he has known for forty-five years are disintegrating and he feels free to be emotionally vulnerable with me.

I'm not worried that my life will fall apart because his life is changing. He can go through a total breakdown and I will still continue to support him. It's been healing for my husband to be with a woman who allows him to be completely vulnerable and totally untogether, a woman who continues to affirm his beauty and worth.

We see our relationship as a container or vessel that can hold growth and change. So whatever happens within the vessel is okay. The vessel stays intact because we each author our own lives. My life is not dependent on what my partner decides to do. I am committed to my

own life *and* to our partnership. I no longer feel that
the man's needs and desires alone shape the
relationship, that his decisions are my decisions,
that his career moves determine mine.

—Rebekah

Relationships of Equality: We Expect Mutuality

A woman who echoes Ntozake Shange's dramatic statement,
"I found God in myself and I loved her fiercely," is saying,
"Female power is strong and creative." She is saying
that the divine principle, the saving and sustaining
power, is in herself, that she will no longer look to men
or male figures as saviors.

—Carol Christ, *Womanspirit Rising*

The power dynamics shift in a relationship when a woman takes her rightful place beside the man. She is no longer available for relationships that are based on a one-up, one-down mentality in which the man's interests take priority. She assumes mutuality. She speaks her mind and expects her partner to listen and acknowledge her thoughts, ideas, and concerns. She expresses her feelings and expects him to witness them without invalidating how she feels. She brings the fullness of her years, her experience, her power, and her wisdom into the relationship and expects her partner to allow his life to be touched, challenged, and changed by who she is.

In the wider world of male colleagues and friends, a similar metamorphosis is happening. The women feel equal to men without thinking about it. They are aware of the gifts of being a woman. They are aware of their capacity to integrate feelings with thoughts in a way that men aren't able to. They celebrate the fact that a woman's way of thinking through issues and speaking about them is different from a man's. No longer do they denigrate themselves. They celebrate being a woman and without shame bring the fullness of who they are into each interaction with friends, lovers, and colleagues. The old way of "one-up and one-down" is dissolving. Instead they are able to delight in the masculine because they've begun to delight in themselves.

In chapter 4, we explored the connection between our religious injuries and the ineffective behaviors we bring with us into adulthood. You were invited to personalize an inventory on the theme: "If God is male, then men are gods" inventory. Now, at this point in our work together, I invite you to update that inventory to reflect the transformation you have experienced. Add your own reflections to the ones below:

"If God is male, then men are gods."

• *The God of my understanding is a shameless woman who is full of herself, a courageous woman who has assumed her rightful place beside the man, and an intelligent woman who values her way of thinking and being in the world.*

"I defer to men in work situations."

• *I am an active participant in work situations. I celebrate the talents and skills I bring to the workplace.*
• *I work with men as partners. I am no longer intimidated by their presence and intelligence.*

"I back down in any argument with a man."

• *Arguments are no longer my style of communication. Arguments involve a winner and a loser. I engage in healthy interactions today. We each present our concerns or issues. Then our challenge is to discover a way in which we both win for the greater good of the relationship.*

"I get quiet in mixed groups, allowing men to dominate the discussion."

• *Today I enjoy the quality of my life, thoughts, and interests. I bring this enjoyment of myself into mixed groups. I expect to be heard with respect. I expect others to be enlarged in their perspective as a result of encountering me.*
• *In mixed groups I look into the eyes of women to acknowledge their presence; I listen to the stories and concerns of women; I ask women questions rather than deferring to the men in the group.*

"I diminish my life and quiet my intelligence so that male coworkers, lovers, and even professors won't be threatened by me."

• *Today I refuse to diminish my life so that others will feel better. I expect peer relationships in which we bring 100 percent of who we are to each exchange. We allow our lives to be enlarged by one another's gifts.*

"A relationship with a man is to be highly desired. He becomes a god. His needs are more important than my children's, my friend's, and my own."

• *I have a full life today that includes special friends, personal projects, and compelling interests. I do not have time to elevate a man to god status.*

"I set aside my own life in order to pursue men and then consider it my duty to meet all of their needs—sexual, emotional, and physical—just as my mother dedicated her life to my father's needs. He was the god of our family."

• *My own life is most important today. I expect men to take care of their own emotional and spiritual needs in the company of other men. I no longer service them. I expect them to bring fullness rather than emptiness to our relationship.*

• *I am drawn to men who have learned to take care of their own practical needs and aren't looking for a mother replacement. And I do not expect a man to be the primary caretaker of my needs. I take responsibility for my own life today. I am the primary caretaker of myself.*

"Men's interests are much more important than mine, and their conversations, careers, and decisions carry more weight than mine. I enlarge my life to learn and grow as a result of their interests. These gods have seldom shown an interest in an idea, a project, or a curiosity of mine. They are superior, and I am inferior. I have never had a healthy and mutual relationship with a man. I think it is impossible."

• *I now know it is possible to have healthy and mutual relationships with men. And this is not necessarily because the men of the world are changing. It is my vision of what is possible that has been transformed as I have come into a loving and respectful relationship with myself. I no longer hate myself. I no longer believe that I am inferior. I walk into any encounter with a man as a whole person expecting respect and mutual enhancement.*

Sitting in a circle, the women share the gifts of their awakening:

The only way I've been able to come into a mutually
satisfying and respectful relationship with men is
through developing a satisfying and respectful relationship
with myself. I have come home to myself, to my body,
and to the validity of my experience, strength, and
hope as a woman. As a result, I don't expect men to
give me an identity or a life. In every arena, I stand next
to men. I am no longer attached to them. Nor do I stand
in opposition to them which I needed to do for
awhile. Now I can be their friend and ally, and I can
allow them to be mine.

—Rebekah

The depth of mutuality I have come to cherish in my
relationships with women has become the measure of the
depth I look for in relationship to a man. I no longer
settle for a relationship that is not life-enhancing for
both of us. Why else would I want to be in a relationship
but to have my consciousness expanded, my limits
stretched, and my interests celebrated?

I want to be with someone who is willing to grow
and expand together with me. One who is willing to be
in a peer relationship. One who is willing to acknowledge
the ways I affect him. In the past I would have
considered such a desire ludicrous. It was the man
who was the teacher and the inspirer. I made no
contribution except as a sexual object. Now that I have
embraced myself, my feminine intelligence, wisdom,
and clarity, I bring that fullness to every relationship.
I expect to be valued and honored for who I am and
what I bring.

—Ferrel

I entered into my marriage feeling that I wasn't as smart
as my partner, and that my education wasn't as
comprehensive as his. I felt one-down all the time. It
was horrible to feel that if I didn't act really smart in
any given conversation, I was going to lose big-time, that
I was going to feel ashamed and stupid.

As my healing deepened and I began to acknowledge

the intelligence of women, I claimed intellectual equality in my relationship. My intelligence is no longer constricted as a result of feeling one-down. I have greater access to it. I readily share my feminine wisdom and insight with my partner. This change has been a source of tremendous relief and comfort for me.

Now when I don't know something or haven't read a book that's being discussed, I accept that I don't have to know everything. Such an admission is an acknowledgment of my limits, not of my inferiority. I don't for a minute think I'm not as bright as my partner or that he is better read than I am. And on a deeper level those measurements or comparisons don't really matter anymore because I have claimed what is truly important to me.

—Colleen

Loving Our Bodies: In the Presence of Men

The masculine and feminine elements, exactly equal and balancing each other, are as essential to the maintenance of the equilibrium of the universe as positive and negative electricity, the centripetal and centrifugal forces, the laws of attraction which bind together all we know of this planet whereon we dwell and of the system in which we revolve.

—Elizabeth Cady Stanton, *The Woman's Bible*

In circles of women we are healing the shame that accompanied our bodies, our natural processes, and our aging. Today we refuse to spend our precious life energy hiding our bodies, disguising the signs of aging, and keeping the realities of our lives secret. Rather we celebrate the accumulation of our years and wisdom, and the changes in our bodies and lives. We choose relationships with women and men who have the depth and the courage to embrace all of who we are now and who we will become in the next decades of our lives. We choose as partners men who have acknowledged their own issues around women's bodies, natural processes, and aging. Men who are not interested in women as ornaments. Men who attract powerful women as partners.

In circles of women we have come home to our own sexuality. Inspired by Mary, we have rediscovered the wonders of our own bodies, their rich erotic potential, and their capacity for sensual delight. We have taken responsibility for our own sexual pleasure and satisfaction, developing self-pleasuring rituals that continue even while we are in a sexual relationship. Through these rituals we grow more in love with our bodies, we discover what arouses us, we develop an understanding of our sexual wounds and armoring, and we deepen in satisfaction and contentment with ourselves. We have come to believe that a personal sex life is an essential prerequisite to sharing healthy sexual intimacy with a partner.

As a result of our sexual healing we expect mutuality in our sexual relationships. No longer is sexuality defined according to the needs and desires of men. We are in touch with our own needs and desires. We bring them with us to our shared bed and we express them. No longer does the man's pleasure take priority. We expect pleasure and satisfaction from our sexually intimate relationships. We are no longer merely spectators who expect men to initiate. We are active participants in each sexual encounter.

Without shame we bring a woman-affirming understanding of sexuality to our partnerships. This understanding moves us beyond the performance orientation of the culture. It includes the expression of the full range of feelings that accompany every intimate relationship, feelings of warmth and caring, of anger and passion, of tenderness and support. We have come to believe that sexuality nourishes the ongoing emotional commitment between partners. That it unfolds gracefully in an emotional environment in which lovers are together because they enjoy each other's company.

I encourage couples to allow the woman's process-oriented understanding of sexuality to deflate the performance pressure that plagues most relationships. As couples let go of orgasm and ejaculation as the primary focus of their sexual interactions, they are free to pleasure each other without a scripted outcome. There is no goal to be reached. No right way to do it. They focus on the sensation of pleasure without a destination in mind. They are free to enjoy each other's touch. Touch becomes an end in and of itself; it is not on the way to something.

They enjoy the warmth and closeness of their connection as it unfolds spontaneously.

Wendy and Richard imagine their bed as a sacred playground that can hold anything. It can hold their woundedness, their attempts at new ways of being sexual, and the rich potential of their healing. It holds every feeling, sensation, memory, fear, and insecurity. Their bed has become a sacred space where they meet to heal the wounds they bring with them to their sexual relationship and to deepen their intimacy as a couple.

I concluded my reflections at Wendy and Richard's wedding with the words below. They were inspired by the women in our circles who have challenged the destination-oriented sexuality of their partners and who are bringing a new vision of sexuality into their relationships.

"Two solitudes greet each other."

To greet is to discover the wonder of simple contacts. Touch Richard as he cooks dinner. Look into Wendy's eyes as she speaks of her day. Greet each other with your eyes and with your bodies. Greet each other with your touch. Greet each other with words and with no words. Greet each other with tenderness, passion, and warmth.

Establish a ritual of greeting early in your relationship lest the pressures of the world crowd out the pure delight of your love. Greet each morning before you rise. Greet at midday to offer support. Greet as you lie in bed in the evening to share with each other the trouble and beauty that each day brings.

Create a sacred time an hour a day, a weekend a month, a week a year to be alone together, to respond to each other in a natural, unpressured, and unscheduled way. Meet in the garden at the fertile border of your solitudes. Come with no expectations. Nothing has to happen. Come with no agenda except to be present in each other's company. Come to look and to listen, guided by serendipity. Come to share the riches of your solitude.

Wendy and Richard, "human love consists in this: that two solitudes protect and border and greet each other."

Sitting in a circle, the women share the gifts of their awakening:

> My husband loves all of who I am, including my body.
> He will put his hands on parts of my body that I find
> it difficult to honor—like my stomach when it gets really

full around my period—and he'll say, "I love this part of you." He supports me to love the parts of myself I have labeled unacceptable.

It's very healing to have such loving affirmations come from the man in my life. I had always assumed that a man could never love me as I aged. Now I know I did not love myself. Through the support of women I have begun to honor who I am. As a result I have drawn into my life a man whose richness and depth allows him to love my body without effort.

—Rebekah

In the past I had no sense of sex as a sacred act. Sex was a compulsion rooted in the incest of my childhood. I was out of my body. I was not available for sexual intimacy. There is a healthy kind of sexual intimacy that I hope to find in my new relationship.

I'm an active participant in our sexual exchanges. I find myself initiating those things that feel good and pleasurable to me. I watch this change in my behavior and I'm astounded because in the incestuous relationship with my father it was absolutely critical that I be completely passive. This passivity carried over into all intimate relationships with men. I always followed their lead. Now I find myself doing things, asking for things, taking the lead. Where did this assertiveness come from? It comes from within me. My life is safe enough for it to emerge. My sexual assertiveness is very empowering.

—Ferrel

I came into the women's circle guarded and ashamed that my partner and I had stopped having sex. We didn't have any desire for it. I felt sexually inadequate. I felt that there was something ugly and distasteful about sex and about being aroused. So I couldn't let myself go into it. I pulled back and maintained a sanitized, pretty, perfect image of myself. I maintained this facade even though I knew I was missing something wonderful and essential.

In the course of the last three years I have acknowledged aloud the pain of being cut off from my body and my sexuality. In the women's circle I affirmed that my body is an essential part of my spirituality and that to accept it was my first step toward healing. It has been such a wonderful gift to name the parts of my body openly and to begin to trust my body's feelings, sensations, and needs.

A Sensual Goddess emerged through our work together. She is a woman who possesses her sexuality. She is loud and spontaneous and earthy. She isn't concerned with her outside appearance. Her only concern is to be in harmony with the deep rhythms of the earth and of her own sexuality. The Sensual Goddess has become a very powerful image. She gives me permission to be earthy and wild and sexual with my partner.

—Colleen

A Circle of Support: No More Knight in Shining Armor

Trust cannot be given carelessly, for there is much woundedness about . . . And yet there are people of honor and places of refuge. One might well ask, what is the alternative to trust? Have we not had isolation enough? Recognizing our longing for closeness, our need for nearness, is not weakness but wisdom.

—Marilyn Sewell, *Cries of the Spirit*

As the face of God changes in our experience, we spend more time in the company of women and less time swirling around men. Women are no longer just fillers in between our relationships. They are the ground of our support. They have become the feminine face of God to us. In circles of women we have searched for and found a God who looks like us. In circles of women we have come to love and accept ourselves. In circles of women we share our common experience, strength, and hope as we venture into the uncharted territory of healthy relationships with men.

We have come to believe that no one person can meet all our needs. Our circle of support has widened. As a result we don't bring unrealistic expectations to our relationships with men. Men no longer determine whether or not our needs and emotions are real, valid, or important. Today we make that determination ourselves. We don't ask men to define and evaluate our emotional health anymore. We take responsibility for our own emotional needs by discerning what it is we really need and who is the appropriate person to fill that need.

Men are no longer the only ones to whom we turn to have our needs met. We find ourselves reaching out to women more often than we do to men. Many of our emotional, spiritual, and intimacy needs are met in women's circles. Women affirm that our needs are valid. They remind us that experiencing a full range of feeling in any given day is natural and healthy. They support our ongoing spiritual journey. They offer us a quality of understanding and acknowledgment that is only possible from another woman. However, there are also times when we ask our partners to meet a need. The difference is that now we're very clear in asking for what we want from them. We no longer expect a partner to read our mind. We take responsibility for expressing our needs clearly.

This widening of support has deflated men's presence in our lives. The shift has been both enlivening and confusing. Some of us can't figure out how to fit men into our lives now that we aren't as dependent on them. Now that we have women's support. Now that we have experienced a quality of closeness longed for yet rarely experienced with men. From this new place we wonder what we want and need from them. We only have tentative answers at this point.

A relationship with a man challenges us in distinct ways. It stretches us beyond what's comfortable and dares us to reach toward wholeness. Their view of the world invites us to be clear about our own. Their priorities extend into the wider world and challenge us to evaluate our overinvolvement with them at the expense of our own priorities and concerns. Men trigger a whole set of feelings that we don't have access to except in an intimate relationship. This allows us to become acquainted with a wider range of emotions, offering us precious information about ourselves and our responses to them. A relationship with a man offers us an opportunity to practice the healthy behaviors we have learned in the company of women.

Sitting in a circle the women share the gifts of their awakening:

> Men are not as big in my life as they used to be. They don't consume me anymore. They don't diminish the fullness of my life as a woman. In the past I had inappropriate expectations. I placed too much pressure on men to fulfill my needs. I now fill myself with the many gifts of power, love, and wisdom I have discovered within me and with the many stories of strength, hope, pain, and challenge that the women in my life bring to me in our honest interactions.
>
> From this place of homecoming to myself and to the circle of women, I am refreshed and made new. I am filled with a satisfaction so great that nothing is missing or lacking. There is no void. In the company of women I have been given back my body, my life choices, my work, my children, and my power. I bring a well-rounded, full-circled woman who celebrates herself, her life, her sisters, and her children to every interaction with a man.
>
> —Erin

> In the past all of my intimate relationships with men were to be kept secret and hidden. A relationship was shameful, and I couldn't even imagine mainstreaming it into my ordinary life. As a result of the healing I've experienced in the community of women, I have a new vision of being in a relationship, and at the same time being with other people.
>
> My longing for connection grows out of my connectedness to myself as a woman as well as to other women. These connections have grounded me and have allowed me to feel connected to the rest of the human race. I view being in a relationship with a man as an expansion of that connectedness. For someone who had lived such an isolated life, this is an incredible

shift. It goes so deep it feels as if it's reached the
molecular level.

—Ferrel

My partner is very spiritual. The paths we have chosen
are different yet compatible. I have embraced a woman-
affirming spirituality and he has found a spiritual
home within Zen Buddhism. His daily meditation
practice is an important part of his life and occasionally
I've joined him in meditation. In past relationships I felt
it was absolutely necessary to do anything the man
considered important in order to prove my love and
devotion and to guarantee the survival of the relationship.
Today I honor the shape of my own spirituality. I learn
from him. He learns from me. I am no longer willing
to abandon myself, to twist any part of my life out
of shape to please a man.

—Emily

As my connections with women have grown, my
relationship with my partner has receded some in my
consciousness. It occupies a smaller place in my life.
My partner no longer dominates my life, thoughts,
and feelings. He has diminished in significance and in
psychological size. I am clearer. I have my own life. I can
do things completely apart from him. I make my own
decisions. I know what I think and feel. My relationship
has changed so much. It's a new and different organism.

In the past I expected him to take care of my
feelings and to always be present for me. I don't have
these expectations anymore. He's just one thread in a big
tapestry of support that surrounds my life. There are many
times when I feel anxious or upset, or when I need
to think an issue through with someone, and I don't
go to him. I'm happy to go to others. My life is full of
people with whom I share myself, my problems, and my
celebrations.

—Colleen

CHAPTER FIFTEEN 🦢

Awakened to a Woman-Affirming Spirituality

Psychological theory, elaborate theologies, and the rhetoric of recovery were not able to reach to the depths of our woundedness as women. Alone they were powerless to heal the wounds and to untangle the patterns of ineffective behavior that had controlled us for years. We hoped and prayed, made resolutions, and tried the advice of one expert after another, but all these efforts to change brought only momentary relief.

In the fullness of time we became entirely ready to plunge into the woundedness of our lives. There we discovered the God of our understanding, a God in our image and likeness. This journey toward a self-defined spirituality involved exorcising the old names and images and embracing of woman-affirming alternatives.

As we immersed ourselves within these new images, we awakened to the spiritual resources that remained dormant within us. This spiritual awakening reached beyond words to the deep wounds of our self-hatred. No longer excluded from the divine, we now celebrate our sacredness. No longer believing that we are inferior, we celebrate our goodness, power, and courage. No longer needing others to validate, legitimize, and save us, we celebrate the richness of our own inner resources.

Awakened to the Power of Language

> We must choose our own kneeling places and not have thrust upon us an agenda foreign to our spirits.
> —Marilyn Sewell, *Cries of the Spirit*

In circles of women, we have tapped into the memories of our religious past. We have sorted through the names and images of God that pursue us into adulthood. We have been offered woman-affirming alternatives to the exclusively male language of religion. Surrounded by women from every age and inspired by their courage, we have ventured into uncharted waters to name and imagine the God of our understanding. In this act we have taken responsibility for our lives, accepted our own empowerment, and stepped into our rightful and legitimate place *beside* men. The following insights inform our woman-affirming spirituality:

1. We have come to believe that the ultimate truth, wisdom, and mystery of the Universe is far deeper, higher, wider, and richer than any name or image we use to refer to it. We know now that every name and image has its limitations and must be held loosely. Mystery cannot be confined within a language.

2. We have come to believe that elevating only one image of the divine is idolatry. It limits the vast potential of our imaginations. We have looked squarely at the wounding of women as a result of the dominance of male God language. As we have begun to glimpse a God who looks like us, our healing has deepened. We are now free to choose which aspects of the God of our religious past we will weave into our unfolding spirituality. God the father has become one among many potentially healing images.

3. We have come to believe that the Universal Spirit reaches out to us in our individuality, enters into our personal histories, and fleshes out its presence in terms of our need. As we have opened ourselves to the Universal Spirit resident within our lives, new images have emerged. The face of God has changed. We honor the changing face of God in our lives.

4. We have come to believe there are many possible options in referring to the divine. Each of us is free to share the God of our understanding in our own language and imagery. In our self-help meetings and women's support circles, there may be a feminist who says "Goddess," a fundamentalist who speaks of "God the father," a Buddhist who shares her sense of the connectedness of all things. Because our own experience is true for us and we trust it, we are not threatened by hearing someone else's truth.

• Some of us have moved beyond the limitations of assigning God a gender. We refer to God in nonpersonal terms, such as *Deeper Wisdom, Higher Power, Wise Energy, Source of Life, Community of Support, Sacred Breath.* For us, the qualities of a personal relationship with the divine are not necessary.

• Some of us choose to retain the personal quality of God language while finding a way to eliminate gender. We use terms such as *Loving Wise One; Creator, Sustainer, and Redeemer; Welcoming Friend; Compassionate One; Nurturing One; Counselor; Seeker of the Lost; Helper.*

• Some of us choose to use exclusively female images. This choice challenges the idols of a religion that prefers men. We use such names as *Goddess, Woman God, Sister God, Sophia, A God with Breasts Like Mine,* and *Mother of All Living.* These names affirm our sacredness, our power, our bodies, and our will.

• Some of us choose to use all genders in referring to God. This choice recognizes that the masculine or feminine, and the singular, alone do not encompass a broad enough spectrum of qualities to support wholeness. Using names such as *Mother-Father God,* we pray for the coming together of women and men in healing and peace.

5. We have come to believe that the male God has not always been faithful to women. That it is a miracle of trust that women have remained within traditional religion at all. We offer our suspicion as a gift to all religious institutions. We tell our stories. We shout out our questions. We release our anger. We give voice to the One whose face has been obscured and whose ways have been distorted. As did the prophets of old, we call the religious community to confront its idolatry of God the father. We call on religion to remember its original lessons.

Awakened to the Feminine Face of God

> There can be no doubt that in the very earliest ages of human history the magical force and wonder of the female was no less a marvel than the universe itself; and this gave a woman a prodigious power, which it has been one of the chief concerns of the masculine part of the population to break, control, and employ to its own ends.
> —Joseph Campbell, *The Masks of God*

We have reclaimed the story that reaches back before the Hebrew and Christian Scriptures were written—before "the beginning" defined by men. We have reclaimed our woman history from the very beginning! We have remembered the time when the divine was imagined as a woman who looks, bleeds, ages, and experiences life as we do.

Inspired by Eve, we reawakened ancient beliefs in a Great Mother who gave birth to the cosmos and its inhabitants, both human and divine. All gestated within her body and emerged in the fullness of time. All that she gave birth to was good. It was very good. We recalled ancient times when women were honored for their intimate involvement in the origins of life. We learned of ancient women who did not apologize for their fertile wombs, pregnant bellies, and full breasts. Women who celebrated themselves as the embodiment of the Great Mother.

Inspired by Lilith, we reawakened ancient beliefs in a strong and capable Goddess who acted on her own behalf and the behalf of all women. We reclaimed those ancient ways that taught women to refuse submission and subordination and that applauded women for their assertiveness. We recalled ancient times when women were honored for their capacity both to nurture and to accomplish great things. We learned of ancient women who did not apologize for their power, courage, and independence.

Inspired by Mary, we reclaimed the ancient ways that celebrated the Goddess and her savior son, her representative on earth who ruled from her lap. We recalled ancient times when virgin meant a woman who was "one in herself," owned by no man, author of her own life, creator of her own destiny. We learned of ancient women who did not apologize for their sexuality and who refused to surrender except to the natural rhythms of life.

Inspired by The Divine Girl-Child, we learned of ancient times when it was from the mother, the giver of life, that the line of the generations was traced. A time when children of the mother were both legitimate and respectable and were given her name and social status. We learned of ancient women who did not apologize for their girl-children. Women who celebrated the birth of their daughters, who believed in the goodness of their daughters, who nurtured the wisdom of their daughters, and who cultivated the power of their daughters.

Inspired by The One Who Shed Her Blood, we reawakened ancient beliefs that celebrated the Great Mother, whose "moon blood" thickened within her and then spilled from her to create all that is. We read of ancient ways that held a woman's blood to be magic, flowing in harmony with the moon. We recalled ancient times when the color of royalty was the dark-red wine color of our beautiful blood. We learned of ancient women who did not apologize for their bleeding time.

Inspired by Tamar and The One Who Was Cut into Pieces, we reclaimed those ancient beliefs in a strong Goddess, who did not stand by patiently as those created in her image were raped, battered, molested through incest, and robbed of their self-love and self-trust. We recalled the ancient times when reverence for the Goddess gave women status, a voice, and fair treatment. We read of ancient ways and laws stating that if a man raped a woman, he was to be put to death. We learned of ancient women who did not apologize for their bodies or their voices.

Inspired by The Wise Old Woman, we learned of ancient beliefs in the Crone Goddess, who changes as we do, who represents old age, winter, and the waning of the moon. We recalled ancient societies that celebrated the accumulation of a woman's years and that respected the menopausal retaining of a woman's wise blood. We read of ancient ways in which only postmenopausal woman could preside at rituals and sacred rites. We learned of ancient women who did not apologize for the fullness of their years and their wisdom.

As we have extricated the stories of Eve, Lilith, Mary, The Divine Girl-Child, The One Who Shed Her Blood, Tamar, The One Who Was Cut into Pieces, and The Wise Old Woman from the all-encompassing story of the male God, we have received the courage to reclaim our own stories. We have gathered more of the fragments, beginning with our birth, traveling through the creation myths and symbols that shaped us, venturing into our body's unfolding cycles and rhythms, exploring our vulnerability to rape and incest, and reclaiming the wisdom of our old age.

Along the way we confronted the taboos found in every religious tradition that set aside our bodies and processes as dangerous and immoral. We have moved beyond these taboos to reclaim the sacredness of our bodies, to explore woman-affirming images, and to creatively reinvent old myths and rituals that once disempowered us.

No longer imprisoned within men's interpretations, speaking now in their own voices, these women of old have become healing images of the divine to us. In their presence we have descended into the wealth of our own lives. Our inner spaces, once cluttered with shame and guilt, have been cleared out and reclaimed as our own. We have become reacquainted with our goodness. We accept all of ourselves as worthy. We accept our vitality, expressiveness, spirit, power, courage, and independence. We accept our bodies, our sexuality, our natural processes, and our wounds. Embracing the whole of ourselves, we move forward as both powerful and vulnerable.

The Perspectives of a Woman-Affirming Spirituality

> Spirituality is expressed in everything we do. It is a style, unique to itself, that catches up all our attitudes: in communal and personal prayer, in behavior, bodily expressions, life choices, in what we support and affirm and what we protest and deny.
> —Anne Carr, *Women's Spirituality*

Inspired by a time that once was, we have rejected a shame-based religion that was shaped by men, for men, and based on men's experience. We have exorcised the disempowering remnants of religion that were deposited within our bodies, minds, and lives through its myths, rituals, and instruction, and by family and societal beliefs and customs. We have embraced a woman-affirming spirituality that recognizes the complexity of the cultural and religious factors that have influenced the unfolding of a woman's life. We allow the perspectives of a woman-affirming spirituality to enhance the quality of our lives; to appraise the merit of religious teachings, therapeutic models, and recovery principles; and to evaluate the mutuality of our relationships to friends and lovers, teachers and therapists, and religious leaders.

With Eve, we reject the dominance of a creation myth that portrays women as the instigators of evil and that excludes the Mother from the creation of the world. We reject the shame-based messages of family, religion, and society that stressed our wrongs, our defects, and our insufficiencies. We embrace a woman-affirming spirituality that celebrates the Mother's intimate involvement in the origins of life and reminds us of our original goodness.

With Lilith, we reject the dominance of religious myths that exiled strong women and portrayed us as powerless victims. We reject the shame-based messages of family, religion, and society that emphasized our inability to function independently in our own lives. We embrace a woman-affirming spirituality that reminds us of our original power, courage, and independence.

With Mary, we reject the dominance of religious myths and theologies that exiled willful and sexually autonomous women. We reject the shame-based messages of family, religion, and society that required the surrender of our bodies and wills to the dictates of others. We embrace a woman-affirming spirituality that reminds us of our original autonomy, willfulness, and erotic potential.

With The Divine Girl-Child, we reject the dominance of religious myths and rituals that excluded the girl-child from the divine. We reject the shame-based messages of family, religion, and society that convinced us of our inferiority. We embrace a woman-affirming spirituality that reminds us of our original divinity.

With The One Who Shed Her Blood, we reject the dominance of religious taboos that denigrate a woman's body and her natural processes. We reject the shame-based messages of family, religion, and society that alienated us from the rich natural resources that are found within our own body's cycles and rhythms. We embrace a woman-affirming spirituality that reminds us of the original sacredness of our bodies and of our original connectedness to all women past, present, and future.

With Tamar, we reject the dominance of religious myths, stories, and theologies that marginalize women's experience and ignore women's stories. We reject the shame-based message of family, religion, and society that taught us to be quiet, to mistrust our truth, and to blame ourselves for anything that happens to us. We embrace a woman-affirming spirituality that reminds us of our original expressiveness, that invites our stories out of the silence, and that supports us in our refusal to carry the sins of others within our bodies and lives.

With The One Who Was Cut into Pieces, we reject the dominance of religious myths, stories, and theologies that assault a woman's wholeness. We reject the shame-based messages of family, religion, and society that cut us into pieces labeled Madonna/Whore; Seductress/Wife; Mother/Working Woman; Nurturer/Achiever. We embrace a woman-affirming spirituality that reminds us of our original wholeness and that encourages us to reclaim every experience of our lives, every precious part of our bodies, every amazing inner resource available to us as Children of Life.

With The Wise Old Woman, we reject the dominance of religious myths, stories, and rituals that excluded the experience and wisdom of old women. We reject the shame-based messages of family, religion, and society that deposited within us a dread of growing old. We embrace a woman-affirming spirituality that reminds us of our original wisdom and that encourages us to fill up the years of our lives without shame.

Epilogue

Imagine a Woman

Now that we have reviewed our work up to this point, I invite you to join us in a meditation, "Imagine a Woman." It matters what you believe about yourself.

Imagine a woman who believes it is right and good she is woman,
A woman who honors her experience and tells her stories,
Who refuses to carry the sins of others within her body and life.

Imagine a woman who believes she is good,
A woman who trusts and respects herself,
Who listens to her own needs and desires
     and then meets them with tenderness and grace.

Imagine a woman who believes she belongs in the world,
A woman who celebrates her own life,
Who is glad to be alive.

Imagine a woman who has acknowledged
   the past's influence on the present,
A woman who has walked through her past,
Who has healed into the present.

Imagine a woman in love with her own body,
A woman who believes her body is enough, just as it is,
Who celebrates her body as a trustworthy companion
     and its rhythms and cycles as an exquisite resource.

Imagine a woman who embraces her sexuality as her own,
A woman who delights in pleasuring herself,
Who experiences all of her erotic feelings and sensations
    without shame or guilt.

Imagine a woman who honors the face of the Goddess
    in her own changing face,
A woman who celebrates the accumulation of her years
    and her wisdom.
Who refuses to use her precious life energy to
    disguise the changes in her body and life.

Imagine a woman who authors her own life,
A woman who exerts, initiates, and moves on her own behalf,
Who refuses to surrender except to her truest self
    and to her wisest voice.

Imagine a woman who names her own gods,
A woman who imagines the divine in her own image and likeness,
Who designs her own spirituality
    and allows it to inform her daily life.

Imagine a woman who values the women in her life,
A woman who sits in circles of women,
Who is reminded of the truth about herself when she forgets.

Imagine a shameless woman who is full of herself.
A powerful woman who has awakened to the truth about herself.
A courageous woman who has assumed her rightful place beside men.
A wise woman whose beliefs about herself are reflected
        in her relationships.

Imagine yourself as this woman as you gather the gifts of your awakening: a freed imagination, a God born of your own experience as
woman, the unfolding images of your spiritual center; a suspicion of the
customary, a courageous rebellion, a commitment to shape your own
life and spirituality; the celebration of your body and natural processes,
the accumulation of your years, the rich resources of wisdom within
you; an affirmation of your goodness, an acknowledgment of your
wounds, an experience of healing into the present.

Gather these gifts and offer them to your mothers, daughters, granddaughters, and nieces. To your fathers, sons, grandsons, and nephews.

Offer them to your lovers and friends. To a world out of balance, estranged from wisdom, and addicted to power.

The feminine has been exiled. She groans through our wounded bodies, our severed relationships, and the broken earth. We call upon her to return and teach us new ways of living and being, new ways of relating to each other. We invite her out of exile as we reclaim our original goodness, power, courage, independence, sexuality, divinity, wholeness, and wisdom. It is through us that she is present in the world.

A Prayer for Our Daughters and Sons

We have taken a careful look at our religious past to bring gifts of awareness, liberation, and truth to our children in the present. Daily we pray for an expanding of the images of the divine and a widening of the inclusiveness of language for the sake of the girls and boys attending religious services this Sabbath, for the sake of the young women and men attending self-help groups this week. May they travel a less turbulent path toward self-love, self-trust, and the creation of healthy relationships with themselves and others. And daily we offer a special prayer for our daughters:

> May they discover the divine within them and love her fiercely. May they see her face as they look into the mirror. Bless her body as they shower and bathe. Celebrate her life in the telling of their stories.

> May they face her without shrinking. She is lovely to behold. May they face her without cringing. She is not their judge. May they face her without drawing away. She offers them the abundance of life.

> May they turn toward her with assurance and determination. She will inspire them to act on their own behalf in their personal lives and to serve with compassion in the world.

Notes 🙖

INTRODUCTION   Beginning Our Journey

1. See the following resources for an in-depth discussion of the inner child and the nondominant handwriting technique:
- Lucia Capacchione, *Recovery of Your Inner Child* (New York: Simon and Schuster, 1991).
- Lucia Capacchione, *The Power of Your Other Hand* (Hollywood: New Castle Publishing Co., Inc., 1988).

CHAPTER 1   Religion's Far-Reaching Effects

1. See Merlin Stone, *When God Was a Woman* (New York: Harcourt Brace Jovanovich, 1976), p. 239.
2. Marianne Williamson, *A Return to Love* (New York: HarperCollins, 1992), p. 95.
3. Ibid., p. 183.
4. The story was adapted from Harry Chapin, "Flowers Are Red," recorded on *Legends of the Lost and Found* (Elektra Records, 1979). The gender of the child has been changed from "he" to "she."

CHAPTER 3   The God of Our Childhood Understanding

1. Robert Coles, *The Spiritual Life of Children* (Boston: Houghton Mifflin Company, 1990), p. 40.
2. *A Catechism of Christian Doctrine,* (New Jersey: St. Anthony's Guild Press, 1961), pp. 17–18. The emphasis is mine.

3. Rosemary Radford Reuther, *Sexism and God-Talk* (Boston: Beacon Press, 1983), pp. 125–126.

CHAPTER 4   Our Wounds and Ineffective Behavior: *Exclusion, Inferiority, and Dependency*

1. *Baptist Hymnal,* "Rise Up, O Men of God" (Nashville: Convention Press, 1956), p. 455.

2. Gregory Baum, *Man Becoming* (New York: Herder and Herder, 1970), p. 195. The emphasis is mine.

3. *Sabbath Prayers* (New York: Bloch Publishing Company, Inc., 1927), p. 38.

4. "Who Is God?," *Life*, December 1990, pp. 47–48.

CHAPTER 5   Our Healing: *The Changing Face of God*

1. See Charlene Spretnak, *Lost Goddesses of Early Greece* (Boston: Beacon Press, 1979), p. 19; Stone, *When God Was a Woman*, pp. 9–10.

2. *The Interpreter's Dictionary of the Bible,* vol. 3 (New York: Abingdon Press, 1962), p. 975: "Queen of Heaven—The object of worship, particularly by women, in Judah in the time of Jeremiah; cakes possibly shaped as figurines were offered to her with libations."

3. F. M. Cross, *Canaanite Myth and Hebrew Epic* (Cambridge, Mass.: Harvard University Press, 1973), pp. 54–56.

4. Alcoholics Anonymous, *The Big Book* (New York: Alcoholics Anonymous World Services, Inc., 1987).

5. *Al-Anon's Twelve Steps and Twelve Traditions* (New York: Al-Anon's Family Group Headquarters, Inc., 1989).

6. *Alcoholics Anonymous Comes of Age,* (New York: Alcoholics Anonymous World Services, Inc., 1967), p. 63.

CHAPTER 6   Fragments of the Forgotten

1. Elizabeth Schussler Fiorenza, "Interpreting Patriarchal Traditions," in Letty M. Russell, ed., *The Liberating Word* (Philadelphia: Westminster Press, 1976), pp. 41, 55.

2. Resources for further exploration of a time when God was worshiped as woman:

- Elinor W. Gadon, *The Once and Future Goddess* (San Francisco: Harper and Row, 1989).
- Marija Gimbutas, *The Civilization of the Goddess* (San Francisco: Harper and Row, 1991).
- Nor Hall, *The Moon and The Virgin* (New York: Harper and Row, 1980).
- Raphael Patai, *The Hebrew Goddess* (Detroit: Wayne State University Press, 1978).
- Merlin Stone, *When God Was a Woman* (New York: Harcourt, Brace, Jovanovich, 1976).
- Barbara G. Walker, *The Crone: Woman of Age, Wisdom, and Power* (San Francisco: Harper, 1985).

3. See Jane Sprague Zones, ed., *Taking the Fruit* (San Diego: The Woman's Institute for Continuing Jewish Education, 1981).

CHAPTER 7   Eve: *The Mother of All Living*

1. Tertullian, "On the Apparel of Women," in *The Ante-Nicene Fathers*, vol. 4 (Buffalo: The Christian Literature Publishing Company), p. 14.

2. Herbert Haag, *Is Original Sin in Scripture?* (New York: Sheed and Ward, 1969), p. 19.

3. Louis Ginzberg, *The Legends of the Jews*, vol. 3 (Philadelphia: Jewish Publication Society of America, 1909), I:67: "Woman covers her hair in token for having brought sin into the world; she tries to hide her shame; and women precede men in a funeral cortege, because it was woman who brought sin into the world."

4. Quoted in Linda Mercadante, *Gender, Doctrine and God* (Nashville: Abingdon, 1990), p. 13.

5. See M. Stone, *When God Was a Woman*, pp. 219–223; John A. Phillips, *Eve: The History of an Idea* (San Francisco: Harper and Row, 1984), p. 3ff.

6. Rosemary Radford Reuther, *WomanGuides* (Boston: Beacon Press, 1985), pp. 38, 62; Marija Gimbutas, *The Civilization of the Goddess* (San Francisco: Harper and Row, 1991), p. 223.

7. B. G. Walker, *The Woman's Encyclopedia of Myths and Secrets*, p. 685.

8. Erich Neumann, *The Great Mother* (Princeton, N.J.: Princeton University Press, 1974), pp. 135–136; Elaine Pagels, *The Gnostic Gospels* (New York: Vintage Books, 1979), p. 56.

9. The United Methodist Church, *Words That Hurt, Words That Heal* (Nashville: Graded Press, 1985), p. 9.

10. An Encounter with Eve: The Original Mother. Resources for further exploration:

• E. Pagels, *The Gnostic Gospels,* pp. 53, 57–58.

• J. Phillips, *Eve: The History of an Idea,* p. 3.

• B. Walker, *The Woman's Encyclopedia of Myths and Secrets,* p. 288–291.

11. An Encounter with Eve; Original Goodness. Resources for further exploration:

• Ecclesiasticus 25:24; I Kings 11:5; II Kings 21:7.

• Robert Graves and Raphael Patai, *Hebrew Myths: The Book of Genesis* (New York: Doubleday & Co., 1964), pp. 26–27.

• Patricia Monaghan, *The Book of Goddesses and Heroines* (Minn.: Llewellyn Publications, 1990), pp. 118–119.

• Phillips, *Eve: The History of an Idea,* p. 3.

• Stone, *When God Was a Woman,* pp. 199–218.

CHAPTER 8   Lilith: *The Rebellious First Woman*

1. Elizabeth Cady Stanton, *The Woman's Bible,* p. 20.

2. Although female subordination seems to be assumed in the second creation account, there are biblical scholars who argue that the second account does not support this assumption. See Phyllis Trible, "Eve and Adam: Genesis 2–3 Reread" in Christ and Plaskow, *Womanspirit Rising* (San Francisco: Harper and Row, 1979). Consider Trible's words: "In creating woman the Lord God 'caused a deep sleep to fall upon the man.' Man had no part in making woman; he was out of it. He exercises no control over her existence. He was neither participant nor spectator nor consultant at her birth. Like man, woman owes her life solely to God. For both of them, the origin of life is a divine mystery."(p. 74)

3. Graves and Patai, *Hebrew Myths: The Book of Genesis* (New York: Doubleday and Co., 1964), p. 65ff; Phillips, *Eve: The History of an Idea,* p. 38.

4. Ginzberg, *The Legends of the Jews,* vol. 3, I: 65–66.

5. Hallie Inglehart Austen, *The Heart of the Goddess* (Berkeley, Calif.: Wingbow Press, 1990), p. 128.

6. Graves and Patai, *Hebrew Myths,* pp. 68–69.

7. An Encounter with Lilith. Resources for further exploration:

• Austen, *The Heart of the Goddess,* pp. 128–129.

• Elinor W. Gadon, *The Once and Future Goddess* (San Francisco: Harper and Row, 1989), pp. 123–125.

• Graves and Patai, *Hebrew Myths: The Book of Genesis,* pp. 67–69.

• Genia Pauli Haddon, *Body Metaphors* (New York: Crossroads, 1988), pp. 37–44.

• Patricia Monaghan, *The Book of Goddesses and Heroines* (Minn.: Llewellyn Publications, 1980), pp. 208–209.

• Phillips, *Eve: The History of an Idea* (San Francisco: Harper and Row, 1984), pp. 38–40.

• Judith Paskow, "The Coming of Lilith," in Christ and Plaskow, *Womanspirit Rising,* pp. 205–207.

• Walker, *The Woman's Encyclopedia of Myths and Secrets,* pp. 541–542.

• Zones, ed., *Taking the Fruit,* pp. 28–31.

8. See American Association of University Women, "Shortchanging Girls, Shortchanging America" (Washington, DC: AAUN, 1991); Lyn Mikel Brown and Carol Gilligan, *Meeting at the Crossroads: Women's Psychology and Girls' Development* (Cambridge, Mass.: Harvard University Press, 1992).

CHAPTER 9   Mary: *The Virgin Mother*

1. Phillips, *Eve: The History of an Idea* (San Francisco: Harper and Row, 1984), pp. 131–147.

2. Rita M. Gross, "Steps Toward Feminine Imagery of Deity in Jewish Theology," p. 245.

3. Rosemary Radford Reuther, *Sexism and God-Talk* (Boston: Beacon Press, 1983), pp. 74–76, 96.

4. Ibid., pp. 125–126.

5. E. Schillebeeckx, *Mary, Mother of the Redemption* (New York: Sheed and Ward, 1964), p. 140.

6. Elinor W. Gadon, *The Once and Future Goddess,* pp. 194–195, 206.

7. Elizabeth Johnson, "Mary and the Image of God" in Doris Donnelly, ed., *Mary, Woman of Nazareth* (New York: Paulist Press, 1989), pp. 31–32.

8. Johnson, "Mary and the Image of God," pp. 31–32.

9. Marina Warner, *Alone of All Her Sex: The Myth and Cult of the Virgin Mary* (New York: Vintage Books, 1976), pp. 47–49.

10. Gimbutas, *The Civilization of the Goddess,* p. 223.

11. Rosemary Radford Reuther, *Mary—The Feminine Face of the Church* (Philadelphia: The Westminster Press, 1977), p. 15.

12. Audre Lorde, *Sister Outsider* (New York: The Crossing Press, 1984).

CHAPTER 10   The Divine Girl-Child

1. James Strong, *Strong's Exhaustive Concordance* (Nashville, Tenn.: Abingdon, 1890).

2. United Methodist Church, *Words That Hurt, Words That Heal,* pp. 9–10.

3. Elizabeth Brumiller, *May You Be the Mother of a Hundred Sons* (New York: Random House, 1990).

4. United Nations, *The World's Women 1970–1990: Trends and Statistics* (New York: The United Nations, 1991), p. 11.

5. American Association of University Women, "How Schools Shortchange Girls" (AAUW Educational Foundation and National Education Association, 1992).

6. American Psychological Association Task Force, Women and Depression (Washington DC: American Psychological Association, 1989).

7. Stone, *When God Was a Woman,* p. 60.

8. Theodore W. Kraus, "Jesus: The Divine Child of The West," *Creation,* Jan.–Feb. 1989, p. 27.

CHAPTER 11   The One Who Shed Her Blood

1. See Leonard Swidler and Arlene Swidler, eds., *Women Priests: A Catholic Commentary on the Vatican Declaration* (New York: Paulist Press, 1977).

2. Adrienne Rich, *Of Woman Born* (New York: W. W. Norton and Company, 1986), p. 106.

3. John M. Smith, *Women and Doctors* (New York: The Atlantic Monthly Press, 1992), p. 2.

4. See Walker, *The Woman's Encyclopedia of Myths and Secrets,* "Menstrual Blood," pp. 635–645.

CHAPTER 12   The Wounded Healers

1. Phyllis Trible, "The Pilgrim Bible on a Feminist Journey," *The Princeton Seminary Bulletin* (vol. XI, no. 3, 1990), p. 233.

2. See Ellen Bass and Laura Davis, *The Courage to Heal* (New York: Harper and Row, 1988), pp. 345, 346, 348.

3. See *The Interpreter's Dictionary of the Bible* (New York: Abingdon Press, 1962), vol. 3, pp. 876–880: "The representative sanctity of the Hebrew

priesthood is expressed in the three-fold hierarchy of cultic officials: High Priest, Priest, and Levite. The lowest grade consists of the Levites, who are set apart for the service of the sanctuary. They represent the people of Israel as substitutes for the first-born sons, who belong by right to God."

4. See *The Interpreter's Dictionary of the Bible,* vol. I, p. 666: "A concubine is a slave girl who belonged to a Hebrew family and bore children. They were acquired by purchase from poor Hebrew families, captured in war, or taken in payment for debt."

5. Mary Beth McClure, *Reclaiming the Heart* (New York: Warner Books, 1990), p. xvii.

6. Claudia Black, *"It Will Never Happen to Me"* (New York: Ballantine Books, 1981), pp. 154–155.

7. United Nations, *Violence Against Women in the Family* (New York: United Nations, 1989), p. 33.

8. Stone, *When God Was a Woman,* p. 59.

9. Barbara G. Walker, *The Crone: Woman of Age, Wisdom, and Power* (San Francisco: Harper, 1985), p. 11.

10. Parts of the meditation were inspired by Baby Suggs, a character in Toni Morrison's *Beloved* (New York: Alfred A. Knopf, 1987), pp. 87–89.

CHAPTER 13 The Wise Old Woman

1. See Genesis 16:1–16; 17:15–27; 18:12–15; 21:1–21.
2. See Luke 2:36–38.
3. See the Book of Ruth.
4. See Older Women's League, "Heading for Hardship: Retirement Income for American Women in the Next Century" (Washington, DC: Older Women's League, 1990). Statements from this document and fragments of women's writings on aging are incorporated into this responsive reading.
5. "Women on the Verge of a Nervy Breakthrough," *Time,* February 18, 1991, pp. 58–59.
6. Barbara Walker, *The Woman's Encyclopedia of Myths and Secrets,* p. 641.
7. Jennifer Barker Woolger and Roger J. Woolger, *The Goddess Within* (New York: Fawcett Columbine, 1989), p. 15.
8. See StarHawk, *The Spiral Dance: A Rebirth of the Ancient Religion of the Goddess* (New York: Harper and Row, 1979).
9. Pagels, *The Gnostic Gospels,* p. 54.
10. Ibid., p. 54.
11. Ibid., p. 56.

12. For further biblical references to Wisdom, see: Proverbs 1:20–21, 2:1–6; Wisdom of Solomon 6:12–21, 7:7–11, 22–26, 8:9; Ecclesiasticus 6:27–28, 15:3. For an in-depth discussion of Sophia see: Susan Cady, *Sophia: The Future of Feminist Spirituality* (San Francisco: Harper and Row, 1986).

13. Adapted from the *Baptist Hymnal,* "There's Power in the Blood," p. 193.

Index

and The One Who Shed Her
Blood, 223, 226–30, 232,
234–35
spiritual awakenings and, 292,
299–300, 302–5, 308, 311
The Wise Old Woman and, 274,
281
The Wounded Healers and, 241,
243, 256–57, 260, 265
and wounds and ineffective
behaviors, 67, 70–71,
74–75, 77
see also specific kinds of feelings
Ferrel:
The Divine Girl-Child and,
195–96
Lilith and, 151–52, 155–56
Mary and, 176–78
and The One Who Shed Her
Blood, 224–25
and reluctance, anger, and
courage, 41–42, 44, 46
spiritual awakenings and, 295,
303, 307, 311
The Wise Old Woman and,
271–72
The Wounded Healers and, 248,
257, 260–61
"Flowers Are Red" (Chapin), 33
Freud, Sigmund, 250

Gadin, Elinor, 236
Garden of Eden, 86, 128–29, 154,
169
Gathering the Fragments process,
11, 103–5
"Gathering the Gifts of Your
Journey," 288
Genesis, 53, 134–35, 140–43
Gilligan, Carol, 144

Gimbutas, Marija, 172
Girl-Child I Once Was, The, 4
Eve and, 109, 113, 117, 133–35
and God of our childhood
understanding, 56, 59, 61
healing and, 82–83, 91–93
Lilith and, 144–48, 152, 158–60
Mary and, 180–81, 184–85
meeting with, 13–14
and The One Who Shed Her
Blood, 209–14, 216–20
our hopes and dreams for, 203
pillows of support for, 16–18
and reluctance, anger, and
courage, 40, 46
The Wounded Healers and, 259
and wounds and ineffective
behaviors, 63–70, 76–78
Gnostics, 277
God, 139–43
author's personal story and, 5–6
changing face of, 10, 79–96
circles of women and, 18–19
dangerous questioning of male
language and imagery for,
58
The Divine Girl-Child and, 192,
194–97, 199–200, 203,
205, 207
Eve and, 109–14, 117–38, 157,
163, 168, 170
and far-reaching effects of
religion, 23–32, 34–36
as female, 5, 8, 34–36, 40–41,
52, 65, 67–68, 74–75,
78–79, 83–92, 94–95,
102–4, 107–8, 110, 114,
120–38, 141–42, 149–50,
153, 158, 161, 170,
172–74, 176–79, 182–83,

Patricia Lynn Reilly offers women's spirituality workshops, retreats, and presentations based on the material in this book. If you would like a schedule of upcoming events, write or call:

Open Window Creations
P.O. Box 8615
Berkeley, CA 94707
(510) 524-3479

Join Our Circle

We invite you to share stories about your explorations of your own religious past with us for possible use in a future anthology. Please send them to Patricia Reilly at the above address.

About the Author

PATRICIA LYNN REILLY holds a Master of Divinity degree from Princeton Theological Seminary, and post-graduate certification from the Women's Theological Center in Women's Spirituality and Feminist Theology.

Ms. Reilly is the founder of Open Window Creations, where she conducts workshops and retreats on women's spirituality, recovery, and the healing ministry. She is also codirector of the Circle of Life Women's Center. She lives in Berkeley, California.